Our Side of the River

Also by Alan Emmet

So Fine a Prospect: Historic New England Gardens

The Mr. and Mrs. Club – A Novel

Our Side of the River

A MEMOIR

Alan Emmet

White River Press
Amherst, Massachusetts

Our Side of the River
© 2015 by Alan Emmet

First published 2015 by White River Press
White River Press
PO Box 3561
Amherst, MA 01004
www.whiteriverpress.com

Book and cover design:
Douglas Lufkin, Lufkin Graphic Designs
www.LufkinGraphics.com

Cover painting, *The River – Late Afternoon*, by Caroline Emmet Heald

ISBN: 978-1-887043-14-4

Photographs from the author's collection.

Library of Congress Cataloging-in-Publication Data

Emmet, Alan, 1927-
    Our side of the river : a memoir / Alan Emmet.
    pages cm
    ISBN 978-1-887043-14-4 (paperback : alkaline paper)
    ISBN 1-887043-14-4 (paperback : alkaline paper)
1. Emmet, Alan, 1927---Childhood and youth. 2. Emmet, Alan, 1927---Family.
3. Saint Croix River Region (Wis. and Minn.)--Social life and customs--20th
century. 4. Minnesota--Social life and customs--20th century. 5. Minnesota--
Biography. 6. Vacation homes--Minnesota--History--20th century. 7. Summer--
Minnesota--History--20th century. I. Title.
F612.S2E55 2015
977.6'053--dc23
                                        2014041294

"Often they swam and as Amory floated lazily in the water he shut his mind to all thoughts except those . . . where the sun splattered through the wind-drunk trees. How could anyone possibly think or worry, or do anything except splash and dive and loll there on the edge of time while the flower months failed. Let the days move over—sadness and memory and pain recurred outside, and here, once more, before he went on to meet them he wanted to drift and be young."

—F. Scott Fitzgerald, *This Side of Paradise*

THE INGERSOLL

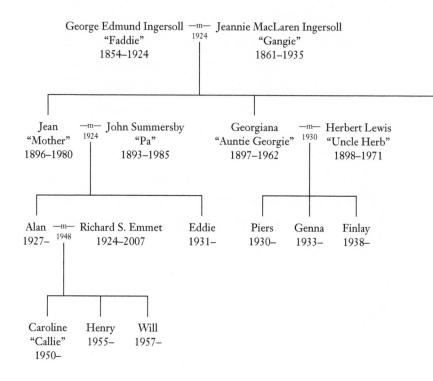

George Edmund Ingersoll —m— Jeannie MacLaren Ingersoll
"Faddie"   1924   "Gangie"
1854–1924   1861–1935

Jean —m— John Summersby   Georgiana —m— Herbert Lewis
"Mother" 1924 "Pa"   "Auntie Georgie" 1930 "Uncle Herb"
1896–1980   1893–1985   1897–1962   1898–1971

Alan —m— Richard S. Emmet   Eddie   Piers   Genna   Finlay
1927– 1948 1924–2007   1931–   1930–   1933–   1938–

Caroline   Henry   Will
"Callie"   1955–   1957–
1950–

FAMILY TREE

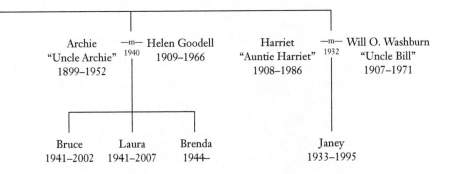

Archie —m— Helen Goodell   Harriet —m— Will O. Washburn
"Uncle Archie" 1940 1909–1966 "Auntie Harriet" 1932 "Uncle Bill"
1899–1952   1908–1986   1907–1971

Bruce Laura Brenda   Janey
1941–2002 1941–2007 1944–   1933–1995

Jeannie with Alan and Eddie – 1933

One day when I was five, my mother read me the story of King Midas. It was supposed to be a tragedy, ending as it did with the King inadvertently turning his little daughter into gold. But I didn't see it that way. I thought it would be wonderful to have the "Midas touch." Maybe my mother did. Every time she talked about the past she applied a shimmer of gold to her grandparents, her family, her whole childhood. I got the idea that they were finer and rarer than other people. It wasn't that they'd achieved greatness as far as the world was concerned. None of them had. But they had style, sensitivity, and auburn hair. The gene for that hair color missed my mother. The heads of her two sisters and her brother were lit with red-gold. My mother's hair was just plain brown, but it reflected the light.

Years later, before my wedding, my mother presented me with a little box I'd seen before. "I think you should have this, Alan." Inside was her mother's wedding ring, a wide gold band. In script almost too tiny to read, the inner surface of the ring was inscribed "Edmund to Jeannie—September 8, 1892." They were my grandparents, the ones who discovered the River and created a sunlit sanctuary for five generations of family.

The River house – 1920

– O N E –

"WE'RE GOING TO THE RIVER," my mother said. "You and Eddie and I. On the train. All the way from New Jersey to Minnesota. Eddie won't have any more asthma." She patted my arm. "And we'll fatten you up so you don't get so many nasty colds next winter." It was 1932; I was five years old.

Going to the River that July was all we talked about for days, while my mother made lists. We went to get sandals for Eddie and me, bathing suits, and new seersucker playsuits. Then she packed everything into two big suitcases and one small one. Everything had to be clean and carefully folded.

"Why can't Daddy come with us?" I asked.

"Oh, he has to go to work. You know."

He drove us to Newark to catch the train. The waiting room of the Pennsylvania Station had a big clock high on the wall, with a round face like the moon. Eddie and I followed our parents and the "redcap" porter who put our bags onto a cart and pushed it along a concrete platform that was so long you couldn't see its beginning or its end.

My mother held tight to Eddie's hand. "Stay away from the edge." Her brown felt hat was like a bowl turned upside down on her head with a feather tucked into its ribbon band. She had on one of those dresses that mothers wore, with a narrow skirt that reached almost to her ankles. I had a hat, too, shaped like hers. Mine was navy blue straw with fake red cherries around its narrow brim.

My father jingled the coins in the pocket of his gray suit. "I'll take care of the porter." He took off his hat to kiss my mother good-bye. "You have the tickets, Jeannie." (My mother had been named after her mother, my grandmother.)

She clicked open her shiny brown purse to make sure.

We saw the train, small and far away, before it came to a gasping stop beside us. A different porter led us to our own compartment.

"Wave to Daddy," my mother said. He was waving to us, looking lonely.

The train began moving, then picked up speed. Eddie and I pressed our noses to the window, the green plush seats scratchy against our bare legs.

We had our own bathroom, tiny, with a silvery basin that unfolded from the wall. My mother scrubbed the toilet seat with a stiff white towel. From her travel bag, she took out a glass medicine bottle and poured syrup into a spoon.

"Time for pink syrup, Eddie." With her thin, white fingers she slid a spoonful of syrup onto his tongue. "Good boy." And then me. We loved that sweet syrup. We'd had it before, every time we'd gone on a trip.

I looked out the window at the tracks converging and dividing beneath us. Another train roared past. We rattled across a bridge. "We're crossing the Delaware River," my mother said.

"Is this river as big as our River?" I'd only been there when I was a baby, so I didn't remember.

"Our St. Croix River is much nicer than this, " she said. "With pine trees, and green hills, and canoes."

"Will we see Indians?"

"No, not anymore. They're all gone. But we'll be with your Gangie, and with Auntie Georgie and Uncle Archie—all your uncles and aunts."

Soon it was time to head to the dining car. But first my mother took another little bottle out of her bag, poured from it into a paper cone, and took three sips. The emerald on her finger sparkled in the late sun. She put her hat on, and slid her purse over her wrist. "We want to be in time for the first sitting."

In the dining car we were led to a table where a woman in a pink dress was already eating her dinner. Our table had a red rose wobbling in a vase. The water swayed from side to side in the pitcher; silverware slid toward the window. The waiter lifted the heavy silver covers off our plates. We each had mashed potatoes in a white dish that was the right size for a doll's bathtub.

The lady in the pink dress asked where we were going. "No, we don't live there," my mother said. "It's our family's summer place, where I grew up."

I bounced on my chair. "It's the River. And we can go swimming."

The woman looked at me. "How old are you, dear?"

I told her I was almost six.

"Can you tell me your name?"

I looked down. "Alan," I murmured.

"I couldn't hear you. What you did you say?"

"My name's Alan."

"Alan! But that's a boy's name, dear."

People always said that, and I hated it.

"She's named for my husband's little brother who died," my mother told her. "I wanted to do something different."

"Hmm. It's different all right."

When we got back to our compartment, it had changed. The upper berth, which was to be mine, had come down out of the ceiling with its own ladder. Eddie had to sleep with our mother, but he was too little to mind. My mother hung up my dress, but everything else went into a green net that hung over my berth. My clothes swung beside me all night.

My mother undressed only halfway, half ready for disaster. She hung up her brown traveling dress and the silk stockings that held the shape of her legs as they swayed back and forth on the hanger.

In the morning she said, "We have to hurry to be ready for Chicago." The porter dusted us off with a tickly brush. From her purse, my mother took some money and gave it to him.

In Chicago we took a taxi to another station. There wasn't much time to catch the Hiawatha, the new streamliner. We ran, but we made it.

In the Observation Car, a round dial on the wall told how fast we were going, which was very fast. My mother fanned herself with a timetable. She gave us each another spoonful of our sweet pink syrup. "Why can we only have the pink syrup when we go on a trip?"

"It's just to take the edge off."

I didn't know what she meant. She began to read her book. I looked out the window, watching the tracks coming together and apart, feeling dozy.

"Prairie du Chien," called the conductor, then "La Crosse, Winona Junction." I looked out at the people who got on or off at places that had nothing but a few plain houses and red barns, each with a silo pointing up to the wide blue sky. Then cows and fields as far as you could see. Our

New Jersey had no fields, no cows, no red barns, and not so much sky.

The Hiawatha took all day. The bright sun was slanting across the water when we rattled over a wide river. "We're crossing the Mississippi," my mother said. "A long, long river, and our river, our St. Croix flows into it. Now we know we're nearly there."

"What will we do at the River?"

"We'll go up to the sandbar in the motorboat, and we'll take the canoe into the slough, where it's very wild, and we might see a beaver or turtles."

"Did you do that when you were a little girl?"

"Oh yes, and sometimes we went up the River to the secret cave where there used to be Indians."

"Will we see Auntie Georgie at the River?" She was the aunt I knew best, the one who sometimes said silly things to me.

"Yes, of course. I told you. And you'll see Cousin Piers— he's just a teeny bit older than Eddie."

The conductor called, "Saint Paul, Union Depot." The porter lifted Eddie down the steps, and my mother counted our suitcases. And there was Uncle Archie hugging us, lifting Eddie and swinging him around. He was my mother's only brother, not much taller than she was, with wire-rimmed glasses like hers and red hair. It was easy to tell he wasn't anything like my father. Uncle Archie was wearing shorts and a brown leather jacket with a zipper. We followed the cart that held our bags through the station, out to Uncle Archie's top-down Ford car.

"You can put your junk up there behind the seat," he said, pointing at my crayons and my coloring pad.

"It's not junk to me," I said.

He laughed. "Who wants to go to the River?"

"I do," I told him, and Eddie said he did, too, even though he'd never been there, either.

Uncle Archie drove us past farms and fields and down a hill into Stillwater. He parked the car. "How about it, kiddos; Coca-Cola?"

I didn't know what it was, but it didn't matter because my mother said, "No, Arch. Not for the kids."

Eddie with Uncle Archie – 1934

After Stillwater we could see our River, not our part of it, but my mother said it was the same water.

"Hey, kids," Uncle Archie said. "There's the old state prison." I could see thick walls and little windows with bars across them. But no roof.

"It's okay," my mother said. "No one's there now . . . slow down, Arch, for Pete's sake."

He flicked his cigarette out the window.

We passed a white schoolhouse, like a little church, with a bell on the roof. "We're almost there." My mother was happy.

The road was not paved after that, just gravel. Uncle Archie turned into the narrow bumpy road that was the driveway. The car started down the steep hill, scary on my side where you could see way, way down. "That's the ravine," my mother said. "We'll walk up the stream one day and see the beautiful waterfall."

As he drove down, Uncle Archie honked, and honked again. "So they'll know we're coming," he said.

We stopped beyond the tennis court under pine trees and got out of the car. The pine needles underfoot were warm and fragrant. In her high heels my mother couldn't walk very well on the stones. I could see the River, wide and still. I tugged at her skirt. "Can we go look at the River now?"

"Oh, we will, but first we have to say hello."

Two people came out the back door, wiping their hands on their white aprons. "Hello, Florence, " my mother said. "I'm so glad to see you! And glad you're cooking for us again." She turned to the other woman, "You must be Florence's sister, Della. I remember your mother."

After they talked, my mother leaned over to murmur in my ear: "They're Swedish people. That's why they sound different."

We walked into the house, through the high, dark living room, following my grandmother's soft voice out to the long front porch where she was sitting with her sewing. Lottie, her old white Sealyham, wagged a stubby tail.

Gangie's gray hair was held back with pins; her dress was patterned with red cherries. She hugged me.

Eddie and I stood there, while the grownups talked. Finally I whispered in my mother's ear. "Now can I go see the River?"

"Oh, yes, let's go. This is what we've been waiting for. Come on, Eddie."

Uncle Archie led the way, holding Eddie by the hand. Gangie stayed in her chair. Down the brick steps we went, and down the big lawn toward the water.

"I'd forgotten how quiet it is here," my mother said. "Look at the maple tree on the bank. When we first came here, in the early days, it was just a little sapling."

Then up the path came Auntie Georgie in her shiny, dripping bathing suit, with curly-haired Piers, my four-year-old cousin. "Well, look who's here! Alan, my skinny little punkins. And Eddie, getting to be an old man. Welcome to the Saint Croix! But I'm much too wet for hugs." She blew an air kiss to my mother, who was still in her city clothes. "Jeannie, we'll get some color on these kids, and a little fat." She patted my shoulder. "Allie, you and I'll find some mischief to get into, won't we? But don't tell your mama!"

With Uncle Archie in his shorts and leather jacket, the three of them stood at the edge of the bank looking out on the wide, shining River. The only sound was the slow, rhythmic creak of oars as an old man in a felt hat rowed by in his weather-beaten scow.

"Any luck, Otto?" Uncle Archie didn't have to raise his voice.

"Coupla small-mouth." The man held up a forked stick with two fish on it. Glistening drops of water fell from his oars.

"I'll be going out later," Uncle Archie said.

And that was how it began, my first visit to the River.

*Top row: Georgie, Herb, Jeannie, Gangie Ingersoll,
with Alan, Harriet, and Bill, on the porch steps – 1934*

– T W O –

THE PORCH WAS GREEN AND COOL—green from
the leaves of the grapevines that clung with curly tendrils
to the screen at the end of the porch. Facing the River,
our St. Croix River, there was nothing to hide our view of
the water and the bright gold of the afternoon sun on the
opposite shore. Gangie was in the wicker chair where she
apparently always sat. The porch was crowded and cozy, with
my mother and all the aunts and uncles filling the chairs,
the dogs sprawled on the straw rug. Everyone was laughing
and talking. I stood by the doorway from the living room,
watching and listening.

"Come on out, Alan, there's room for you."

I squeezed in between Auntie Georgie and Auntie
Harriet on the green-and-white striped glider. They each
put an arm around me. "It's like a swing," I whispered. I felt
safe and snug at this place where we all belonged together.

"Alan, you can take your shoes off," Uncle Archie said. I looked at my sandals and striped socks. "You're at the River."

Florence appeared at the door. "Would you like the iced tea now, Mrs. Ingersoll?"

"Yes, please, Florence," my grandmother said. "And some of your wonderful walnut wafers."

"How about a glass of milk for our skinny little Miss Alan?" Auntie Georgie's bright brown eyes pulled me close to her. No one else looked at me like that. She patted my knee, and I knew I loved her.

My mother stood up. "I've just got to get out of these traveling clothes. Oh, it's so good to be back here at last."

Living with aunts and uncles that summer at the River was like having five extra parents. Except that they weren't parents; they certainly weren't like my mother, who was usually serious with me and strict about my manners. "Mrs. Kirk is coming for tea," she might say one day. "And I want you to be sure to make a nice curtsey when you say how-do-you-do." I adored my father, but he wasn't like these uncles. I couldn't picture them going off every morning in a gray suit and hat the way my father did in New Jersey, walking to the train that took him to his office.

The aunts and uncles were different in many ways. Unlike my mother they let me get away with things. I was the first of the new generation, born before Eddie and the cousins. Maybe that was why. If Auntie Georgie told me to pick up my clothes I knew she didn't really care. When Auntie Harriet said, "Little girls oughta be in bed by now," she laughed, and I knew I could hang around, listening. If I didn't want to play at Monnie's house when her mother invited me, Auntie Harriet said, "Tell her you're much too busy." When Piers bothered me, Uncle Bill told me I should give him "a poke in the snoot." They hadn't learned yet how parents are supposed to act.

All of them were usually barefoot because it was summer. Uncle Archie played tennis and drove his car with bare feet. The uncles wore shorts and no shirts. Auntie Harriet was the youngest sister, so she wore a slinky bathing suit, unlike my mother and Auntie Georgie's flowered ones with little skirts. Sometimes out in the sun when it was just us, Auntie Georgie peeled off her checked shirt, leaving only her white bra.

As a child in the 1930s, I was never taken out at night. Except once, that first summer when I was about to turn six. Not only was it dark, way past my bedtime, but it was raining hard. I sat on my mother's lap, squeezed into the back seat of the car, between Auntie Georgie and Auntie Harriet. Two uncles sat in front. No one had told me where we were going. Uncle Archie was driving. The wipers swung back and forth, thunk-ker-thunk, thunk-ker-thunk. The aunts and uncles talked and joked and laughed. I felt warm and dozy against my mother. Her silky, creamy dress was smooth beneath my cheek. I felt the motion of the car through her. Her brown hair was soft and silky, too, when I reached up to pat it. I touched her necklace, crystal beads alternating with golden ones, tiny beads at the soft nape of her neck, bigger ones at the hollow of her throat.

Then the wipers stopped. The car stopped.

"Why are you stopping, Arch? What's wrong?" Auntie Georgie's voice had a new edge. My mother's lap was not soft any more. I stiffened, too, and sat up. We were not there yet, wherever we were headed.

Uncle Archie was not talking. He was trying to start the car. Ooga-ooga-ooga-unh. Ooga-ooga-unh. Nothing. Uncle

Bill was talking floods, and flooding, chokes, and spark plugs.

"I see a light; we could walk there." My mother and my aunts had ideas.

"Why don't we flag down the next car—here comes one—oh, too late . . ."

Our headlights were still on, burning into swirls of mist and rain.

"Won't the lights run down the battery, Arch?" My mother's voice was shrill. Her body beneath me felt like a rubber band stretched, ready to snap.

"Use your head, Jeannie. We don't want some idiot to come barreling into us, for God's sake." Uncle Archie sounded cross, not at all like the Uncle Archie who was teaching me to swim.

I began to cry. "Why don't we go home? I don't like this; I want to go home."

But we couldn't go home. And I knew then that the grownups couldn't fix everything. The world was dangerous, out of their control. And certainly out of mine. I was not safe even in my mother's lap. Sitting there, ramrod straight, I was terrified.

Uncle Archie and Uncle Bill were going to check under the hood. "Here Bill, take the umbrella!" cried Auntie Harriet.

The rain fell harder. The sound of it was louder when my uncles opened the doors. They folded back the hood. Light shone off my uncles' wet dark slickers and Uncle Archie's wire-rimmed glasses as they bent over the engine. The black umbrella above Uncle Bill's head had the shape of a witch's hat. I cried harder. Auntie Harriet pulled me onto her lap.

"Once upon a time," she began, "there were three sisters. Their names were One Eye, Two Eyes, and Three Eyes. They lived with their stepmother in a little house . . . The stepmother and the sisters were mean to Little Two Eyes, who had only cast-off clothes to wear, and leftover scraps to eat. She was sent into the fields to take care of the goats. One day an old woman appeared, and taught her a magic verse to say whenever she was hungry:

'Little goat, if you're able,

Pray deck out my little table.'

The words were scarcely out of her mouth when a beautiful table stood before Little Two Eyes. It had a white cloth and plates, and knives and forks, and silver spoons, and a delicious dinner, piping hot . . ."

I had stopped crying. I could see that little table that appeared so miraculously in the wilderness. I still can.

The rain had eased up a bit. Now it sounded like the soft hum of bees in Gangie's garden. My uncles were tying a stout rope from the bumper of our car to the rear bumper of another. I was falling asleep in Auntie Harriet's lap.

That summer I never saw Gangie, my grandmother, in bare feet, or going for a swim. No matter how hot it was, she wore one of her pale silk dresses, stockings, and soft white shoes with laces. She sat on the screen porch with her sewing on her lap.

She worked on a linen bureau scarf one day, her needle traveling slowly around each scallop. Another day it was a baby pillowcase that she'd hemstitched, to which she was attaching a modest frill of French lace. "The women in France make this lace with their hands," she told me. She could have done that, too, I thought. Her hands were as white as the linen she worked on. She dropped her gold thimble. I scrambled under her wicker chair to pick it up. (That golden thimble was inscribed "J F McL" in tiny script, with a date, 1879, the year she, its first owner, turned eighteen. Inside a worn leather box lined with blue velvet, made especially to hold a thimble, this small memento of my grandmother's diligent labor nests now, these decades later, in my sewing basket.)

Whenever I went into the warm kitchen, Florence was usually beating eggs at the table in the middle of the room. She had blueberries floured and ready to fold into the batter. I watched her spoon the batter into muffin tins. A blast of heat came from the oven when she opened the door and carefully put the tins inside the hot, black cavern. I had my finger ready, but Florence handed me a teaspoon to scrape the tan mixing bowl.

At the sink, Della was chopping cabbage with a crescent blade in a wooden bowl. Florence was the pretty sister, with her crown of curly blonde hair. She told me she and Della lived on a farm with cows and chickens and a bunch of little brothers and sisters. "Would you like to come there some day?"

"Ooh, could I?"

"Ja, if they'd let you. Our mamma would fatten you up quick, put some meat on these little bones." Florence patted my back.

The kitchen floor had red and black squares. I stepped on only the red squares with my bare feet, past the big tank that made hot water, and out the screen door onto a patch of concrete, always damp under bare feet, and smelling so moldy and old that I had to pinch my nose. Another screen door opened into the dark, dank storage pantry. Cans and boxes lined the shelves. I did not like going in there, but sometimes I had to because—especially when it was my birthday—there might be a wooden case of bottles: fizzy orange pop, cream soda, or root beer, cool on the wet floor. But I had to ask first.

The door wheezed shut behind me as I skittered through the kitchen. "Slow down, missie," Florence said.

"Oh, ja; be careful," called Della.

Gangie was still sewing on the porch, with Lottie, her old Sealyham, asleep at her feet. Auntie Georgie had come in, and they were talking. I forgot what I'd wanted to ask. I liked hearing them talk, their two voices, even though I had no idea what it was about. I flopped down on the green glider. It was like a sofa, only better. You were supposed to sway gently back and forth, but the fun was to swing as far and as fast as you could.

"Not so hard, dear," said Gangie in her mild way.

The screen porch ran all across the front of the house. From the porch you could see Gangie's bright flower garden, alive with orange and yellow butterflies, her rock garden, the sloping lawn, and then the wide river. An old white pine and a giant sugar maple framed the lawn above the riverbank. I went out to sit on the brick steps in the sun, where I could still hear the murmur of their voices. Then I saw a hummingbird, hovering, putting its needle nose into the red mouth of a hollyhock.

Gangie was my MacLaren grandmother. Although she'd lost that name, becoming an Ingersoll when she married my grandfather, the name MacLaren has had its own long half-life in my family, chiefly as a middle name for girls. It was bestowed on my mother, on me, and later, on my daughter and several cousins. The men in the family used to have MacLaren tartan neckties. Everyone apparently thought it was romantic to be connected to a Scottish clan. "Probably a bunch of Highland sheep rustlers," teased Uncle Herb.

"Do you really think that Cousin Hattie Richards' story is true?"

I sat in warm sun on the brick steps one morning, by the porch where my mother and Auntie Georgie were talking.

"Oh, I do," said Auntie Georgie. "No one would make it up."

I didn't know what the story was. But I sat still and listened.

"It was just about a hundred years ago, the 1830s, when the letter reached the Caledonia parsonage in upstate New York. Can you imagine how stunned those MacLarens must have been, getting a letter all the way from Jamaica?"

"Especially from someone who claimed to be a cousin, descended from the MacLarens of Balquiddar."

"And he said his family was important in Jamaica."

Then I heard the rest. The writer of the letter had been about to embark on a tour of the United States and wished to meet his American cousins. He named the day he expected to arrive in Caledonia.

The New York MacLarens got ready for his coming. The six children kept a lookout for the arrival of the stagecoach. When it finally drew up, the family rushed out to greet the cousin. A tall, handsome young man stepped out of the coach. He was elegantly dressed with a derby hat and furled umbrella. He advanced, bowing, while his cousins retreated in shock. Their guest was black.

The Reverend Donald MacLaren promptly informed his Jamaican cousin that in our country the "Color Line" was rigidly observed and that, all things considered, it would be best if the cousin from Jamaica made his visit as brief as possible. This, of course, he did. None of my forbears set eyes on him again.

"But according to Cousin Hattie, somehow the story was passed on," my mother said.

Auntie Georgie recounted the ending. The MacLaren cousin was said to have gone to Paris, married a "blue-blooded" Frenchwoman in a festive ceremony at the Church of the Madeleine, and lived happily ever after. Apparently the "Color Line" was not drawn as rigidly across the French or the Jamaican populations as it was in the young American democracy.

"Such an incredible story," said Auntie Georgie.

"But we must never tell Aunt Katharine," my mother said. "It wouldn't fit her image of the family at all."

My great-grandfather, Robert MacLaren, was a son of that clergyman in upstate New York. After college he'd traveled across the country until he was ready to settle down.

He and his bride Anna McVean, daughter of another Scottish Presbyterian family, went out to Red Wing, Minnesota, on the Mississippi River. When the Civil War began, Robert volunteered for the Army's regiment of Minnesota Volunteers. They were not sent to fight for the Union, but stayed in the northwest to defend the new settlements from wild Indians.

Georgie, Piers, Gangie, and Harriet by the River – 1934

My mother and Auntie Georgie told me stories they'd heard from their mother. I learned about the long months when Robert MacLaren led an expedition with General Sibley up the Missouri River and along the valley of the Yellowstone, to fight the "hostile Sioux." A year later Colonel MacLaren went West again, that time to patrol the plains of the Dakota territory.

Meanwhile, Anna MacLaren and their three small children were left home in Red Wing. Jeannie, my grandmother Gangie, who was then four or five years old, remembered how it was when they'd spy the Indians approaching their lonely little house. "Run! Run," her mother would cry to the children. "Go. Quickly!" Jeannie and her brother Archie, who carried Rob, the baby, would dart behind the house to the asparagus patch. They'd crouch there beneath the pale feathery foliage. There were no trees; that was the only place to hide. They'd huddle there, terrified.

(Sometimes I crawled into our bed of ferny asparagus at the River, imagining that I was hiding from fierce Indians in that frail shelter. Whatever drove me there would have to occur in the summer, I thought, when the asparagus had shot up into its haze of green.)

The children's mother had no choice but to greet those Indians at the door (her husband being far away fighting other Indians), and let them in. Cruising silently through the house, eyes swiveling right and left, the Indians picked up things—once they took a heavy buffalo robe, at other times they took blankets or the bag of sugar—then they'd be on their way.

In 1863, Colonel MacLaren was made a general and commandant of Fort Snelling, which sat high above the confluence of the Mississippi and the Minnesota rivers on land that had been bargained away from the Indians by President Jefferson's emissary. The fort had long been a center of the fur trade, and was for many years the northern-most U.S. military outpost. Now sandwiched between the cities of St. Paul and Minneapolis, Fort Snelling was still a lonely spot during the Civil War years when my grandmother was brought there as a child.

Moving from Red Wing to St. Paul and the fort, the MacLarens traveled by steamboat up the Mississippi. Auntie Georgie once told me about the heroism of a young boy in the family; perhaps it was her Uncle Archie. A child—was it baby brother Rob?—tumbled off the bow of the boat into the dark, rushing water. Archie, moving fast, pulled him by his hair through an opening in the deck, just seconds before the child would have been sucked into the great churning stern paddlewheel.

Both of my mother's grandfathers came to Minnesota in the same year, 1857. Not that they knew each other, or had a thing in common—they just arrived there. Minnesota was not yet even a state, just a territory. And St. Paul was only a rough little town. Indians were still a factor.

Occasionally, when I was growing up, my mother would flip open the supposedly secret panel on the top of the mahogany bureau in which my father's starched white shirts were kept. She'd pull out a few precious artifacts to show me. The best treasure—better than my grandmother's cameo choker, more valuable in my eyes than the five-dollar gold piece— was wrapped in tissue paper. Carefully unfolding the packet, my mother slid a tiny, pearly thing shaped like a fish into my palm. "An Indian chief carved this out of a clamshell from the Mississippi River," she said. "He was a prisoner in that circular stone jail at Fort Snelling, where your grandmother lived when her father was the general." The fish, cool and smooth in my hand, was proof that the long-ago past was real. These were not made-up stories; this was true. The Indian had made the fish, and had handed it through the bars to the general's little daughter, my Gangie. I envisioned a swarthy black-haired brave, in fringed leather, confined to jail for years, but still with his sharp whittling knife, and my little five-year-old grandmother, allowed to wander past the barred cells and visit with the prisoners.

My great-grandfather commanded the fort when the last two Indian chiefs were hanged. This is what his obituary proudly announced. Little Six and Medicine Hat. Had one of them carved the fish?

I don't have that little fish. My mother, a good citizen, decided that the tiny historic artifact should be in the public domain. She gave it to the Minnesota Historical Society, surely a worthy institution, but I wish she hadn't. I imagine it perfectly preserved, diligently catalogued, accurately numbered, wrapped in acid-free something, tucked in the back of an archival drawer, seen by no one, its story left untold.

My mother kept a scrapbook during her teen years. She called it her "Memory Book." I loved looking through it: her life so thrilling, I thought, mine, so drab. In 1911, just over fifty years since Minnesota had become a state, the St. Paul Art School put on an ambitious "Pageant of Minnesota History." The pageant program, pasted into my mother's scrapbook, lists nine acts and an enormous cast, most of the names doubtless known to my mother. The scenes ran from an Indian war dance (performed entirely, of course, by non-Indians), the smoking of a peace pipe, "Coming of the Voyageurs" and the fur trade, Indian treaties, lumbermen, and immigrants. The penultimate act was entitled "Passing of the Indian," featuring five St. Paul debutantes performing a "Dance of Indian Spirits." Spirits were about all that was left by then of Minnesota's Iroquois and Ojibwa. It hadn't taken long. A Dr. Charles Eastman, in fringe, feathers, and tawny make-up, played the part of the "Last Indian."

Alan, Eddie, and Piers – 1933

– T H R E E –

MY LIFE AS A CHILD was divided between New Jersey winters and Minnesota summers. Summer, I thought, made up half the year. After I learned otherwise I wished it were true. I was a different person in summer, braver, and later, possibly even pretty. In summer people liked me.

When my brother Eddie and I got back to New Jersey at the end of the summer, the afternoons darkened earlier, and thick, tired foliage shut out the sky. Our house seemed dim and quiet. My school clothes—plaid dresses, brown lace-up shoes, scratchy wool sweaters knitted by my grandmother—cast a gloom over the dwindling days. I missed my bare legs of summer, my bare feet. Summer seemed hopelessly far off in time and space. I pined for the River.

My mother and Gangie took me with them to Bermuda for ten days the winter I was six. Waving to my father as the Queen of Bermuda slid away from the New York pier, my straw hat with the cherries blew off, food for the fish.

Gangie and I shared a room in a little hotel in Bermuda. I caught a glimpse of intricate pink girdle when she pulled her pale polka-dotted dress over her head. Later she waded, barefoot and laughing into the sea, holding her hat in one hand and the lifted hem of her skirt in the other.

She died that spring. We were in New Jersey. Early one morning, when darkness shrouded my room and a crack of gray daylight framed the window shades, I heard footsteps and talking. I tiptoed to the top of the stairs. Down below I saw my mother in her tea-rose wrapper, strangely huddled over the telephone. It was a tall black phone. You had to speak into its flaring mouth, and hold the hearing part up to your ear.

My mother was listening and asking questions in a muffled voice. I heard her sob. When finally she looked up at me I saw the tears and the splotches of red on her face. I'd never seen her cry. Grownups never cried; only children. But she was crying. I felt an emptiness in my middle. I went back to my room.

My father was off on one of his business trips to Omaha or Buffalo. I was alone with the morning glories on my wallpaper.

Soon my mother came and put her warm arms around my shoulders, rocking me as if I were her baby still. She went away, though, for many days because they had a funeral for Gangie. We got a puppy when my mother came home, one of Lottie's babies. We named him Mickey, but he got run over in Ashland Road. I heard the loud squawk of brakes, and saw the wheels go over him. Some men were fixing the road. They put our white, dead puppy in a burlap bag, and brought him to us. The man who held the bag cried. I saw the tears sliding down his brown cheeks. This was what grownups did if someone died, or a dog. "I should have put his leash on when we came to Ashland Road," said our nursemaid Anna. But she didn't cry.

After my grandmother died, her Victorian sofa came to our New Jersey living room, where it never looked to me as if it belonged. I remember the time when someone poked a hand into the crevice between the seat and the arm, and came up with a tiny pair of golden scissors. "Mother's sewing scissors!" exclaimed my mother. They were shaped like a bird, the two parts of its long bill forming the blades. The scissors have disappeared. Again.

Once in a while, during the winter in New Jersey, my mother let me see the plates that her grandmother had painted, that same brave woman who sent her children to hide in the asparagus patch when the Indians came. My mother kept these dishes behind glass doors on the top shelf in the butler's pantry. We never used them.

"China painting was a hobby for ladies back in those early days," my mother said. "They could buy plates or cups of plain white porcelain, and the paints and brushes they needed. But our Gangie MacLaren was a real artist."

Perched precariously on the green kitchen stool, stretching her arms to that high shelf, she lifted the plates one by one, and laid them in a row along the black counter by the copper sink. "Be careful," she said. "Just look."

Now I've inherited these plates, eight of them, and two little cups and saucers. Each one is different, painted with botanical decorations, such as hepaticas, bluets, and single wild roses with thorny stems. All the plates have a stylized "McL" for MacLaren in the center, and an edging of gleaming gold. One plate painted with violets and a pale blue ribbon bears a date on the bottom: 1883.

After my grandmother died, the whole family—aunts, uncles, cousins—shared the Big House at the River, and the little green Guest House. The whole place seemed the same at first, only without Gangie. But soon it was noisier, more cluttered, a different place. Even the maids' voices were louder.

My mother didn't stay all summer with us at the River. She had to go back to New Jersey to be with our father, who only got two weeks of vacation from his job. After our mother left, Auntie Georgie was the boss of Eddie and me.

Uncle Herbert, her husband, was Managing Editor of the *St. Paul Dispatch*. At the River, Uncle Herb seemed planted on the porch, reading, puffing on his pipe, or telling stories about newspaper people, the city room, and then later, Paris before the Germans came, and London in the Blitz. He tilted his wicker chair back on two legs, laughed his jolly booming laugh, along with us all. I hugged my bare knees, always listening. I only was interested in the newspaper on Sundays, when Eddie and I and our cousin Piers raced up the hill to grab the fat bundle from the box. I gripped most of the paper under my arm while we each grabbed a sheet of the "funnies." We held our pages out in front of us, reading as we walked slowly, slowly down the hill, each of us immersed in "Tarzan" or "Li'l Abner" or "The Katzenjammer Kids" until it was time to trade.

Uncle Herb bought himself a movie camera. He occasionally followed us around with the thing held up to his face. "Hi, Allie! Piers . . ." We'd turn and wave at the camera. "Look this way, Genna; Eddie . . ."

The tennis court was as far from the porch as Uncle Herbert liked to go. He'd once been a serious player. In white shorts, furry bare chest and round tummy, unlit pipe still in his mouth, he ambled out to help us with our backhands, or to hit a few perfect balls himself, his feet rarely stirring from the service line. "Use your whole arm, Allie; don't let that wrist flop." Uncle Herb called me "Allie"—he was the first one who did. He made me feel like a valuable person.

Only the most extreme heat wave could get him into the river. Roaring like a walrus, gripping his pipe in his teeth, he launched himself into three or four splashing side strokes, and then emerged, sputtering and blowing, shaking himself like a dog as he headed back to his safe haven on the porch.

That long front porch was the most important part of the house. There was the cozy sitting end, and at the other end, behind the tan canvas curtain, two iron beds and an Army cot. That was where I slept, along with Eddie and our cousin Piers. When Auntie Georgie came to kiss us good night, we each had our turn to blow out the kerosene lamp that hung on the wall.

The swing—a ship captain's hammock—was in the center of the porch. Our grandfather Faddie, had brought it back long ago from some tropical isle. It was like a bed, though no one ever slept on it, no one since the ship's captain. It was made of creamy old canvas, with polished carved wood at each end where the ropes were attached. We pushed each other in it until our toes touched the rafters, arguing all the while whose turn it was. "Okay, kiddos—skedaddle," said Auntie Georgie when she happened to notice us. "Go on outside to play. It's a beautiful, sunny day. You'll turn into moles hanging around in here."

Auntie Georgie and Uncle Herbert slept in Gangie's old room, painted white, with its own fireplace. Another room had a fancy carved double bed, a bureau, and dressing table that matched, with red printed curtains at the windows. This was the guest room for grownups.

A narrow hall with dark brown walls of vertical tongue-and-groove boards snaked around to the black-and-white tiled bathroom where a rack over the sink held all our toothbrushes. There was also a claw-footed tub with a scary dark place beneath. We cousins never used the tub because swimming in the river was supposed to make us clean. I always preferred to wait for the bathroom than venture to the dank wooden outhouse, in spite of that dark place under the tub. "Hurry up, Allie," Uncle Archie would call when he thought I was taking too long. All the towels were different. Some had "University Club" written on them. I had a towel with my name on it in blue script.

No one ever sat in the dusky brown living room during the day. The long mantel shelf held an array of faded photos in narrow frames, pewter candlesticks dripped with wax, some dog biscuits in a square blue dish, a flurry of postcards, and other propped-up mementos. Slipper chairs and a soft saggy loveseat were covered in faded flowery chintz. Rough straw matting covered most of the floor. Shelves along the walls held my grandfather's sets of Dickens and Thackeray, George Borrow's accounts of life among the gypsies, Xenophon on the Persian expedition, and a sheaf of books about the American Civil War. His big oak desk by the window had a fat brass oil lamp with a tall glass chimney and a row of pigeon holes stuffed with old papers. The back of the battered leather Morris chair could be moved so you could sit up straight, or almost lie down if you wanted. It was still called, "Faddie's chair."

"Faddie always had a book: here, in town, on the train, wherever he went," Auntie Georgie said, shaking her head. "Imagine him reading Thucydides in the evening out on the sheep ranch in Montana."

Uncle Herbert chuckled. "I can imagine it."

In the bookcase Faddie's dim, brown volumes were covered by a colorful, ragged blanket of Auntie Georgie's books—H. G. Wells, Aldous Huxley, George Meredith, and the modern poets. Open books were often left upside down on tables around the room.

A ladder stood flat against the wall by the wood box and led to a small mysterious door that opened into an attic that stretched all the way to the end of the house. The attic floor had loose planks; you had to be brave to go up there.

One day Piers climbed up. "Hey, look at all the bats," he shouted.

When I followed him up the ladder I could see bats hanging from the rafters. They seemed to be sleeping. Piers poked at them with an old tennis racket. He was three years younger than I was, but he always had a way of scaring me with a spider or a frog down the back of my shirt. Now it was a drowsy bat. I screamed; he laughed.

I escaped through the little attic door and down the ladder. But not before I had seen the trunks and boxes and piles of grown-up books up there.

"What's in those old trunks?" I asked Auntie Georgie later.

"Oh, it's all Faddie's junk; his letters, his diary, stuff about his time out West. Maybe when you're a little older . . ."

But I couldn't wait. So she started to tell me about Faddie, but first she wanted to talk about his father.

"Your great-grandfather, Daniel Wesley Ingersoll, was about forty when he got a bad cough. He decided he was dying of consumption. That was what they used to call tuberculosis. He and his doctors had read some articles that said the pure air of Minnesota was the best medicine for people like him, people with lung disease. Our grandfather—old D.W., your ma and I call him—he wanted to check it out. So the next summer, 1855, he said goodbye to his big family in Irvington, New York, where they lived along the Hudson River. When he reached Minnesota it was warm and sunny. It seemed like paradise; he had no idea how cold and icy it would be in the winter.

"When he got back to Irvington, he told Harriet, his wife, 'We're moving.' She went to work and packed all their household stuff, their furniture, their clothes, everything. She and their housekeeper got the nine little children ready for the great migration. She arranged for their horses, their carriages, and their sleighs to be shipped to Minnesota, too. Faddie, your grandfather, was three years old."

"Keep telling," I said.

"D.W., Faddie's father, insisted that he had to travel on a stretcher. He just lay there, giving orders. He was a director of the Erie Railroad, so they all traveled on that train to Detroit, then took another train to Chicago. They continued west on the Rock Island Line to the big Mississippi River. Then they all got on a steamboat—the "War Eagle"—that took them 400 miles up the river to St. Paul.

"Before they had a chance to get settled, our poor, exhausted, little grandmother Harriet, the mother of all those children, got sick. She died. They put her thin body in a coffin and shipped it all the way home to Brooklyn, to be buried in Greenwood Cemetery next to the graves of her parents and her little first baby." Auntie Georgie paused, then said, "That's enough story for now; it's too sad. Go on, tell Beverly it's time for her to take you all swimming."

My mother and Auntie Georgie had never known their grandfather, Old D.W. I could tell they didn't think much of him, but they liked to tell stories about him.

One morning, Auntie Georgie was on the brick steps painting her toenails red. My mother sat next to her, looking at a small, framed oval photograph of D.W. They didn't seem to mind me listening. We had two kittens that summer; one purred in my lap, a peaceful small roar.

"I guess Minnesota agreed with D.W.," my mother said. "He got well pretty quickly after our poor grandmother died."

"Do you remember Faddie talking about his stone building downtown? D.W. had his first dry goods store on the ground floor; upstairs was the first public library; and on the top floor was Ingersoll Hall where they had concerts. It was all torn down before we came along."

Auntie Georgie with Genna and the dogs – 1935

"I remember Faddie telling us how D.W. used to boast about Ingersoll Hall: 'The easiest to sing in, in America; the best seats in the State; the best ventilated hall this side of Italy; and the best lighted in the World.'" The sisters laughed. "But the store kept going in another building."

"It still does," said Auntie Georgie.

D.W. flourished, too, I gathered. After his wife died he built a fine new house for his family, married their housekeeper, fathered six more children, and lived another thirty years, outlasting most of his first set of offspring. I have a photograph of D. W. with his new bride. Though his upper lip is clean-shaven, he sports a long white beard that looks fake, like a department store Santa Claus.

"I remember Faddie telling us that old D. W. bought a place in Tallapoosa, Georgia, where he used to go hunting. That was where he died."

"Yes," my mother said. "He died in 1894. He would have been eighty-two, a pretty good age back then."

I was thinking about D.W.'s new wife and the six more children. "So the six children were your new aunts and uncles? How come we never see them?"

Auntie Georgie sniffed. "Most of them are dead now. The second litter."

"But they all had children. Our cousins," my mother said. "Not that we ever see much of them."

"That's fine with me," said Auntie Georgie.

"But after all, Georgie, what could the man have done but marry his housekeeper?"

Later that day they were still talking about their grandfather.

"He owned a stable filled with horses," Auntie Georgie said. "And all those parcels of rich farmland in southern Minnesota."

"I still resent that old lawyer-cousin who conned Mother into trading all that valuable Ingersoll farmland for some worthless, run-down tenement in the wrong part of St. Paul. Don't tell me he didn't know what he was doing. Those cousins of ours ended up with far more of D. W.'s fortune than we ever did."

"Oh, yes, Jeannie, I know. And they still get a good income from those farms."

(But I'm now the lucky one who inherited their grandfather's hefty silver dinner forks, marked with the initials D.W.I. in flowing script.)

Another day my mother and Auntie Georgie were reading some typed pages written by their Uncle Fred Ingersoll, an uncle from the first litter, a year younger than my grandfather Faddie.

Apparently, when D.W.'s sons were growing up, he'd taught them how to shoot. There was no need to go far from home to bring down plovers by the dozen, "a very good eating bird," according to the pages that Uncle Fred had written. The sky was dark with passenger pigeons, and these too they shot. "All the wild pigeons and plover must have been shot in those days," Fred wrote, "for we do not see any of them now . . ." They saw none because there were none. Extinction had come in his lifetime.

Of his childhood in St. Paul, my same great-uncle wrote, "Indians were pretty troublesome in those days." To a small boy in about 1860, they must have seemed terrifying. At night, Fred and his brother Ed, my grandfather, sometimes peeked through the slats in the hastily fastened window blinds to see Indian braves gathered in front of their house, in war paint and feathers, brandishing tomahawks and dancing around a fire, while others beat on their tom-toms.

Whenever their father decided the war dance was veering out of control, he'd lead his large family to the cellar. From there, one by one, they'd escape through a tunnel to an exit concealed beneath a long grape arbor at the far corner of their property. There they were bundled into a carriage and driven at a fast pace to safe refuge in the Merchants' Hotel downtown until the danger passed.

These Dakota (or Sioux) Indians had been driven off their own lands. They'd been paid—in whiskey and a pitiful bit of cash—for thousands, then millions, of acres. These were the acres claimed by speculators and immigrant settlers who wished to farm or cut timber. The Dakotas and the Ojibwa had been herded onto reservations, inferior land where they were expected to stay and take up an alien existence as farmers. Chased out of St. Paul in 1862 by U.S. military might, a band of Dakotas traveled west along the Minnesota River. They burned houses and massacred as many as 350 settlers who were nothing more than interlopers to them.

"Farmers in the St. Croix River Valley were terrified for their lives, too, fearful every day that the Ojibwa would join the marauding and the slaughter," my mother said. "Faddie often told us that."

"But that was the beginning of the end for the Indians," Auntie Georgie shook her head. "Some of them were caught and imprisoned; many were hanged. The U.S. Army expelled the rest out of Minnesota, further and further west, far beyond the white invaders like us, so far that the Indians would never, ever, see their homeland again."

George Edmund Ingersoll, "Faddie" – 1917

– FOUR –

MY GRANDMOTHER WAS JUST "MOTHER" to their three children, but "Faddie"—well, that's what they called him. George Edmund Ingersoll, Ed to his friends.

My mother loved to tell stories about Faddie. "When he was young he went out west with his friend Charlie Spencer. They bought a ranch in 1877 near the town of Great Falls, Montana, and started out to be sheep ranchers."

"Tell about the snowstorms," I said.

"Whenever it began to snow," she said, "the sheep got edgy. They huddled together, baaing and blatting beneath the dark sky as the white flakes flew. Following each other, round and round in a roiling mass, those frenzied sheep would come closer and closer to the edge of a precipice." My mother's hands went around in circles. "Your grandfather and Mr. Spencer rushed to stand below in the whirling snow, ready to catch the sheep, as one by one they toppled over the edge."

"Keep telling."

"Okay, one last story for tonight. Then you have to go to bed. Well, Faddie gave up on the sheep before long, and went to work in Montana for James J. Hill. He staked out the route of the new Great Northern Railroad all the way to the Pacific. Faddie designed the tunnels, and he told the workmen where to lay the tracks." I knew about James J. Hill; his ugly stone mansion in St. Paul was the biggest house I'd ever seen.

Faddie wrote loving letters to Jeannie MacLaren from Montana. Hers in return were few, with tantalizing references to parties and sleigh rides. He went back to St. Paul as often as he could to pay court to Jeannie.

"Your Gangie had a glorious soprano voice," my mother said. "She went to Paris in the 1880s to study with Madame Somebody-or-other, a famous opera coach. Hers was a light-opera voice, a Puccini-Madame Butterfly voice. She was a serious student, not thinking of marrying anyone." My mother paused. "And then a French doctor took out her tonsils, using a fancy new French technique that burned her throat and ruined her voice. She came home, her opera career over before it began."

"I remember her singing the chickadee song," I said. But my mother made me go to bed.

I heard more another day.

"It took Faddie ten years to win your grandmother. They were married in 1895. Her satin wedding gown had come with her from Paris."

My grandmother needn't have worried that she'd have to fold her wings. She and Faddie did not settle down. They went first to Montana and the new frontier town of Helena, where he and his friend Archie Griffith had been hired to lay out streetcar lines. "'Griffith & Ingersoll, U. S. Deputy Mineral Surveyors:' that was their letterhead."

My grandmother had left her Paris trousseau behind in St. Paul when she went to live in the primitive back of beyond. A Paris trousseau! "The ladies of Helena were furious," my mother said, "when they learned that the new bride, with her tiny little waist, had brought only her second best dresses to Montana." Helena's social life was intense. Tea parties, ladies' lunches, theatricals, and gossip: life on the frontier. A scattering of dashing, fortune-hunting, English "remittance men" added spice to Helena society. My mother tried to explain the English law. "In England, only the oldest son inherits their family's home or money. He gets everything, and the younger brothers, nothing."

In 1900 my grandfather was engaged to operate a gold mine near Ashland, Oregon. There were three little Ingersolls by then—my mother, sister Georgiana, and baby brother Archie, each a year apart. Accompanied by Lydia, a fourteen-year-old Wisconsin farm girl who'd been hired as the children's nurse, the family traveled west by train from St. Paul with a wicker hamper stuffed with food. Their train would have run along the tracks across Montana that their father had laid out.

Ashland lies in the hills of southern Oregon, surrounded by forested wilderness. The Ingersolls settled into a high-gabled house on one of those hills, with long views in every direction. A rope hammock hung from a tree laden in summer with sweet white cherries that the children popped into their mouths. The garden was surrounded by rose bushes. One day, as my grandmother was going out, she told her children not to pick the yellow roses that were just coming into bloom.

Taking it as a challenge, my mother plucked off every single rose she could reach. I felt a frisson of perverse pleasure to hear that as punishment she'd had her hands spanked with a hairbrush.

With their horses, Biddy and Daisy, harnessed to the carriage, they'd all go off for picnics near the mineshaft or at some scenic spot in the countryside. Their father, who loved fishing, went off with friends now and then for a day or two. He'd come home with a mess of glistening brook trout or a great salmon from Upper Klamath Lake. The children stared as their father slid the fish out of their gunnysacks and laid them on the front porch to be cut into steaks and shared with friends.

Anna McVean MacLaren, my great-grandmother, was a widow. After the death of her younger son, she went to live with the family in Oregon. During her last years, she suffered from crippling and painful rheumatoid arthritis. My grandmother looked after her. Each day the old lady walked slowly up and down the garden, leaning on her daughter's or Lydia's arm, trying with exercise to defeat the arthritis. (It didn't help; before they left Oregon she was in a wheelchair.)

All too soon there turned out to be no more gold in the gold mine. Or else there was no more money to dig it out. After three years, Faddie had to make another fresh start, not quite as easy now, encumbered as he was with three children and his invalid mother-in-law.

The old lady was the only one not sad to leave Oregon. She no doubt knew Santa Barbara would be warmer, better for her. Better also because her elder son lived there with his family, and he was a physician.

On their first day in Santa Barbara, Nurse Lydia took the children out for a walk. The two little girls, Jeannie and Georgie, dressed always as twins, wore brass-buttoned blue coats and leghorn hats with streamers down the back. Their brother, Archie, in his sailor suit, sailed his boat in the basin around the municipal fountain. Georgie, the naughty one, jumped in fully dressed.

Before long they had to move again. Faddie had been hired to superintend the installation of electric carlines around Los Angeles and Pasadena. In Los Angeles they leased a house, rather than buying: Faddie still wasn't putting down roots.

My mother remembered hearing newsboys calling on the streets in 1901, when she was five: "Extra, Extra! President shot by an assassin." McKinley was dead.

In 1904 the family joined the crowd along the street to greet Theodore Roosevelt, who was campaigning for the presidency. "He took off his hat," my mother told me, "and bowed low to our grandmother, because she was such a distinguished-looking old lady, sitting there in her wheelchair."

Her grandmother may have looked fine, but she was the bane of my mother's childhood years. The family was so often on the move that the three children were not sent to school. The old grandmother, the grownups thought, was just the one to teach them to read and do their numbers. The children knew her only as short-tempered and strict. In constant pain from arthritis, it apparently hurt her even to be touched. "If one of us accidentally brushed against her," my mother said, "she would flinch and snarl at us, baring her teeth."

My mother dreaded lesson time. She and Georgie learned to read from *The Sun Bonnet Babies' Primer*. Both sisters came later to love reading and books with an ardent passion. Arithmetic was a different story. My mother was so terrified of her grandmother that she could never come up with the right answer, or indeed any answer. If she and her sister were unable to tell their grandmother how much two plus three equaled, the old lady would rap the children's knuckles with a ruler. As a result, my mother formed a block against arithmetic that lasted for life. After they were married, my father had to take care of anything to do with money or counting. I remember that she'd even turn to him to help her keep track of the number of stitches to pick up or cast off in the sock she was knitting.

The California interlude lasted no longer than the time in Montana or Oregon. Maybe St. Paul was to be home after all. Faddie, having lined up a job there, went on ahead to start work and find a house. The packing up, closing the Los Angeles house, reserving space in the sleeping car, and getting the family onto the train was left to my grandmother. Her mother's condition had deteriorated. Now the children's grandmother was confined to a stretcher; only the sleeping car's single "drawing room" would have enough space.

On the last day, my grandmother, her old mother, the three children, Nurse Lydia—and all the luggage—were taken in horse-drawn taxis to Union Depot. "They had to take a window out," my mother told me, "to get our grandmother's stretcher onto the train." Essential Lydia helped them board. "I'll be back in just a minute," their mother told the children. They saw her edge through the crowd on the platform, then hurry back into the station on some last minute errand. They waited.

"All aboard!" called the conductor. The train began to move. "Mama! Mama!" The children screamed. Lydia rang for the porter. The train picked up speed. The conductor came. The children cried harder.

"Mrs. Ingersoll has our tickets," Lydia told him, surely near tears herself. "She . . . she missed the train."

"You have no tickets?" The conductor looked stern. "I'm sorry, but you'll have to get off at the next stop." He looked at the weeping children, the invalid old lady, the piles of bags. "I'm sorry. That's the rule."

Lydia pleaded with him. "Oh, please, sir! We don't even have any money."

They were put off at South Pasadena, the old lady stiff as a board on her stretcher, carried out onto the platform. The train went off without them, trailing clouds of steam.

The motherless family spent all day in the South Pasadena station. "A kind women gave us three bananas," my mother said. "That was all we had to eat." Finally, late that afternoon, their mother arrived and rescued them. (Lydia had somehow managed to get word to her.) She'd thought she'd have to follow her family the next morning. Why she had missed the train was never clear. Perhaps it was an early instance of the charming vagueness I used to hear about. Charming? "She was easygoing," said my mother, who wasn't.

They all returned to Los Angeles until the whole venture could be rearranged. Finally they were on their way, chugging through the mountains and across the dusty desert. The children had been exposed to measles before their trip. As soon as they reached St. Paul, they all got sick, one after another, the old grandmother, too. "That Santa Fe Railroad conductor lost his job," my mother said. "He shouldn't have thrown us off." She loved to tell this story, but always ended it then by saying, "That's enough for now."

I hated to have her stop.

Sunbath: Piers, Eddie, and Genna – 1937

– F I V E –

AUNTIE GEORGIE DECIDED that we children should
lie out in the sun every morning with nothing on. The sun
would make us brown and strong, she said. It would keep us
from getting colds or worse in the winter, maybe even stave
off Eddie's alarming attacks of asthma. Auntie Georgie was
the monitor of our sunbaths. Eddie and Piers and I, and soon
our younger cousins, lay on scratchy, wool blankets on the
big lawn, while our "monitor" read aloud to us from Kipling.
The tropical atmosphere of *The Jungle Book* was enhanced
by the heat of the sun on our bare bodies, and the steamy air
we breathed through the sweet, warm fibers of old yellowed
Panama hats. We were carried away to remote outposts of
Empire, to Mowgli the Man-Cub brought up by wolves,
fearsome Shere Khan the tiger, and the foolish, chattering
Monkey-People. All this not by the shores of "the great, grey-
green, greasy Limpopo River, all set about with fever trees,"
but on the banks of our own placid, tea-colored St. Croix.

From beneath my hat I could see Auntie Georgie's sharp, narrow nose in profile. Her fingers that held the book were as slim as my mother's; her shoulders were dotted with freckles. She wore wide-legged pants of faded denim, her feet were bare except for dark crimson polish on her toenails. I was mortified whenever she stripped off her shirt, exposing her white bra and her freckled shoulders to the sun. What would Mr. Bruett think if he happened to come then to deliver ice? What if Harlan Gabrielson looked over while scything the meadow?

People heard about our bare-naked sunbaths. Once I turned my head under the straw hat, and saw Hendrie Grant standing at the edge of the lawn, with Skipper Hardy beside him, just watching. When I was nine I begged to be allowed to cover up just a little. Auntie Georgie was scornful: "Oh, Alan, don't be such a silly-billy." But after that I—and I alone—was allowed to keep my underpants on.

During "rest-time" after lunch or before bed, I read to myself. Auntie Georgie fed me books. She had no use for some of the "junk" I liked: the Oz books or Nancy Drew. "Try this," she said, handing me *The Man-Eaters of Tsavo*, a thrilling tale set in a far-off jungle. Jean Webster's saccharine *Daddy Longlegs* passed muster, probably because she'd once loved it. The story was told through a series of letters from a girl in an orphanage to her fatherly benefactor, the man who sent her candy, and the book ended with the surprising last page revelation of a romantic liaison between the two. I was only eight, and I was horrified. But Auntie Georgie was partial to romance in almost any form.

Sometimes I flopped down beside her, while she read me incomprehensible snatches of poetry until I was almost hypnotized by the sound of her voice. Auntie Georgie was infatuated with the English pre-Raphaelites, had me listen to Christina Rossetti's "Goblin Market" and a tragic ballad about Sohrab and Rustum. She read me snatches of Swinburne,

whose overheated rhythm and rhyme were captivating, even
if I didn't know what on earth he was talking about:

> *She waits for each and other,*
> *She waits for all men born;*
> *Forgets the earth her mother,*
> *The life of fruits and corn;*
> *And spring and seed and swallow*
> *Take wing for her and follow*
> *Where summer songs ring hollow*
> *And flowers are put to scorn.*

Auntie Georgie was also captivated by A.S. Neill's *Summerhill*,
an account of the progressive English boarding school he'd
founded. "It's a revelation, Jeannie," Auntie Georgie told
her. "You really should read it. The kids there are so free."

I thought Summerhill as she described it sounded scary—
no rules, no punishment, and often, apparently, no clothes.

"Oh, Georgie, he's a crackpot!" my mother said.

Except for our nude sunbaths, Auntie Georgie didn't
actually follow Neill's preachings; her regime was, in fact, far
more rigid than my mother's. Under Auntie Georgie's care we
lived by a panoply of rules, schedules, competitions. During
children's dinners at the round table on the back porch we
raced to see who could clean his plate first. Who could choke
down that watery summer squash? The bitter, chewy Swiss
chard? Or what Auntie Georgie called "D.V.O.T.," a creamy
hash of chipped beef? After I learned what those letters stood
for, I wouldn't touch it. The "D" stood for "dog;" the "V"
was too gross. The "O.T." stood for "on toast," which made
the image even more disgusting.

She tacked up a chart on the wall: stars for good
eating, prizes for the most stars. We had bed-making races,
swimming races, and contests to see who could spot the
most birds. We cheated when we could. We had our ways. A

chipping sparrow? I could hear "chips" all day long, so I put a check next to chipping sparrow every week. I really did see the yellow-bellied sapsucker. He lived in the silver poplar, where we had our tree house. That became one of our favorite taunts: "You moron! You yellow-bellied sapsucker!"

Whichever one of us had checked off the most birds in a week won a prize. As the oldest, I was often the winner: a flashlight once, a box of saltwater taffy another time. Each sausage-shaped piece of taffy was wrapped in wax paper, twirled at the ends. The cover of the box showed all the colors of the rainbow, but it turned out that each color tasted just like every other. Still, I tucked this prize under my pillow.

"You have to share," said Beverly, lingering over the "r," making her pronouncement especially harsh. Beverly was our babysitter that summer, a college student. Tall and strident in her red-checked, one-piece playsuit and rimless glasses, she seemed to me as old as any grownup.

When my mother had gone back to New Jersey, she and my father sent Auntie Georgie $100, presumably by prior agreement, "for kids, board, maid, etc." Georgie, in turn, sent reports to our parents on Eddie and me. "I think it is good for your kids not to have you but to have Beverly supervising them. Both A. & E. have responded by being always good." I "played well" with other children, she wrote, and "ate well" (very important). Eddie, at four, was "noisier, freer, easier" without his mother. He "laughs more, squabbles more, runs like the dickens." (I wonder how this made our mother feel.)

There was more: "He seems so pathetically to need building up this summer. . . ." She thought Eddie had rickets. He did not, but had always been afflicted with asthma. There were so many things he couldn't eat; no wonder he was skinny as a victim, with knobby knees and his little torso striped back and front with rib bones. His asthma was terrifying to our

Eddie with Beverly – 1936

parents. They followed every minutia of our pediatrician's advice, every proscription against dust, feathers, and a whole shelf's worth of foods. Eddie was seldom sick in the summer; our mother and Auntie Georgie were convinced that summer was the time to fuel him up against the onslaught of winter. Plenty of sunshine and as much of the right food as he would eat—it all would add up to health insurance for Eddie, and for me, too. This was serious. Auntie Georgie weighed us every other day at the River. My mother kept a running weekly tab of our gains (and our losses) in her red leather-bound, five-year diary.

"Dear Mommy and Daddy," I wrote the summer I was seven: "This is Camp Sunshine. Auntie Georgie christened it." I listed the camp rules; I loved the rules:

1. If you are asked to do an errand and you don't do it, you get another chance. You have to do 2 errands, if you don't do them you don't get candy after supper.
2. Nobody can go in the river without life belts on, strictly enforced.

3. And you cannot wear dresses or suits.
4. You have to have on sun suits when the sun is shining and it's warm enough.
5. You can't go near the River by yourself.
6. You cannot go near the road on the hill.
(Both 5 & 6 were to be strictly enforced.)
7. You can't go wandering off by yourself.
8. Never tell secrets in front of anyone.
9. Go to bed at 7:30, Get up at 7 o'clock.

"If you mind these rules you get a prize at the end of each week. I have two. Already I am the brownest one here."

There were six of us then, Piers, Eddie, and me, and two little girl cousins who didn't really count yet, and Mike Pettee, two years younger than I was, and not a cousin at all. His mother was Auntie Georgie's best friend, and his father was off being a Commander in the Navy. Sometimes Mrs. Pettee lived with us, too, and Little Mary, Mike's sister. Mrs. Pettee taught us card games and how to shuffle. She and Auntie Georgie sat in those long chairs on the lawn, looking at their red toenails and laughing. Auntie Georgie said things in French when she didn't want me to understand. Commander Pettee came now and then. His tan uniform was soft, with stars on the shoulders, but I didn't know how such a small, quiet man could be a Commander.

Auntie Georgie's Piers was a year younger than Mike. He had yellow curls all over his head, and a knack for tormenting me: "Why don't you swim across the river, then, if you think you're so good?" He pulled a wood tick off Ballou, Auntie Georgie's rust-colored chow, and put it on my arm. "Ha-ha, now you'll catch Rocky Mountain Spotted Fever."

Eddie followed Piers by almost a year. He had our father's pale blue eyes. His front teeth overshot his lower lip, as did mine. Every breath he took had a faint asthmatic wheeze. We all dressed in similar fashion, a pair of shorts, a red- or

blue-and-white striped T shirt—we called them "jerseys,"—
and bare feet. The summer I turned eight I always wore my
navy-blue Best & Co. shorts, with sailor buttons and white
stripes up the side. Sometimes Eddie still wore a special
sort of playsuit, probably patented, called a "Klad-E-Zee,"
that was held together by a belt attached to a convenient
drop seat. Our mother bought these and our striped Buster
Brown socks, from Mrs. Pellett, a mournful woman who
came to our door in New Jersey. "We have to help poor Mrs.
Pellett," my mother said. She lived near us with five children
whose hair was never brushed and whose father never came
home anymore.

Auntie Georgie dreamed up projects to get us occupied.
"Out of my hair!" she said, with mock ferocity. "It's a
beautiful sunny day. Go on out now; dogs, too." She sent us
off on "nature walks" with Beverly the sitter. We raced up
the hill, trying to scare Beverly by teetering on the edge of
the ravine, then dashing out past the mailbox to the Soo Line
tracks. We loved walking along the tracks. We had to slow
down, carefully stepping only on the ties, or, with our arms
spread for balance, walking the rails. I was always darting
off to pick the wildflowers that grew in profusion along the
tracks—white daisies with yellow eyes, pinky-lavender Joe-
Pye weed. When we heard the distant whoo-whoo-wa-whoo
of the steam whistle, we slithered down the bank, away from
the approaching train, hoping we wouldn't land in stinging
nettles at the bottom. Clickety-clack, louder and louder.
Sometimes the engineer gave a little toot if he saw us waving.
We had to wait until all those freight cars rattled past—Rock
Island, Northern Pacific, C B & Q, Great Northern, Soo
Line, C & O,—and finally the red caboose. We always got a
wave from the caboose.

One day Auntie Georgie invited Roddy from across the
River to come over and dissect a frog. "This will teach you
about frogs," she said. Roddy had just completed a semester

of high school biology. He came with his little kit of scalpels and probes. And a dead frog. We were impressed. "Ooh," we said, and "ick," until Auntie Georgie made us shut up.

Beverly watched Roddy, too. She looked different that day, with pink lips and a white ribbon bow tied to the barrette that held back her brown hair. She was wearing the red checked playsuit that she usually wore at the court on Sundays to watch the uncles and Roddy play tennis. We were all leaning in close to see what Roddy was doing with the frog. "This is its heart," he said, pointing with his little sharp knife. I happened to look up then at Beverly's long legs, the checkered playsuit, and her wistful face. Her eyes were not on the frog, but on the top of Roddy's head, his sun-streaked brown hair and the tanned back of his neck. I couldn't understand why she'd be dressed up, especially for Roddy and the frog, but still I hoped Piers wouldn't notice. It turned out all right, though, because after Roddy had wiped the frog's blood off his hands, and packed up his kit of scalpels, Piers was the one chosen to take the remains of the frog, wrapped in newspaper, and set them on fire in the stone incinerator where our paper trash was burned. "You kids, stay out of my way," he said. Stinky black smoke spiraled upwards.

Roddy walked back to his boat to row home. When I went inside to change for swimming, I heard Beverly sniff. I looked at her. "What are you staring at, Alan? I think I'm getting the sniffles." She put the hair bow back in the top drawer.

We were supposed to learn from live animals, too, from kittens, dogs, the noisy flock of chickens, and a bad-tempered goat named Heidi. We stood around watching one morning, while Lottie the Sealyham bore her puppies in the living room. As if it were a show just for us.

The vegetable garden was Auntie Georgie's province. She had Fred Rosengren spade it up for her, but she did the weeding, always it seemed on the hottest days, in her skirted bathing suit on hands and knees beneath a wide straw hat. Our job was to eat a bite or two of the mostly loathsome vegetables she produced. She didn't grow corn, the only vegetable everyone loved. The sweet corn for Sunday lunch came from Theresa's farm, beyond the railroad tracks.

I flourished under Auntie Georgie's charts and her orchestrated learning experiences, but my mother's way was different. She espoused her own version of benign neglect as far as Eddie and I were concerned. Boredom, she believed, was a spur to the imagination. "Go on out now, outdoors. Play," she'd say, and we would. One thing my mother claimed not to believe in was praise, at least for children, although now and then a compliment might accidentally slip out, and I knew she loved me. My mother was appalled at how Auntie Georgie fussed over Piers, her oldest, saying marvelous things about him while he was right there. Piers was destined for greatness, she claimed: "They told me he has the highest IQ they've ever seen . . ."

This infuriated my mother. She refused to boast about Eddie, her own tiger cub and not even a year younger than Piers. I heard her tell our father, "I can't stand the way she goes on about Piers; she's ruining him. He'll be so spoiled." As the oldest of the cousins, I was safe. I had no rival.

My cousins Genna and Janey were exactly the same age, almost twins, six years younger than I was. Genna was Piers's little sister; Janey belonged to Auntie Harriet and Uncle Bill Washburn. Everyone referred to them as "the little girls." They were always together. Janey was pink and white like her father, with his blue eyes and a crown of tight blonde ringlets. In the summer, she, like Eddie and me, spent most of her time under Auntie Georgie's purview. This left Auntie Harriet and Uncle Bill quite free from the boring aspects of being parents. They whirled around in snappy cars to parties and clubs with Archie and their dashing young unmarried friends. They were avid fly fishermen as was Uncle Archie, and often took off for a day or even a week of trout fishing. Auntie Georgie complained regularly about the frivolity of their lives.

The summer that the little girls, Genna and Janey, were four, they took to wearing their ballet-lesson tutus all day, every day. Even in swimming they wore those filmy tutus, long since gone limp and ragged, faded from pink to the non-color of dirty dishrags. Even I, staunch proponent of modesty, would have preferred to have them wear nothing. I was embarrassed to have Uncle Archie's stylish friends see them.

Sundays were special because the uncles didn't have to go to work; they were all there. Uncle Bill brought "dry ice" for the peach ice cream. The dry ice smoked and steamed as if it were hot.

"Don't touch it," he said. "It'll burn you." He packed it into the wooden churn, all around the metal container that held the peaches and sweet cream. Squatting on the grass, Uncle Bill let us turn the crank.

"Le'me try," said Piers.

When it was my turn, I could hardly move the crank.

"Okay, kiddos, let's let Della finish it." He carried the churn into the damp pantry by the kitchen door, where Florence and Della took turns cranking. Uncle Bill opened a bottle of Hamm's Beer, and ambled out to join the other aunts and uncles on the front porch. I stayed to watch the churning so I could lick the dasher.

Five cousins at the River – 1936

– S I X –

IT WAS ONE OF THOSE RARE, perfect June days when the sky is as blue as the Mexican glasses from which my cousins and I drank our milk.

Even at the River my mother was usually busy with all the things that always occupied her days: calling Roy Strand from the wall phone in the back hall with the grocery order, counting sheets in the linen closet, making lists. Auntie Georgie was not like that. She could pause whenever she felt like it, to plunk herself down and read or talk or tell a story. Anytime. But on this rare June day my mother was somehow able to allow herself not to be busy.

"Come on, Alan, let's go for a walk. We'll pick some wildflowers for the house. You'll need your sneakers. And tell Florence we want to borrow the kitchen scissors. Don't forget to say please."

We started off past the tennis court. "No, we don't want the dogs to follow. Piers! Put Baloo inside. And Lottie, too."

My mother and I climbed the steep hill, coming out by our big mailbox onto the Otisville road. It felt like a special outing, just my unusually carefree mother and me. "'Watch Out for the Cars.'" I read out loud the words on the weathered wooden sign at the railroad crossing. "Why does it say that?"

"It means watch out for the train. Trains have cars, too, you know."

There were white Xs by the crossing, but of course everyone could hear the whistle long before the train came down the track. Even down by the River we heard the whistle, a romantic sound especially at night, when I was snug in my cot on our sleeping porch.

"That used to be Charlie Ekdahl's store," my mother said as she pointed to a small, weathered building whose windows had been boarded up. "Now it looks ready to fall down, but we used to come here every day when we were not much older than you, to get the milk and the mail. Back in the early days."

My mother loved to talk about those early days. "The train used to stop here then. Charlie would wave a red flag to signal the engineer. I remember one day we went into Charlie's store when he wasn't there, and cleaned everything up. We put all the Ivory soap on one shelf, and the cans of kerosene together, and the baking powder and the bags of flour in one place . . . and Charlie was furious. . . ."

My mother and I started walking along the track. "I haven't done this for ages," she said. "We used to walk here all the time, and I'd bring flowers back for the house, a big bunch for the living room, and some to decorate the table whenever your Gangie was having one of her ladies' lunch parties."

"What if a train comes?"

"Don't worry, dear. We'll just go down the bank if a train comes along. If you put your ear down on the rail you can feel a train when it's far away."

I put my ear against the warm metal rail, but I felt nothing. My feet went from one tie to the next as we walked along, pausing when my mother stopped to cut flowers. She told me their names: "Bouncing Bet, Sow Thistle . . . and Turk's Cap Lily, that wonderful orange . . ." Each name made a picture: Butter and Eggs, Queen Anne's Lace. She cut a few of almost everything. "But not that lovely Blue Lobelia. There's not much of it; it's too precious. And not this dear little Bottle Gentian—look at it, here where the soil is quite moist."

"We shouldn't pick any blue flowers?"

"It does seem they're especially rare. But look at all the yellow ones we have, and white, and lavender . . . I think we've got a pretty good bunch. When I was about your age, Auntie Georgie and I went for a walk one day with our nurse Lydia, and she spanked us for holding our bouquets upside down."

I flipped our flowers up, even though my mother said it didn't make a bit of difference. "As long as we put them in water the minute we get home."

We heard the whistle of a train, far, far away.

My mother was still reminiscing as we walked down the hill toward home.

"When I was a little girl, Alan, we used to go to White Bear Lake in the summer. We took the electric train from St. Paul. All our friends went to White Bear too, so Auntie Georgie and Archie and I played with the same children we played with all winter."

"But why didn't you come here?" I asked. "This is the best place." We could hear the water rushing over the falls in the ravine.

"Oh, we didn't even know about the River, then. I was seven or eight, and I loved White Bear. We rented a different house every summer. Sometimes we were invited to go out for a sail, or to the Yacht Club. But Faddie never liked White Bear."

"Why didn't he?" I realized I was holding our flowers upside down, and quickly turned them up again.

"Oh, it was much too civilized for him. I've told you: He loved the West, Montana, the sheep ranch, laying out the railroads, the gold mine—and fishing. It was his friend Dr. Foster who discovered the St. Croix. The Fosters bought the old log house. And then Faddie bought this place in 1912, and got carpenters to build our house. There used to be a sawmill here, where they cut up the big logs of white pine and floated them down the River."

Suddenly I started running down the hill toward the house, my feet skidding on the loose stones, still clutching our flowers. I could see the River through the trees.

I listened whenever my mother and Auntie Georgie reminisced about those early days. They talked in the car sometimes, or while we were swimming, or in the canoe.

"We were the only families on the River then," sighed Auntie Georgie one morning. "Just the Fosters and us. Now there're so many people all around us. I loathe the summer colony atmosphere. Don't you feel that way, Jeannie? Our solitude is gone, the peace, the privacy. . . ." She shook her head.

They were sitting on the rocks in their towel robes, ready to go for a swim. I hugged myself, shivering in my cold blue bathing suit, still damp from yesterday. My mother didn't respond to Auntie Georgie's lament. It turned out she was recalling something else. "Remember the old steamboat, the Olive S.? It used to stop at Log House Landing. We took it a few times, down to Marine or up to Taylor's Falls. Once it got stuck on a sandbar—do you remember, Georgie?—and we all had to climb out so they could drag it off."

Another day I followed them up along our wooded stream. "Look at all the maidenhair fern," my mother said. "And those brilliant cardinal flowers! We never pick them."

I liked the snakegrass; you could take its telescoping segments apart, and then fit them back together.

"Jeannie, it's been years since we did this! Oh, Allie, wait till you see the waterfall."

"We used to call it 'Fairy Falls' . . ."

I heard the waterfall before we could see it. Then around the next bend, there it was, so high, way over our heads. Water cascaded in rivulets over steps in the rock. On one side of the falls the sandstone rose in a vertical wall, with tufts of fern sprouting from every mossy crevice.

"You can go right underneath the water, Allie; walk across the rocks . . ."

"But it's so cold . . ."

"Keep going . . . that's right; stand close underneath, behind the water . . . you'll be surprised . . ."

I stood with my back to the wall of rock, behind the icy cold water pelting down around me. My striped jersey wasn't even wet, nor was my hair. A secret place. Auntie Georgie and my mother knew. Now I knew it, too.

Just below the falls was a flat spot, green with moss, from which three giant white pines reached up to the sky. My arms went only halfway around them, the biggest trees I'd ever seen.

"The old lumbermen left these trees; they couldn't get them out," my mother said. "They cut down all the others."

The timber harvest in Minnesota had begun around 1850, and lasted more than half a century. With big two-man saws, lumberjacks cut down the old trees, some of them two-hundred feet tall with trunks four or more feet in diameter, leaving a wasteland of stumps and brush. They stripped off the branches, heaved the logs onto wagons or huge sledges. Teams of horses hauled the high-piled loads to the bank of the River. Water helped preserve the wood, and the River was their highway.

My mother and Auntie Georgie remembered the last log drives. "Enormous tree trunks covered the River all the way across, as far up and downstream as you could see, the water was solid with logs. We'd watch the lumberjacks with their great long pikes hopping over the logs, keeping them moving when they got jammed up."

"And they built wing dams, too, to keep the logs going, piles of rocks that angled out into the main channel . . . you can still see some of those old wing dams."

"Those log drives went on for days. Do you remember, Jeannie, how we used to picnic on top of the log boom?" The log booms, she told me, were stacks of logs that the lumbermen put up to keep the logs moving the right way.

"Sometimes we even walked onto the floating logs," my mother said. "We'd be slipping and shrieking . . . it was so dangerous."

"But Jeannie, none of us ever fell in."

The other side of the River
(photo by Andrew Summersby)

– S E V E N –

WE HAD A FANCY NEW DEVICE in our house in New Jersey: an enormous radio-phonograph, a Magnavox, in shiny walnut veneer. It anchored one end of the living room, where it became for my family the closest thing to a household shrine. No one else had a record player that was automatic. You could stack three or four 78s on its spindle and watch as the needle dropped gently onto the top disc. After playing that record the machine would click and groan and send it hurtling off into a felt-lined cavity. The needle would then descend again—all by itself!—onto the next disc. Despite what sounded like brutal treatment, it was only occasionally that one of those fragile black records would end up with a crescent-shaped bite taken out of it.

Our living room was dim and gloomy, shaded by a stand of lank rhododendrons outside the windows. One day, my mother and I were alone. We'd just come from our summer at the River, where the sun was always shining. She put on a little stack of records and turned up the volume. "This is my favorite," she said. "The Moldau. It reminds me of the River." She sighed.

The music began with a sound like trickling water, swirling and bubbling. As we listened the music grew louder, deeper, and wider. It did seem like our River, our far-away St. Croix, always rolling, flowing on by forever. I wished we were still there.

One morning the next summer Auntie Georgie and my mother lay back on the striped canvas sling chairs on the lawn. In their laps were ribbon-tied bundles of my grandmother's letters. I sat on the grass behind them, so they might forget I was there. One of Lottie the Sealyham's puppies wriggled in my arms. Listening to them was how I learned about life, about the past, the present, and how things really were. With each other, it seemed to me, the sisters spoke more honestly than with most other grownups. And my mother certainly talked more freely to Auntie Georgie than to me. I tried to take it all in, another form of nourishment.

"What on earth shall we do with all these?" my mother asked.

"Jeannie, we can't throw them away."

My mother untied one bunch. "These are from her time in Paris. Here she's telling Faddie about her voice lesson. Who's ever going to care about that? Really, Georgie."

"Read it."

"Oh, all right. 'Last night we heard Il Trovatore. The Opera House is very grand, with crystal, gilt, and crimson velvet. We were seated in the Dress Circle.' Now who else would ever be interested in that? And poor Faddie was out west in the wilderness, trying to figure out where the railroad should go."

I spoke up. "Read more."

My mother and Auntie Georgie both turned to look at me. "Oh Alan, do you really want to hear more about Gangie in Paris?" My mother seemed surprised.

She read one or two other letters. (I have never seen them since that day. Perhaps they're still sitting in Auntie Georgie's attic.)

Auntie Georgie was the only person I knew who had pierced ears; it simply wasn't done. But she'd inherited long dangles of gold and semi-precious stones from their grandmother and an old aunt. Of course Auntie Georgie wore the earrings, no question. They seemed almost as much a part of her as the bright brown eyes that looked right into you. She was different from my mother in so many ways. That was why I loved listening to their talk.

"Mother and Faddie used to have fits over you, Georgie, especially Faddie," my mother said. "Remember when you had those breeches you were so proud of?"

"I only wore them on canoe trips. He was just as upset when I wanted to go the U., instead of some sedate, ladylike place, Smith maybe, or Vassar."

"I guess he thought boarding school was enough."

They had shared three years at St. Mary's Hall, on the banks of the Delaware River in New Jersey, where they'd been introduced to girls who had grown up in the East, whose families had more money and different customs. My mother always said they were sent to St. Mary's because it was cheaper than a more stylish school like Miss Porter's, where their friend Alida went, or St. Tim's, where Cousin Carrie's parents sent her. An older cousin, Kitty MacLaren, had the even more expensive and exotic experience of finishing school in Florence.

Their friend Scott Fitzgerald had a similar reaction to the Catholic boarding school where he was sent. "Oh, Jeannie, Scott was like us. Do you remember that story of his, about the shame of being one of the poorest boys in a school of rich boys?"

"Well, it was a big expense for Faddie, to send us off," my mother said. "Most of our friends' families had old money, unlike us. But I never felt ashamed."

"Hmm. I did."

"I adored our trips on the train, going east, and then home for Christmas. We'd see all our friends—and then we changed trains in Chicago. We were special, the ones going further west . . ." My mother sounded wistful.

"I must have Scott's story somewhere, the one where he talks about seeing us on the train, 'the Ingersoll girls.' I loved those train trips . . ."

When his daughters went east to St. Mary's Hall, an Episcopal Church school, Faddie wrote Mrs. Fearnley, the principal: "My daughters are not to be subjected to any Episcopal proselytizing whatsoever." As a result, the sisters had to walk to the local Presbyterian Church, being let off only in case of rain. Still, there was enough Episopalianism at school to spill over onto the Ingersoll girls. Wearing white handkerchief veils, they stood and knelt with the other girls in the school's Gothic chapel, ardently singing with the choir. My mother loved it. "I felt like a nun," she said once.

Another morning my mother brought out her old black album, the one with photos of their boarding school days. I turned the black pages carefully, peering into my mother's and Auntie Georgie's world before they became mothers or aunts. On "Field Day" running girls flashed by the camera, in their white middy blouses, baggy black bloomers that covered their knees, and black stockings. I have the silver cup my mother won in the 1916 "Gymnastic Contest." With two handles, it looks like a trophy you might see on display at some golf or yacht club, except that hers is three inches high.

There's Georgie on the next album page, costumed for a play in a tight buttoned jacket, little pillbox cap tilted at a rakish angle, wide trousers, feet apart, hands on her hips. "What play was it, Auntie Georgie?" I held the book open for her.

"Look at us; how killing! Oh, that was Patience, Gilbert and Sullivan. I was always chosen to play a man's part. Unlike your mama, who got to wear nice frilly dresses."

And there is my mother, dressed not for a play, but for church, perhaps. She's wearing a stylish little hat, with a fur scarf around her neck and an enormous fur muff. "We all had those, then," she said.

"I wish you still had yours," I said. "You look like grown-up ladies. Did you always get dressed up like that?"

"Our skirts were down to our ankles."

My mother had been elected President of the school after her first month. She thrived at St. Mary's Hall, unlike Auntie Georgie. "Mr. Fearnley told us that one girl was so outstanding that he hoped we'd be wise enough to elect her," my mother recalled. "After I won, I never knew whether Mr. Fearnley meant me. Or not." She smiled, shaking her head.

Because they lived so far away, my mother and Georgie were often invited by friends for holidays or an occasional weekend. At Princeton for the Yale game (19-14, Yale) they saw their old St. Paul friend, Scott Fitzgerald, a Princeton freshman. Thanksgiving found the sisters being called for by a classmate's brother in his sporty auto. "I remember their beautiful old house, and being served breakfast in bed." My mother smiled.

"That happened in our house only if we were sick!" Auntie Georgie said.

"Before we sat down for the fancy Thanksgiving dinner— remember, Georgie?—we heard Bea ask her mother, 'Are we wearing hats today, Mummy?'" The sisters laughed. People in St. Paul never wore hats for dinner.

I piped up. "Did you have to?" They were still laughing, but they couldn't remember.

Another time they visited their rich relatives, the Richards, on Park Avenue in New York. Cousin Hattie Richards was their mother's first cousin. The sisters slept late, shopped for new dresses. "We had lunch at an Automat."

"Do you remember our weekend at Adelaide's, in their lovely old house? Here it is, Alan." She held out her album. I saw terraced lawns up to the front door, the walk lined with small trees pruned like lollipops in neat beds of iris and peonies.

These places they saw were like nothing in St. Paul or White Bear, even the grandest rail magnate's vast Victorian pile. The Ingersoll sisters were being introduced to older families and places, to old money. My mother lapped it up, while Georgie was already starting down her own path.

My mother did not consider attending the University. Nor did any of their St. Paul friends. Auntie Georgie was the only one.

Georgie's racy streak went beyond wearing "breeches" on canoe trips. When some young man brought a bottle of Gordon's Gin to one of their picnics, Georgie tried it. Prohibition—the Volstead Act, named after a Minnesota congressman—enhanced the allure of cocktails for Georgie and her new friends.

She started smoking cigarettes. In her diary she wrote about an evening of dancing at the St. Paul Hotel. Archie and Georgie's friend Honor dared Georgie to light up. "Honor giggled hysterically but I kept brazenly on amid the stares until the manager told Ted that ladies were 'not permitted to smoke here.'" She loved the image of herself as "brazen." Faddie blew up at her afterward for smoking—with men.

Georgie bobbed her glorious auburn hair, and took on the attributes of a jazz-age flapper. She dreamed of becoming a writer, and working in publishing or on a newspaper. She yearned to travel "abroad," which meant Europe, and struggled with Faddie before he'd allow her to go. She and her friend Mary K. sailed to Cherbourg in 1923 on the RMS Majestic, dancing, sipping bouillon in their deck chairs, and Benedictine with the captain.

In Paris, a Jewish road builder in Africa whom they'd met on the ship, took them to dinner at the Ritz, dancing in Montmartre, the Folies Bergère, "with champagne at each place. To his rooms at the Ritz for a highball. Taxi home with him at 6 A.M! He kissed me."

After Paris, they went by train to Vienna, Budapest, and finally Bucharest, where they spent a month with old St. Paul friends, Honor and Don Bigelow. Don was with the Foreign Service. Georgie and Mary K. had a high time at concerts and balls, dancing with consular officials and dashing naval officers. Georgie described a party at one legation: "liquor, no lights, necking in every corner, danced till 4:30."

During their travels, they occasionally met up with dependable St. Paul stalwarts, old school friends and their mothers, a virtuous balance. Auntie Georgie was brought to heel in Florence by her expatriate Aunt Anna Ingersoll, Faddie's older sister, then 76. Aunt Anna told Georgie her skirts were "too short, colors bad, hat wrong," and that she should "try to appear the well-bred lady I was" and avoid bright colors in favor of black—"or they'll know you're American."

After she was back home, Georgie typed up her travel memoirs, omitting the racier bits. Six pieces appeared in the St. Paul paper.

I remember another day when my mother and Auntie Georgie—in their flowered bathing suits—were talking on the lawn, in the sun. They weren't paying any attention to me.

"Faddie would have hated it, Georgie, when you went to work at the paper."

"I know, Jeannie, I know. He would have been furious. A daughter of his in that grubby newspaper world—so unladylike. Oh dear, I guess it's lucky he was dead by then."

"Well, maybe you wouldn't have taken that job while he was still alive. Or perhaps you would; you always pretty much did what you wanted."

"You think I'm just selfish, Jeannie. But St. Paul has always been so stuffy, so smug, so close-minded. I'm sure people were appalled when Herb and I got married. Faddie would have really have had a fit about that, me marrying a Jewish newspaperman from a small town in a southern part of the state . . ."

"That's all water over the dam, Georgie. Herb is just so wise and wonderful. You know we all love him, we always have. And Mother adored him, too. You know that."

"Aunt Katharine probably thought I was disgracing the family."

"Stop, Georgie, stop it. All that's over."

Uncle Archie with his catch – 1936

– E I G H T –

THE LONG BACK PORCH at the Big House was more than just our dining room. There was that barrel-shaped straw hamper stuffed with tennis racquets, a high shelf for the cans of tennis balls and the wooden ice-cream maker. Every ledge and shelf was cluttered with reels, bass lures, tackle boxes, and all the old hats we wore for our sunbaths: straw farmers' hats, cowboy hats, topees, and a sombrero. Raincoats and dark oilskins dangled from hooks. Fishing rods hung horizontally along one wall. Landing nets and more rods leaned into a corner.

One wall was reserved for recording our heights. Each summer we cousins took turns being measured. With our backs to the wall, Auntie Georgie would place a book on our heads—"Stand up straight, Piers"—and make a mark with a pencil. If that was a competition, I, the oldest, always won.

"Yay! Uncle Archie's here." We cheered when we heard the toot of his car horn, and rushed out to see him. Sometimes on the weekends he came out with his friend Smiley Randall, or Ralph Clark, and one or two willowy ladies. Usually they brought a big white box of fancy Maude Borup chocolates. The candy was for us children. We always checked first thing to see if there were three layers or only the ordinary two. With Uncle Ralph, as we called him, we could count on three. We were each allowed one piece after lunch, and one after supper—but only if we cleaned our plates, which often entailed slipping the horrid beets or Swiss chard into our paper napkins.

It was Uncle Archie who taught all of us to swim. He stood in the water with us, up to our chests beside the floating dock, among schools of darting minnows. Each in turn, starting with me, the oldest, he aimed us toward a great black boulder on the shore. "You can do it," he'd say, as with clenched teeth we dog-paddled madly toward that rock.

Archie's own early exposure to swimming was rather different. The Ingersoll family had still been spending summers within the formal confines around White Bear Lake, before they had their own more rustic place on the River. Faddie, dressed in a summer suit, necktie, and straw boater, tied a rope around his children's middles, and walked with it up and down the pier while Jeannie, Georgie, and Archie kicked and splashed in the water below.

By the time he was twelve Uncle Archie was a strong swimmer. My mother used to tell me about their first Fourth of July at the River, 1912. The Ingersolls had just moved into the new house in Otisville and were ready to set off firecrackers, when Georgie and Archie rescued their two maids from drowning. Amanda and Marcella, young farm girls, giggling and carefree, with no idea how to swim, decided to try the water. The River drops off steeply in front of the house. Right away the girls found themselves sucked into the current, and sinking beneath the amber water. When he heard their screams, Archie dove in fully dressed. One of the girls weighed 160 pounds, according to an account in the St. Paul paper, and Archie, who was only twelve, yelled to Georgie for help. She came running down, plunged in, and with Archie grabbed the shrieking girls by their long hair. They pulled them—gasping and coughing—to safety on the rocky shore. Faddie had taught them how to save "drowning persons," according to the newspaper. And this was the family's first day there.

When it was time for Eddie, the cousins, and me to learn our strokes, Uncle Archie guided us to coordinate the flutter kick with our arms and our breathing, until we mastered the crawl, then the back-stroke and the side-stroke. Boasting to my far-off parents, I wrote, "I can really dive off the dock where it is over my head." A major rite of passage was the swim across the River—four or five-hundred yards?—accompanied by Uncle Archie in a rowboat, cheering us on. It seemed to take forever to gain that far shore. Once or twice a summer, after we were swimming like fish, Eddie or I ran onto the dock and dove in, realizing too late that our metal-rimmed glasses, his or mine, were now at the bottom of the River, drifting away with the current. "There goes another fifteen dollars," our mother said.

Uncle Archie sometimes engaged in dangerous pursuits involving us. "Arch . . . for heaven's sake!" my mother and Auntie Georgie cried when he rigged a rope to a tree and started us jumping off the rope into the River.

He had always been a risk-taker, always skirting the cusp of disaster. At fifteen he tooled around on his motorcycle and tobogganed down the steepest hills. When he was seventeen he confided in his sisters, making them promise not to tell: "Arch told us of two unknown trips on freights to Duluth last summer!" Duluth is 150 miles from St. Paul.

He usually drove too fast. Barefoot, wearing only shorts, he used to race his old green Ford along dusty back roads, trying to beat the afternoon freight from the railroad trestle to the next grade crossing. One day he took a bunch of us kids down an empty gravel road between wide fields of corn. The canvas top was down; my hair streamed straight back. "Ninety-six!" shouted Uncle Archie.

We just laughed at our friend Hendrie when he stammered, "M-m-my f-father never drives this f-fast."

"Sissy," Piers said.

One hot day Uncle Archie stopped the car beside an isolated railroad water tower. He led Eddie and Piers, then seven and eight, up the ladder and into the dark tank for a brief swim. I didn't want to climb up there. I stayed on the ground, in the bright sun, listening to the grasshopper hum. "Sissy," said Piers when they were down. But I didn't follow Uncle Archie onto the Soo Line Bridge either. (This was a swing bridge, ready in theory to open up for some tall-masted boat to pass through. That never happened.) But Piers and Eddie walked carefully after Archie, stepping gingerly from one tie to the next, looking down at the water far below. Suddenly Uncle Archie dove, plunging thirty feet into the roiling river current. When I saw him go I couldn't breathe. I stood there on the bank, clinging to a pine tree. The boys, alone now on the trestle, looked thin and small. They turned and walked slowly back across the ties, holding tight to the frail guy wire that served them as a railing. Eddie looked white; I thought he'd be sick any minute. We three watched in silence as Uncle Archie popped up to the surface with a triumphant "Whoo-hoo!" He swam in his confident crawl back to the riverbank, scrambling up on hands and knees until he reached us at the top.

"OK, kiddos," he said, "let's get out of here before the afternoon freight comes through." We four walked back along the track to the green Ford. Uncle Archie had all the timetables in his head, it seemed. I remember him looking at his gold Bulova as he fastened it around his wrist: "The Empire Builder is just pulling into Spokane." He knew exactly when the train to Duluth would be leaving Lake Elmo, when it would reach the flag stop at Copas, and when it would reach the bridge over the River. Just as he started the Ford, we heard the whistle and the long train of cars clattering across the bridge.

When Eddie and Piers were a little older, Uncle Archie sometimes took them off for three or four days of fly-fishing in northern Minnesota or Wisconsin. They fished the Namekagon, a little river that fed our St. Croix. Sometimes they canoed down from Danbury, camping overnight. Always they came home with a mess of fish, forty trout one time. That night we had a fish fry outdoors.

Fishing had been Archie's chief bond with his father. Fly-fishing had always been Faddie's passion. He'd taught Archie with care and patience, until Uncle Archie—with a quick flick of his wrist—could drop the fly precisely into the shadow beside the rock where a trout or small-mouth bass lurked. Little sister Harriet also learned the art of fly-fishing. She remembered Archie and Faddie, unwashed and unshaven, coming home from long fishing weekends, Faddie for once proud of his son, both pleased with each other, laughing and full of stories.

I have photos of Uncle Archie, cigarette dangling from the corner of his mouth, holding up a string of trout, or a salmon from Oregon's Rogue River. I used to linger by a lampshade in the Big House that was festooned with flies Uncle Archie had tied. He kept them there, ready to be taken out and flicked over a wary brown trout or a rainbow.

My mother was proud of her skill at paddling the old green Mueller canoe, holding it steady, close to a little pool on the down-stream side of a fallen maple tree, while Faddie or Archie cast out a tiny fly from the bow seat. Uncle Archie wrote a heartbroken letter to his mother after Faddie died, remembering their fishing trips together, trips that would never happen again.

We cousins wished Uncle Archie could be at the River every day, but he had to go in town for work. After two years of Beverly, our first college-girl babysitter, we had Dorothea. She was not at all like Beverly, quieter, and, I realize now, less confident. Piers and I were quartered in the Guest House that year, along with Dorothea. He and I slept under old striped blankets on twin beds on the porch, while she had the other room, the only real room in that cottage. We brushed our teeth at a tiny sink that had a black iron hand pump. A path through the woods and a plank laid over a marshy patch thick with ferns and pale yellow touch-me-not led to our outhouse, with its fresh sweet smell of new pine boards.

Dorothea's room had whitewashed walls, a Franklin stove, built, I believed, by Ben Franklin himself, and a writing table. One day Piers and I raced up from swimming to change, arriving breathless at the Guest House ahead of Dorothea. On the desk was a half-finished letter that caught my eye. I was a good reader, a skill still beyond Piers, and I began reading the letter aloud. I suppose it was to Dorothea's family back on the farm. Her words, or a few of them, are still engraved on my brain: "Even the swimming is no fun here, because I have to watch these little spoiled brats. I can't wait to get home . . ."

Brats? Us? How could she not like us, not even like the swimming? I looked up. There at the door in her shiny blue bathing suit stood Dorothea. I was standing by the desk with her letter in my hand. I put it down.

"Do you think it's nice to read other people's letters?"

Silence. I had no answer. We got dressed, with clean striped jerseys for supper. The next day Dorothea was gone.

My mother said she wanted to talk to me. I hung my head, waiting to be scolded.

"Tell me what Dorothea said in her letter. Tell me what you remember, Alan." My mother wanted to know. I would rather have had her punish me.

I heard her later telling Auntie Georgie about the letter. "Silly girl," Auntie Georgie said. At first I thought she meant me, but from the way they talked I realized it was Dorothea.

In our orange lifebelts for my birthday picnic on the Auk – 1936

My birthday, which happened in August, was always the occasion of a grand celebration. All the Otisville children came. If I was lucky Uncle Archie was there, too. We put on our best and cleanest clothes—I even wore a dress. We played games on the lawn: Red Light-Green Light, Statues, Giant Steps, the games everyone knew. "Still Pond, No More Moving," called the one who was "It."

The birthday parties ended with a wiener roast. Uncle Archie made a fire between the rocks at the bottom of the lawn. "Watch out," he commanded. "Stand back, or you'll get burnt." We each grabbed a pointed stick and speared a wiener to scorch over the fire. As it grew dark we threaded marshmallows onto our sticks, and held them over the glowing coals.

For my ninth birthday, Auntie Georgie hired the Auk, a boxy little craft powered by an outboard and able to hold us all on benches inside, on the open front deck, or up on the flat roof. We chugged up to the big sandbar where we swam and had peanut-butter sandwiches, orange pop, and watermelon.

My mother's birthday was the day after mine. We both opened presents sent from New Jersey. My father had had Miss Benn, his secretary, pick them out: fancy embroidered handkerchiefs for nine-year-old me, and slithery rayon pajamas. I kept these things safe and new in my bureau drawer.

"I still remember what I got for one birthday," my mother said. "I was older than you: a photo album, a box of candy, a Roman sash, a tennis racquet." She blew out slowly.

When all the aunts and uncles were there, we had family picnics up the River. My cousins and I still had to buckle on those loathsome orange life jackets before we squeezed into the boats. The outboard motors caused endless trouble. It always required many cranks of the rope to get them started, while we drifted rapidly downstream.

"Choke! Choke!" shouted Uncle Bill from the bow.

"It must be the magneto," said Uncle Archie, out of breath from pulling the starter rope. "I think we're flooded."

When we finally got underway, we putted upriver to the motor's deafening roar of sound, following the white Xs on the trees that marked the channel. Summers in the 1930s were dry and hot; the River was too shallow for our clumsy, heavy-laden motorboats. When the propeller hit bottom, the motor bellowed in pain. Then silence, as we began to drift down, one good reason why we always headed upstream to picnic.

"Sheared a pin, dammit. Do we have a spare?" demanded Uncle Bill.

"Look in that little drawer," called Auntie Georgie.

I was allowed to sit up on the bow, my bare toes trailing through the water.

"Watch for deadheads, Allie," said Uncle Herb. Deadheads were partially sunken logs, relics of the old logging drives, and a hazard to navigation. I was proud to have a job.

It was still hot later that day when we cousins were having supper on the back porch. Our shoulders and faces were watermelon-pink. "Ow," said Piers when his mother laid her cool fingers on his neck. She smoothed creamy Noxzema over our burning skins, and we inhaled its soothing, spicy smell. In bed that night the sheets felt hot, and it was hard to sleep.

During the July heat wave in 1936, the thermometer hovered around 100 degrees, climbed to 102, and one day reached 105. There'd been no rain for weeks. The River had become so shallow that I could stand up even out in the middle. Mr. Edquist and another farmer walked their cows from the bare, brown pastures down to the water. It seemed strange to see those big, tan Jersey cows amble all the way across the River to find green grass and fresh leaves on the watery islands.

The grownups were afraid of fire in the woods. Almost everyone smoked, of course, so a match or a cigarette flicked out of a car window was hazardous, even though Uncle Archie sometimes did that. When we went anywhere in the car we saw the road lined on both sides with an ugly blackened strip from the little fires that were supposed to prevent a forest fire. When you came to where the burning was, you saw those men in striped prison clothes, their faces black from smoke, slowly moving their rakes to keep the flames from spreading.

Another grown-up worry that frightened me was a bad sickness, the "White Pine Blister Rust." Bad for the pines, anyhow. White pines were the most common trees in our part of Minnesota. Crews of men came through our woods putting string and little stakes around the patches of wild currant bushes that, according to Uncle Herb, were the "host plants" that caused the dreadful Blister Rust to spread. We walked carefully around these marked patches. But the wild currants never went away, and I worried that the stakes and the string wouldn't stop that disease.

Uncle Herbert told us one day that a man named Henry Otis had died. "He was ninety-three, one of the last of the old lumberjacks. He was wounded in the Civil War."

"He spent every summer in his tar-paper cabin on the island over there . . ." my mother said as she pointed across the way. "We used to paddle over to see him, back in the early days. We all thought he was an old, old man then."

Otisville got its name from Henry Otis's father, but it was another man who'd planned to build an actual town along the River. Uncle Herbert pulled open one of the little drawers in the desk that had once been Faddie's, and took out a folded-up paper.

"This is it, kiddo, the plan for Otisville." I was the only one there, except for my mother. We cleared everything off the desk so Uncle Herb could spread out the plan. The paper was dry and stiff; the ink lines on it were faint. "Careful, careful," he said.

"Charlie Ekdahl owned all this land then." My mother spread her arms wide. "The Ekdahls came here all the way from Sweden, almost a hundred years ago."

By this time Uncle Herbert knew as much about the River as she did. "It was around 1900 when Charlie hired a surveyor to plan the town. You can see where all the streets were supposed to go."

"And the buildings, too," my mother said. "Can you see,

Alan? Here's the church, the post office, shops, all the house lots. And a hotel, even; can you imagine, Herb?"

"The main street, Washington Avenue, would have gone along the brow of the hill, just where the road actually is. And look, here's Water Street—running right along the edge of the River." He pointed.

"But it was only a 'paper town,'" my mother said. "And it never happened, thank goodness."

"And it never will," said Uncle Herb. "Your grandfather, Allie, was the only one who wanted to buy any of Charlie Ekdahl's land."

"I bet Charlie was happy when Faddie came along. He was the man who kept the store on top of the hill, back in the early days," my mother said. But I knew all about the store where they used to get milk and stuff. And their mail.

"After Gangie died," Uncle Herbert said, "We got Benno to have Water Street 'vacated.'" Benno Wolff was the family lawyer. "Of course, it was only a paper street, but someone could have caused trouble. And it ran right across our lawn." I felt comforted when the grownups talked about Benno. They always seemed to be worrying about money or property, and Benno, I thought, was the one who would come to our rescue.

Like most of Faddie's ventures, his new property at Otisville came with a small flaw. The story goes that only later did he discover that the land he'd bought from cagey old Charlie Ekdahl was in fact a fat doughnut surrounding a tiny hilltop parcel, three-quarters of an acre, that a sharp-nosed lawyer named Morgan had purchased for five-hundred dollars from Charlie. Faddie foolishly signed a piece of paper—legal jargon and fine print—granting Mr. Morgan and his heirs a ninety-nine year easement across his land, right down to the River's edge, with the right to keep a boat there.

My mother complained regularly. "Faddie was so gullible."

Auntie Georgie in knickers – 1924

– N I N E –

"AS YOU ARE PROBABLY TIRED OF HEARING each year," wrote Auntie Georgie in June to my mother, who surely was tired of it, "I think your kids look badly. Why are they so white and thin? Does their life at home put a great load on them or what? But now they are already sore about the shoulders from sun . . ." a good thing in Auntie Georgie's opinion.

Despite the supposed health benefits of Camp Sunshine, Eddie's frightening asthma attacks grew worse. He struggled to breathe, mouth half open in his little narrow face. A steamer in his room made the air damp, heavy, and sweet, the smell of asthma. The only possible solution, said his doctor in New Jersey, was to take him to Arizona for the winter. I can imagine our father reluctantly saying, "Well, Jeannie, I guess we'll have to do it." Eddie had another bad bout of asthma in September. That clinched it.

I was nine then, and Eddie was five. Of course I had to go to Arizona then as well. But not Daddy; he had to stay at his job. We kissed him good-bye as we set off on a really long train trip, four days and four nights to Tucson and a little rented house.

My mother knew a thing or two about using fierce tactics to defeat a hostile illness. I was all ears whenever she and Auntie Georgie began talking and laughing about the famous long-ago year when my mother was faced with TB. They made it sound so romantic and exciting that I wished I'd been there, too.

My mother's trouble had cropped up suddenly when she and Georgie were in their twenties, not yet married. "No, it wasn't TB," she always said. "I just had a spot on my lung."

Her treatment was drastic. She had to spend a whole year in an unheated house at the River, doing nothing but rest, and checking her temperature and pulse each day. Doctor's orders. Fresh air—cold air—was then the recommended treatment for TB. Auntie Georgie stayed with her, looked after her, and shouldered the endless task of keeping them from freezing to death. They might have: Minnesota winters are notoriously long, snowy, and cold.

"We couldn't stay in our own River house," they told me, "with our long steep driveway and all the snow." My mother, Georgie, and their little dog Jude the Obscure lived in the neighboring Clapp Cottage from September 1923 until the following August.

Tuberculosis was still a fearsome disease, striking with particular malevolence at young women, Henry James heiresses among them. Two of Faddie's sisters had succumbed to consumption, as they called it, each at the age of twenty-two. Heredity was thought to play a role.

Jeannie and Georgie weren't left entirely alone. "Your father used to come out every week, no matter how snowy or muddy," Auntie Georgie told me. "He was so proud of that car, his first one, with its electric starter, and windows that rolled up and down . . ." She and my mother laughed. "Archie came out, too, and Faddie with Mother when the weather was good, bringing clean laundry, and more blankets."

I have a snapshot from the Clapp Cottage year. There is Auntie Georgie sitting on the doorstep, cross-legged in corduroy knickers and sensible shoes. It's almost spring, no snow. She wears a striped cardigan over a blouse with a ruffled collar. Tendrils of hair blow around her face. She looks up with an impish grin, brown eyes sparkling. Across her lap, enfolded by her arms, are two dogs: Jude—a black-and-white mutt, his head tilted at a rakish angle—and a sedate-looking brown terrier whose name I don't know. Auntie Georgie was always flanked by dogs.

The dogs were part of their lives that winter. Every morning the water in their dishes was frozen solid. Georgie got the fires going in the stove and the fireplace, while my mother stayed snug under the green Hudson Bay blankets with their trademark black stripes. Faddie's old buffalo robe seemed to give off extra heat of its own. Soon they heard the farmer's boots squeaking across the snow, and the scrape of his shovel. He stomped in with another load of firewood.

Georgie melted snow on the stove for brushing their teeth and making tea. After breakfast she pulled on her galoshes, coat, fur hat, mittens and scarf, and set off for Charlie's store.

They read a lot that winter, often aloud. I see them beside the fire, each with an oil lamp at her shoulder, Georgie curled up in the Morris chair with Huxley's *Antic Hay*, my mother on the sofa, brown hair pinned back, wire-rimmed glasses sliding down her narrow nose, and the newest volume by Edna St. Vincent Millay.

"We read *The Magic Mountain* that winter. Do you remember?" Auntie Georgie asked. "Maybe we wished we were there, in that hothouse of a sanatorium." Both sisters laughed.

"Oh, we had the time of our lives that year," my mother said. "The dogs, too."

Our year in Arizona was not much like the sisters' winter in the Clapp Cottage. My mother knew a few people in Tucson—others from St. Paul with health problems. Her constant companion was Mrs. Power, who'd rented a house near ours for her two asthmatic sons and herself. Eddie and I heard too much of Mrs. Power's whiny voice, always complaining. Everyone we met that winter was there because of a family member with asthma.

The walls of our house were tan stucco, inside as well as out. Everything in it was brown, including the prickly velour of the overstuffed sofa and armchair that scratched the back of my legs. The massive Philco radio on twirly legs broadcast scary news reports about all the people who'd been shot on a nearby mountain. "I used to go up there with one of them fellas," said Della who came to cook for us. I worried about gas fumes from the space heater, after warnings from our landlord—whose name was Mr. Fume, an unpleasant word I'd never heard before.

East Fourth Street, where we lived, was wide, unpaved, and ended just past our house. Beyond lay trackless, barren desert. We'd been there about a month when a new house across the street blew up in the middle of the night. I slept through the explosion, but we went the next day to look into the hole where the house had been. "That was the gas," said Della.

"A little girl used to live there," I said.

"Yeah, well . . ."

Eddie's sunbath on the army cot behind our Tucson house – 1937

Eddie and I made friends on East Fourth Street. Ginny Lent lived next door; her father had asthma. Ginny caught ringworm. She had to have her pigtails cut off and her head shaved. After that she wore a red kerchief. I'd never heard of ringworm.

Eddie played with Walter Joe, who lived at the end of our block. They played in an old milk truck with no wheels that sat behind Walter Joe's house. The truck and other expired bits of equipment once used by his father were scattered around their small patch of desert.

My mother set up a canvas army cot behind the house where Eddie and I were to lie in the sun. Of course. This was what had brought us all the way to Arizona. Each day she noted in her diary when she "gave" us our sunbaths, making it sound like medicine. My brother and I lay head to toe on the cot, toasting one side and then the other. Eddie still wheezed occasionally, perhaps from the constant dry, dust-laden wind.

My mother walked with me on my first day at Sam Houston School. I had to be interviewed by the principal. "Fourth grade?" she asked. "Let me hear the nine-times table." No smile. I failed; we hadn't gotten to the nine-times in New Jersey. This was not New Jersey.

"4-B," said the principal, and I knew this was way below 4-A. She marched me to an enormous classroom, perhaps forty children. The teacher sat me at a desk in the back row. I couldn't decipher the chalk hieroglyphics on the blackboard. No one had told me I was nearsighted.

When the recess bell rang I walked with my seatmate Eula Mae across the hot, bright, dusty playground to a spot of shade beneath the lone pepper tree. When we reached the pepper tree the bell rang, and we walked back.

I didn't last long at Sam Houston. Over the telephone from New Jersey, my father said yes, they could afford to send me to little, rarefied Old Pueblo School where Eddie went to kindergarten.

I loved Old Pueblo. Mrs. LePine, the grandmotherly headmistress, took me to the thatch-roofed, open ramada that was to be my classroom. Third, fourth, and fifth grades— eight children—shared that ramada with our teacher, Miss Meigs. The only solid wall held the blackboard; the space was so small that I could read the board perfectly.

The 3 Rs were of minor concern at Old Pueblo. We learned to make baskets. At lunch in the pink adobe house where the boarders lived, we drank milk from blue Mexican glasses. My new friend was Mabel Ringling, whose father ran a circus. Every afternoon we all went riding at Mrs. Walker's stable. I rode a Shetland pinto pony named Dolly, who was so small that my feet almost touched ground when we cantered down the dry riverbed. Mabel rode bareback and did tricks on her big bay mare.

At home in our little house I sat at the table and designed ranches with crayons and paper: bunk house here, tack room there, and the corral. I tried to draw horses, but they never came out right. Their legs are extremely difficult.

On weekends my mother, Eddie, and I often rode at Los Cerros, a dude ranch where divorcees outnumbered the horses. Gerald Elliott, the owner of Los Cerros, was a

Alan rides bareback at Mrs. Walker's stables in Arizona – 1937

dashing early prototype of the nineteen-sixties Marlboro Man. My mother surely alarmed my father when she wrote him about some of Mr. Elliott's guests, including "shy Mrs. Dillon" who had gone "off to Nogales for 4 days with a man in a business suit."

At Christmas my father came out to spend a week with us. I was given a black cowboy hat, and other western accouterments. But no cowboy boots. "You'd just outgrow them," my mother said. So I had to ride in my shameful brown school shoes. I was embarrassed by Eddie, who wore an aviator helmet and bounced along on Peanuts. I tried to convince my father that we should buy a ranch and stay forever.

My mother and I were hoping that Uncle Archie would come to Tucson to see us. Whenever he walked away from a job—or had been asked to leave—Archie traveled. I imagine now that he must have been selling a few shares of stock each time he wanted to finance a trip. He'd been traveling out west that year, and then sailed to France on a fancy new liner, the SS Normandie. Now he was in Mexico, not very far away, I knew. I learned how to say "Popocatepetl," the name of a high mountain he had climbed. "A volcano," said my mother, shaking her head.

In February he wrote to my mother from Mexico City, telling her his adventures. He'd driven there in his 1932 Ford V-8 convertible, 800 miles along a rough, steep road. "Some people in those mountains had never seen an automobile," said my mother. He didn't come then to visit us in Tucson. Not until three months later, when our situation was quite altered.

My mother took Eddie and me to a small traveling circus in March. For years afterward she was convinced that in the stuffy, crowded tent during that tinselled performance, Eddie and I picked up the germs that nearly cost us our lives. By the middle of April we were both very sick.

Eddie was down first, with swollen glands and a high fever. Two days later I was ill, too. Within another day or so we were in adjoining private rooms at St. Mary's Hospital, with special-duty nursing sisters around the clock. We were diagnosed and misdiagnosed with measles, meningitis, polio, scarlet fever, and finally, a streptococcus infection. The unfamiliar word itself compounded our mother's living nightmare. Penicillin was not yet in clinical use in 1937; antibiotics were as unknown to the floundering Tucson doctors as was our disease itself.

Dr. Carrell, Dr. Mikell, Dr. Patterson, Dr. Seacrist, Dr. Gore, Dr. Harper, Dr. Storts: between them, they operated on Eddie's throat, and gave each of us multiple blood transfusions.

As my fever climbed, the crucifix on the wall opposite my bed became a key that I tried feebly to reach. Sister Clotilde and Sister Therese fluttered around my bed in their long white habits, urging me to take sips of water, and trying to comfort my frantic mother.

Dr. Carrell called in all his colleagues. Attempting to drain and purge me of infection, they operated three times on my abdomen, before deciding that they were wasting their time and perhaps shortening mine.

By the middle of May, the outdoor temperature in Tucson was 102 and rising, as was mine. I was moved from my $6.00-a-day room to one that was air conditioned, for an extravagant daily rate of $8.50.

Transcontinental phone calls were strictly crisis-related then, certainly for my family, but that was the only way to keep our father informed. As Eddie began to improve, I weakened. My parents despaired. My father flew out from New Jersey, all day on a DC-3.

My fever reached 106. Delirious, I didn't know my parents. One day I had "a bad chill and a sinking spell;" my face turned gray, my blood pressure plunged. The local doctors seemed to have given up. Uncle Archie drove up from Mexico in his battered Ford. My mother wired Georgie, who flew out from St. Paul.

"We've got to get Birnberg out here," said Auntie Georgie. Dr. Birnberg was their St. Paul pediatrician. They all hoped I could hold out until he arrived. The nursing sisters prayed he might be a new Messiah. Auntie Georgie and my father met his plane.

Shocked by my condition and inadequate medical care, Dr. Birnberg turned things around during the 24 hours he was there. He ordered another blood transfusion, intravenous glucose, and infant formula by the teaspoonful. "If you don't feed your patient, you lose your patient," he thundered. He prescribed a brand-new drug called sulfanilamide, just then emerging from the laboratory where it had been developed. Birnberg ordered special blood serums flown in from Los Angeles and Denver. Uncle Archie sped back to the hospital from the airfield with the chilled serum beside him on the seat of his Ford.

By the time I began inching toward recovery, Auntie Georgie and my mother had come to loathe Tucson. The cruel sun blazed hotter each day; the constant, dusty wind was punishing. I was comforted by Auntie Georgie's accounts about daily life at the River in cool, green Minnesota. Each day I begged her to "tell me about the River." Each day she repeated the same stories. The house was being painted, she said, gray with dark red trim. Fred Rosengren was planting seeds of cosmos, nasturtiums, forget-me-nots. Lettuce, Swiss chard, and peas would soon be springing up in the vegetable garden. The seats in the green Mueller canoe were being recaned; the maids' room had new blue-checked curtains; and the tennis court, new tapes. Lottie would soon be having puppies. Again. "Tell me about the River," I'd say. Auntie Georgie made it real. The River became my Mecca, my holy grail, the place I had to reach.

The Tucson doctors, surely anxious to be rid of us, finally announced that it would be safe for me to be moved to St. Paul. My mother and Auntie Georgie hugged each other, dancing around my bed. By then I had lain in that hospital for five weeks.

For three frantic days of unbearable heat and blowing dust, the sisters worked toward our "getaway," as my mother termed it; "our escape from that outpost of civilization." They packed trunks and crates, sold the car, gave away any remaining food and the "lawn" chairs. My mother wrote that when everything had gone, our house "looked just as dismal as it had the first day I saw it."

I was taken to the train station by ambulance on May 23rd, accompanied by Miss von Wert, the nurse who was to travel with us on the three day trip. Dr. Birnberg was not told about the move until we were already on our way. He was furious at those Tucson doctors: "She'll never stand the trip. They're going to kill that child!"

They almost did. At Kansas City a doctor came on board to check on me, after I'd told Miss von Wert that my chest hurt. A lung had collapsed; the doctor said that I now had pneumonia. He told me about his little girl, who had her own pony. I envied that little girl. My temperature had risen, but he let us continue our journey.

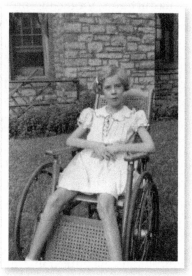

Alan at Children's Hospital, St. Paul – 1937

Our arrival in St. Paul was ceremonial. An ambulance and all my mother's family were there to meet us. The three sisters cried. My mother wrote that she'd never known such joy and relief. At last she was home, home with her family, her oldest friends, and doctors she could trust. "Those Tucson doctors were incompetent," my mother said. Dr. Birnberg nodded.

I spent another month in the hospital in St. Paul. Dr. Birnberg was there to see me through each setback: the lung collapse, the drainage wounds that wouldn't heal, a kidney infection. But now my mother felt safe and happy. I was happy. Everything was different. This was Children's Hospital, and soon I was well enough to meet other children, and to be pushed out onto the lawn in a wooden wheelchair.

My mother's old friends brought me presents. Mrs. Evans, my day nurse, dreamed up projects for me. As a surprise for my mother on her birthday, I compiled a cookbook cutting out recipes from the *Ladies' Home Journals* that Mrs. Evans brought in. I chose only those that sounded delectable, pasting them into a brown spiral-bound notebook. Some I copied in pencil, but by the time I reached "Bake at 375 for 20 minutes," I'd fall back on my pillows, exhausted. Skinny to start with at 59 pounds, my weight had fallen to 46. I looked like a skeleton, but thinking about food got me eating again, as Mrs. Evans had planned.

Meanwhile this extraordinary nurse sat beside me, making miniature furnishings for the new dollhouse that, unbeknownst to me, my father was building, back in New Jersey. She made the frilly curtains, the little upholstered sofa, the wing chairs, and crocheted rugs that I still have. Auntie Harriet brought me a tiny chest with five drawers that opened, each filled with lemon drops.

Auntie Georgie and my mother went downtown one day to Bullard Bros., St. Paul's best jeweler, to pick out the gold watch for Dr. Birnberg, a gift from my parents and all the aunts and uncles.

I was gaining weight. "No ribs show, no collarbone. What a heavenly relief," wrote my mother in her diary. "Let A's afternoon nurse go, for first time in 3 months!" My father came to St. Paul at the end of July. I staged a surprise for him. "Guess what, Daddy. I can walk!" And I took a few shuffling steps across my hospital room. A week later Dr. Birnberg said I could leave the hospital.

Eddie was at the River with Auntie Georgie and Uncle Herb, having moved out with their family in June. On the great day of my release from the hospital, I rode with my parents to Auntie Harriet and Uncle Bill's house in town, a distance of little more than a mile. The trees and houses seemed to whip past us with frightening speed.

The trees seemed so tall and the grass so green at Auntie Harriet's house, and all so quiet inside the high brick wall between their property and the silent Visitation Convent. Janey, my three-year-old cousin, and I played and laughed in her wading pool until it was time for lunch and naps. The rooms in that house were wide and cool, with soft carpets and pretty colors. When Uncle Bill came home, the grownups had their highballs on the terrace.

"The long-awaited day has come for Alan," wrote my mother in her diary, after another week. Uncle Archie drove us to the River. I was almost sick again, but that time with excitement.

The River looked wider, the Wisconsin Hills higher, and the whole place was so quiet. Eddie and the cousins came out to greet me. Their voices seemed to float on the air.

And there was Auntie Georgie, in her soft, floppy, old River pants, her arms out to hug me. She lifted me off the ground. "Oh, my darling, you're here. " She took my hand for a short walk around to see everything that was new and everything that was the same.

My mother and I had the Guest House to ourselves. I slept for an hour or more each afternoon, but battled fiercely to resume my normal life. "Do you really think you ought to be turning somersaults, dear?" inquired a well-meaning friend of Auntie Georgie's. "That can't be good for you." I shot her a look, and turned three more.

"Alan, show Cousin Margaret your scars." My mother summoned me. Scowling and furious, I had to comply. I pulled up the edge of my navy blue shorts, exposing one corner of my tummy so that everyone could marvel at the evidence of what we had endured.

My mother was more traumatized than I was by the ordeal from which we'd at last emerged. It was years before

I understood how difficult it had been for her. At the time I wanted only to move on to normal, everyday life. But that wasn't possible. My mother could hardly speak of anything else. For at least a year she talked to absolutely everyone about everything that had happened to me. Even from another room I could hear her telling her friends, people who worked for us, and even my friends the entire, deadly saga. "Come, dearie," my mother would say, "let Mrs. Quinn see your scars. She just wants to look."

She bought a flowery chaise longue for my room at our house in New Jersey. Did she really imagine that, at ten, I would lounge upon it? Yes, she did. But I did not.

Uncle Archie on the dock with all the cousins – 1938

– **T E N** –

MY PARENTS GAVE ME a Box Brownie camera for
my August birthday the year I turned ten. We were at the
River, as usual. I had finally recovered from my near-fatal
strep infection, although I was still emaciated, still made to
take naps.

It never occurred to me to ask Eddie and our cousins
to "hold still." I just held up my black box, peered into the
viewfinder, and clicked. The results—at least what were
probably the best of my pictures—are fastened with those
little corner tabs to the black pages of a family album. Some
of my deckle-edged snapshots are fuzzy or off-kilter, but
there are Eddie and the cousins Piers, Genna, and Janey,
all younger than I was. Fin was not even born yet. They lie
sprawled on a woolly steamer rug on the big lawn, buck-
naked for the compulsory sunbath, while Auntie Georgie in
a halter top and flaring slacks reads from the *Just-So Stories*.

Lottie the Sealyham is lying there, too, head between her paws, waiting for some action.

Now they're all sitting in a row on the edge of the dock, toes in the water, bare from the waist up. Only Janey, who hadn't yet learned to dog-paddle, still wears one of those fat orange life jackets. Standing behind them, hands on hips, is Uncle Archie.

My Box Brownie could snap eight pictures with each roll of film. I had to learn how to open the camera after number eight, seal up the precious roll, and ask my mother or Auntie Georgie to drop it off at Strands' Store. I had to wait a whole week before I could see my pictures.

The same album includes some bigger, brighter, better pictures, too. I wish there were more. These are Uncle Archie's photographs, taken with his Leica. The compact, lightweight German Leica was a status symbol in the 1930s. With reason: it worked for amateurs like Archie as well as for professionals like Walker Evans and Henri Cartier-Bresson. Uncle Archie was always intrigued by well-made machines that had a certain cachet attached to them: the best Gokey fly-rod, with a Hardy reel, a late-model Ford convertible roadster, a brand-new Lincoln Zephyr. Or the Leica. In my mind's eye I see one of his photographs that I cannot find. It shows the backsides of my aunts and uncles and my mother as they all leaned out a window at Miller Hospital in St. Paul, where my cousin Finlay was being born. Auntie Georgie, the new baby's mother, is not in the line-up. I try to imagine what they were seeing in the wing across the way. It can't have been the delivery room, or perhaps it was. Maybe they are peering into Auntie Georgie's hospital room, hoping to spot the nurse holding the newborn. Even in this view of their rumps, the spying aunts and uncles convey a festive atmosphere. It's a party, and Uncle Archie was there.

The arrival of "Baby Fin" kept Auntie Georgie in town for much of the summer, leaving my mother in charge, for once, at the River. She was responsible for Eddie and me, three cousins, Auntie Harriet, Uncle Bill, Uncle Archie, Archie's friend Al O'Toole, Uncle Herb occasionally, a household staff of three, and three family dogs—Hamish the black Scottie, Lottie who was white, and Baloo, a fluffy red Chow. My mother was the one who planned meals, ordered the food, kept track of everyone's comings and goings, and settled our arguments.

Grown-up party on the lawn: my father Jack,
Auntie Harriet, and my mother Jeannie – 1938

The grownups had parties at the River every summer, real parties, and we got to go. I remember one party when Florence and Della carried potato salad and fancy grown-up food out to the round white table on the lawn where one of the uncles had put the whiskey bottles and tall glasses. The white iron chairs were spread around, and Uncle Bill made a fire in the special place between the rocks. We kids stuck our wieners on the long forks, and sizzled them over the fire while the aunts and uncles and the friends sipped their highballs.

The grownups were laughing and talking in their party voices, not like the daytime voices when they told us what to do. Auntie Georgie had on a striped dress that went to a V at the front. She wore her dangly inherited earrings, and high sandals with laces twirled around her ankles. Auntie Harriet's auburn hair was piled on top of her head. Her dress was white, with straps over her bare shoulders. My mother had on the silky pale blue dress that I loved, with puffy sleeves and her fancy brown-and-white shoes. She wasn't wearing her glasses because it was a party. With her different voice, she didn't seem like my regular mother. Uncle Herb and Uncle Bill wore white shirts and white pants, but Uncle Archie had on his ordinary shorts and bare feet, same as always.

The cousins and Eddie and I got to toast marshmallows. As it got dark we started running around, trying to scare each other. Genna and Janey ran back to the fire and their mothers. Piers and Eddie and I burst into the cluttered kitchen, now reigned over by a new housekeeper, the magisterial Dena. Piles of dirty dishes filled the black sink and covered every surface. We were hopping with excitement.

"We need some jars! To catch lightning bugs. Please. Please!"

"All right, all right, all right." Dena pulled three jelly jars from the cupboard above her head. "Go on, now. Off with you; outta my way, kids."

Softly, on bare feet, we crept through the dewy grass, trying to scoop up those tiny flickering yellow lanterns. In the jar they still kept on winking, on and off, on and off.

It was a dark night, and no one made us go to bed. We finally just did.

That was the summer when Uncle Archie took over the Guest House with Al O'Toole, a bald man with a fat stomach. "He's a mathematical genius," Archie told my mother and

Auntie Georgie and Uncle Herb. Al O'Toole was developing a "system" to beat the stock market.

I didn't like Al O'Toole. He never brought us candy or anything, and he kept Uncle Archie from swimming with us. We had to stay away from the Guest House in the mornings while they worked. My mother described the scene to my father: "Al has piles of papers and something called a 'comptometer' on the table where he works all day, monkeying with the grain market." She was baffled and amused by the title of his university thesis: "On Symmetric Functions and Symmetric Functions of Symmetric Functions." "It's all very funny—Arch in such company—," she said, "but I'm suspicious, too."

At night, from my bed on the porch, I heard my mother and Auntie Georgie and Uncle Herbert trying to talk Uncle Archie out of risking his small inheritance by playing the stock market. Their voices rose and fell, murmuring along quietly, then loud enough for their words to reach me.

"You just don't get it, Jeannie," I heard Uncle Archie say. "We stand to make a fortune. Al knows all the ins and outs; he's a genius at this stuff. You're married to a businessman: talk to Jack. He'll understand. You'll be missing a rare opportunity if you don't . . ."

"It's a little hard to explain," Al O'Toole said solemnly. "Of course a math background helps."

Herb knocked the ashes out of his pipe. I could hear him filling it with the sweet-smelling tobacco from his can of Balkan Sobranie. "Math would be fundamental, I should think," he said with a short laugh. "I've had a fair amount of math myself." He put a match up to his pipe. "So tell me: how are you planning to accomplish this amazing feat?"

Then Auntie Georgie's voice: "You're crazy, Arch. This sounds like a racket!"

Then my mother, her voice low and tragic, said, "Oh, Archie, be careful."

Uncle Archie almost shouted: "Well, okay, okay. Hang on to your Mining shares, then, both of you. You'll never be rich. I'm going to get myself another drink." I heard his feet slap the bare floor as he walked through the house.

Later, on the porch by themselves, the two sisters sighed and exhaled. "Oh, Lordy."

"Faddie'd be turning his grave. How can Archie . . .?"

"That Al, that ghastly man . . ."

Then I heard Uncle Herb's weary voice from their room. "Come on, Georgie. Time for bed."

Eddie, Alan, and Piers in Indian costumes for the Fourth of July parade – 1938

That year, 1938, marked the centennial of the founding of Marine, the nearest village to us, and the oldest in Minnesota. We were all caught up in the grand parade that Fourth of July. Eddie, Piers, and I were going to be Indians in the parade, along with a few other Otisville kids. Otisville is three miles above Marine on the River, but still considered itself part of "greater" Marine. Mrs. Stutz, an Otisville dowager, designed and, with the help of other ladies (not including Auntie Georgie), made our costumes. In Uncle Archie's photographs, we look absurd, hideous, and pale. All three of us wear black skullcaps with dangling braids, a lone feather sticking up from our headbands, and streaky orange makeup. I am dressed in a baggy tan garment that was decorated with mystic symbols and had a fringe around the bottom. The two little boys wear fringed sort of loin cloths tucked into their bathing trunks. They both scowl fiercely over their bows and arrows as they aim at the invisible enemy. The arrows are tipped with suction cups, the better to avoid putting out the eye of some innocent bystander. Their skinny little torsos look awfully white. I, being a "squaw," naturally have no bow and arrow, only a strand of beads. All three of us are wearing white sneakers.

I've seen a snapshot of our neighbor Mr. Fuller in the parade, dressed up as the prehistoric "Otisville Man." He's clad in a furry sort of toga that leaves one shoulder bare. Brandishing a huge bone, he's dragging a large stuffed dummy with hair of yellow yarn. The grownups laughed when someone said that the dummy represented Mr. Fuller's wife, Emma. I imagine that his toga had been fashioned from one of Emma's old fur coats.

We cheered when we saw Uncle Archie. He came marching along with Al O'Toole, dressed up as trappers, with someone's old fur pieces around their heads, and snowshoes slung across their backs. They held opposite ends of a pole from which a large cardboard deer was suspended. The closets of these Otisville matrons apparently held a boundless supply of frayed furs.

My mother and the aunts and uncles went on to a grownup party that night, by the pool at the University Club in St. Paul. "Archie dove in with all his clothes on," my mother told us the next day. She smiled and shook her head.

The next week was Uncle Archie's fortieth birthday. His friends came trailing out to the River all afternoon, laden with food and drinks. They swam and had their highballs. We all had supper on the lawn. No one seemed to talk much with Al O'Toole. We cousins were left behind when the grownups drove off to Wisconsin for more partying. My mother stayed in bed with a headache the next morning.

A few days later my mother had a letter from my father, saying he would not come to the River that year; they couldn't afford the expense of his travel. "Oh, poor Daddy," I said. Eddie and I were sad. That night, when the long-distance rates went down, my mother called him on the telephone in the hall. I heard her say, "Oh, Jack, please come—I'm sorry—I don't really care about all these silly parties—you're the one I love." He came, late in August, for his paltry two weeks.

Wisconsin was wide-open compared to Minnesota. In Wisconsin, you could buy fireworks, strong beer, probably stronger alcohol, and stay out drinking later. The village of Somerset had a nightclub and gambling; that was where Uncle Archie's birthday party wound up. Even children could play the nickel slot machines in Somerset. My cousins and Eddie and I were taken more than once in the daytime to float down the swift little Apple River on inner tubes. The Apple was a tributary of our River. A truck belonging to the nightclub would carry us back to where we'd started, where we'd eat our sandwiches and play the slots. The machines had pretty little pictures of oranges and lemons. Now and then, with luck, a little pile of nickels would come shooting out.

Uncle Archie looked like pictures of his father, the same sturdy build, strong nose and chin, receding hairline. Like everyone else in the family, he was nearsighted and wore glasses. That summer, while he was closeted with Al O'Toole and the comptometer, my mother and the aunts worried about Uncle Archie. I heard them talking one morning on the porch.

"Remember how furious Faddie would be when Archie neglected his chores?" my mother was saying. "Fishing was really the one happy bond between them."

"He was the gay little bird in our family when we were growing up," Auntie Georgie said. "So many friends; he'd be out every night."

"He hadn't a trace of snobbery in him," said Auntie Harriet. "He knew the farmers, the farmers' sons, the guys who worked on the railroad. One time when we went fishing up north, the car broke down. We went into a bar looking for help, and next thing everyone there was Archie's friend. He could charm a bird out of a tree."

My mother remembered a story about Archie's last year at school. "The boys in his class were told to wear dark coats, white pants, and white shoes to the spring dance. Archie didn't dare ask for white shoes, but a friend offered to lend him a pair. But oh, no, Faddie would never allow that. Pride. So Archie made up some excuse, and didn't go."

"He wasn't much of a student," Auntie Georgie recalled. "But he loved the military drill at the Academy and their mock rifles."

"Then Arch left without graduating," my mother said. "So foolish. Of course it was the War. He enlisted, remember? Got his army uniform, went off to training camp, and two months later, the whistles blew, and it was the armistice. So he never got a chance."

"Yeah, he always felt he'd missed out," said Auntie Georgie. "He went right to work at Faddie's old firm."

"That didn't last long," Auntie Harriet remembered. "He couldn't stand that Mr. Borchert. Mutual, probably."

Auntie Georgie chimed in: "But he was a terrific salesman. He liked that part. He could talk you into buying anything, a Ford car, anything."

"Remember the smoke alarms?" That was Auntie Harriet. "'They're guaranteed,' he told us. 'Absolutely foolproof. Could save your lives!' And we all bought 'em."

"He sold them to everybody," my mother said. "But don't forget, he was fired there, too. He argued, never followed the bosses' orders. So of course he got fired, over and over. 'For no reason,' he always said." She shook her head.

One morning I trailed after Auntie Georgie and my mother as they walked down to the dock. They sat on the edge, dangling their feet in the water while I waded in the shallows, looking for agates and listening.

"Archie's always wanted to have money," my mother was saying. "That's nothing new. Remember how he envied all the rich families we grew up with? Everyone had a lot more than we did."

"Yeah, and Scott Fitzgerald felt that way, too. Remember how they used to be so jealous of poor old Aunt Georgie Clark and the Herseys and the Weyerhausers? Even though they didn't quite trust most of them, either."

"Well, I sort of envied those people, too, Georgie. I used to wish Faddie had gone into the lumber business, or started a railroad like Mr. Hill."

"Oh Jeannie, I didn't envy them. Sure, they had those big ugly houses and fancy cars, but the parents were so shallow and snobbish; all the wrong values."

"I remember how Faddie looked down on Mr. Ordway who had that plumbing business. But then it turned into Minnesota Mining—now they're calling it 3M."

"Archie worked there once," Auntie Georgie murmured. "For a couple of months anyhow. Got himself a few shares."

"He got Mother to buy some. We all did. That was lucky. Never sell your Mining stock: that's what I always say."

I didn't know what it meant, but I'd often heard my mother say exactly that.

"But darling, foolish Archie always thought he could do better." Auntie Georgie looked as if she might cry. She stood up.

My mother got up, too. "Of course he blew it in the end. And the '29 crash took the rest. We better get back, see about lunch and all."

Uncle Archie with Helen on her first visit to the River – 1939

– ELEVEN –

OUR MOTHER SENT EDDIE and me off to the River ahead of her in June, 1939. She seemed to have had no scruples about asking favors of people. This time she'd prevailed on an old St. Paul friend of her mother's to chaperone us from New Jersey on the train. We had root beer as we rode the afternoon "Hiawatha" from Chicago. Mrs. Foster said she would wait and have supper when she got home, but I told her I thought we had better have ours on the train. So we did.

The aunts and uncles met us at the station in St. Paul. Uncle Bill took us on a tour of his family's Balm Argenta factory the next day, and then to the University Club to see

Uncle Archie. Was he surprised! He asked us to have a swim with him in the swimming pool.

When we arrived at the River, Auntie Georgie said, "Guess what we have here." She'd bought a little white goat. I wrote my parents, "Heidi is nice & she bleats all the time. I can hear her now. We keep her tied up in the meadow because she eats all the flowers."

That summer, the boys slept on the porch as usual, but I was given a room of my own. It was an inside room with windows that opened onto the porch. You could climb through when you didn't feel like walking around. The pine walls in my room had been painted white, and the floor, dark green. My closet, like all the others in that house, consisted of an alcove hidden behind a curtain. Blue and green checked cotton matched the curtains billowing at my window. In the afternoon, stretched out on the narrow bed for my "rest," I gazed up at a watercolor farm scene by Jean Taylor until I was almost in it.

Jean Taylor was a daughter of the Taylors whose rustic cottage my mother would soon obliterate when she set about building her dream house on the land she inherited. The watercolor paid homage to the cubism of Picasso and Braque even as it illustrated the prototypical Minnesota farmstead, possibly one of the very Scandia farms that I knew so well. There was the white house, plain and tall, the big red barn and cone-roofed silo, brown hens scuffling in the dirt, the curly-tailed mutt, stately Holstein cows. But all the shapes were stylized, the cows squared, the sky vertically bisected into two shades of blue, the red barn flat pink where the sun struck it, the cornfield a green and gold triangle.

Sometimes on a summer morning I'd escape to a high perch in the fork of the great sugar maple that stood at the foot of the lawn on the bank above the River. The dark branches of a pine tree were embraced by the maple and formed the ladder by which we climbed to this leafy nest.

My dangling legs hugged a thick, comfortable limb, while I leaned against the rough ridged bark of the trunk. I could hear the regular squeak and splash of oars as someone unseen rowed deftly across the water. From the house came the pulsing swish of Dena's broom across the wooden floor of our eating porch. Two long rings, two short, the faint chime of the phone sounded from the dim inner depth of the house. "I'll get it," came Auntie Georgie's voice, clear and near from the front porch. A screen door banged, followed by the steady creak of the ropes as some cousin embarked on the old hammock swing, whose creamy canvas and smooth mahogany never failed as transport to the tropical seas and palmy isles of my imagination. Then came the slumbrous buzz of the lawnmower, as Fred Rosengren began pushing its neat curving blades in stripes across the broad slope of grass. From the top of the hill, through the trees, two faint beeps of a car's horn meant someone was about to arrive.

Later, down on the shore in the warm noonday sun, Piers and Eddie and I waited for Beverly to come so we could swim. We tried skipping stones across the water: I flicked my wrist and sent off a small flat pebble, hoping it would bounce two or even three times. We kept trying. Then Harlan Gabrielson, at work in the upland meadow, put down his scythe and came to join us. On his first throw the stone made ten, eleven, twelve plops on the surface before it disappeared almost halfway across the River.

The uncles took charge of our fireworks on the Fourth. Piers and Eddie and I were allowed to have sparklers, a slim box each. We took turns touching one precious sparkler to the glowing stick of punk held by an uncle. After a first, tiny whoosh, the sparkler, held well out in front of us, sputtered with a soft, satisfying hiss, shedding a twinkling shower of light into the gathering darkness. We waved them in loops and parabolas, sometimes dangerously close to our own and each other's eyes.

"Stand back, kids. Watch it, now." Uncle Archie sounded almost fierce. He and Uncle Bill and Uncle Herbert had rigged up a wooden trough at the edge of the big lawn, above the River. They had a paper bag filled with red-wrapped fireworks, decorated with strange writing and pictures of flowers and sunsets. "Made in Japan," Auntie Georgie said.

Uncle Herbert laid a Roman candle in the trough, and touched the smoldering punk to its wick. "There she goes!"

He turned and ran back. I'd never seen Uncle Herbert run before; usually, he even walked slowly. The Roman candle arced into the sky, emitting puffs of green sparks, then pink, then green again, before it disappeared into the dark water. Uncle Herbert's white shorts, his white shirt, glowed in the night. Laughing, elated, he handed the punk to Uncle Bill.

"Piers! Eddie! Get back," called Auntie Georgie. She and Harriet were sitting on the grass, trying to keep the little girls, Genna and Janey, out of the danger zone. Janey shrieked with excitement; Genna squirmed in her mother's arms. Piers and Eddie and I ran around waving our sparklers, pausing each time an uncle set off another glorious cascade of light.

Uncle Bill, a head taller than the other uncles, scampered back on his long bare feet from the brilliant pinwheels he'd released into a rolling rainbow over the water. Then he paused, panting, laughing, swatting at the mosquitoes that converged on his half-bald head. "Hey, how did you like that, kiddos?"

Uncle Archie was barefoot, too, as always. He grabbed the punk to touch the fuse on a skyrocket. These shot up higher than any of the others, sending out twinkling cascades of white sparks, best of all, I thought.

The uncles took turns, running back and forth, laughing, excited. They seemed different, not at all the way they were in the daytime.

After the fireworks had ended, and I was lying in bed by the window that looked out to the porch, I saw something dark whir through the air just over my head.

"A bat! Herb, Herb," called Auntie Georgie from the other end of the porch, the sitting end. The grownups were still up, of course, talking softly and laughing. I'd heard the ice tinkling in their highball glasses. Now they sprang up, noisily.

On his cot, Piers sat up out of sleep. "What's going on?"

"Bill, get him! Do something, Arch!" shrieked Auntie Harriet.

The bat darted over us again. "Use a racket, Herb," called Auntie Georgie.

I got up to watch. So did Piers. The three uncles were flailing about with wooden tennis rackets, swatting at the air and at the screens. "Open the door, H! Maybe he'll fly out." The aunts sat huddled in their chairs, with towels over their heads.

"Got 'im." That was Uncle Archie. I could hear the wicker chairs creak when they all sat down. "Back to bed, Allie. You too, Piers."

"They're not really interested in your hair, girls," I heard Uncle Herbert say. "You know that's just an old wives' tale."

After a few summers of sharing, Uncle Archie and the three sisters decided they should formally divide the River property their mother had left them. Archie, still single, still carefree, wasn't ready to be tied down. "You girls work it out," he said finally, after one of their interminable late-night discussions. They were to reimburse him for his share of the place. "Don't lose it all on the stock market, Arch, for Pete's sake," pleaded my mother.

The sisters drew lots—wooden matches, actually—one night when my cousins and I were meant to be asleep. They were laughing, as if it were a party game. Grownups always seemed to have the most fun. Except when they argued; that was scary. Well, they weren't arguing that night, and they each ended up happy, finally, at the way things turned out.

Archie and the sisters conferred with their lawyer, Benno Wolff, to arrange trade-offs and boundary adjustments, to make sure that each was treated fairly in the settlement. I never met Benno Wolff, but I used to love hearing his name, imagining someone bearish, wolfish, shaggy, but reassuring. And of course wise, too.

Auntie Georgie wound up with the Big House, the oldest, the biggest, and the best. Auntie Harriet got the Guest House, in a lovely grove of pines, and a larger piece of land. My mother ended up with the Taylor House, a ramshackle cottage built ten or fifteen years earlier by the family of Uncle Archie's fishing buddy, Mouse Taylor. My grandparents had allowed the Taylors a long-term lease on a little bluff overlooking the water, upstream from the Big House, with the right to build a cabin. The Taylors' lease on the land conveniently expired that year. The Ingersolls paid the Taylors $400 for their ratty little house. That's what my mother got, a cottage with ceilings so low my father couldn't even stand up straight. But she got more land than the others, plus the tennis court, and a special bonus: the deep rocky ravine, with its high sandstone cliffs and two tall, sparkling cold waterfalls.

After my mother and her sisters had settled which house and land each of them was to have, they spent the whole rest of the summer dividing up the contents of the houses, every single thing from beds to books to saucepans. Afterwards we called it "the dividing summer." They spent days drawing straws— using matches, again—to see who would get what. They did it by categories: choosing from all the kerosene lamps, say, or all the ancient blankets, or the platters, accumulated miscellany of years of family life. They divvied up all the old books: "69 volumes for me," my mother said, including Faddie's old Xenophon and his beloved George Borrow.

One morning they lined up all the straight chairs on the front lawn, more than twenty of them. Eddie and Piers and I watched from the porch steps as the three sisters circled the chairs in the wet grass. It looked as though they were playing Musical Chairs, except there was no music. They took turns sitting in the chairs, then picking them up, turning them over, checking for cracked rungs or cane seats that were about to burst apart.

I remember them out there another day, pummeling pillows, old ticking-striped pillows with feathers leaking out, blowing around them, floating in the sun. They started laughing, two redheads and my brown-haired mother, but somehow they all knew which pillows held real goose down.

"The war & all the horrors seem impossible. We feel very, very remote here at the River," wrote my mother that summer of 1939.

"The condition here is appalling. That monster Hitler." This was the news from 86-year-old, half-blind emigré Aunt Anna Ingersoll on the French Riviera at Menton. Auntie Georgie was reading her letter aloud. "What would you say if I were to marry? Strange enough there have been several men who want to marry me."

"Maybe they're onto something," said my mother.

Auntie Georgie had resurrected the old River logbook. It became her record of what went on, rather than the guest book it had been in the early years. "Changed our name to Herbert Lefkovitz Lewis," she noted in 1940, a reversal of

Uncle Herb's middle and last names. Our mother tried to explain this to Eddie and me. Ever since I'd learned to read, she'd given me moralistic pamphlets written for children: we were all brothers under the skin; ethnic or religious differences were irrelevant; prejudice was wicked. Some of my parents' friends in New Jersey—the Bronisches, the Solmssens, Jon Ladenberg—had had to flee Germany or Austria. I thought it was because of their names. We knew that Adolf Hitler was trying to get rid of people who were Jewish. Maybe the names were his clues. Uncle Herb was Jewish, my mother said. He and Auntie Georgie didn't want their children to be held back by the name of their father's father. But, I thought, if it doesn't make any difference, then . . . why? I liked their old name better, anyhow.

Minnesota was different from New Jersey. There didn't seem to be any families who had fled Hitler. Nor in my sliver of experience had I seen anyone in Minnesota whose skin color was darker than mine. But even at the River we sometimes heard Hitler's incomprehensible rants booming out of the arched-top Philco. Piers and Eddie and I drew cartoons of his face, that toothbrush mustache and the angled sweep of his hair.

I remember the first time Uncle Archie brought Helen out to the River. They came with candy for us, but it wasn't the same candy. Nothing was the same. Helen was too dressed up. Her high-heeled sandals sank into the lawn. She had on too much perfume, too many beads. Her upswept hair ended in too many tight curls on top of her head. Her dress was in two parts, revealing on purpose a sausage of pale flesh around her middle. I wished she were prettier.

We were all gathered on the lawn in front of the Big House, grownups in the chairs, cousins on the grass. Uncle Archie tried to act the way he always did, but it wasn't working. Everyone was talking in a funny way, as if they didn't know each other. Helen's voice was husky, so low that you practically had to lean on her soft, plump, bare arm, into the haze of her cigarette smoke, to hear anything she said. She sounded as if she came from a different place. The other ladies who used to come out with Uncle Archie and his friends had uttered soprano shrieks and shrill cascades of laughter. They often took off their shoes, and sometimes wore culottes. But Uncle Archie didn't take Helen swimming; she didn't look like a person who liked to swim. Sometimes he called her "Helene." Finally the grownups had drinks, even though it was before lunch.

That evening, after Uncle Archie had taken Helen back to town, I listened to my mother and her sisters talking about her.

"Oh, Lordy," my mother said.

"Oh, Archie, Archie." Auntie Harriet shook her head.

"B.P.O.E.," said Auntie Georgie, with a sniff. This was one of her acronyms. My mother told me later that it stood for "Benevolent Protective Order of Elks," which I'd never heard of. To Auntie Georgie it conveyed scorn for an object or for someone whose taste was common and, well, tasteless. Anyone she considered a social climber was definitely B.P.O.E.

Helen came out with Archie almost every week that summer. The sisters referred to her as his "ladyfriend." I was sad because he didn't swim with us as much anymore. Eddie and Piers and the little girls and probably even Baby Fin soon knew that we had pretty much lost our best uncle.

Trees along the River
(photo by Andrew Summersby)

– T W E L V E –

"GO ON, KIDS; scram. Go on outside; it's a beautiful day."

Every morning, after breakfast, after our chores, Auntie Georgie prodded us out of the hammock, off the porch, up from our books. "Come on, you little moles; how 'bout a swim."

We raced down the lawn, down the steps by the big sugar maple, across the bouncy planks to the dock, and dove into the current, one after the other, I remembering or not remembering to tuck my glasses into the ledge on the big rock. We all wore little rubber nose-clips to keep the water out of us; Dr. Birnberg's orders. The deep channel ran past the dock, but if you swam out a little way, the River was shallower, and your toes could touch the sandy bottom.

We could go anywhere at the River, and no one would know. I could have drawn a map of my River landscape, those places we went to often, and others we visited once a summer. And the places to avoid.

Our side of the St. Croix, the Minnesota side, was warmed by brilliant morning sun, but by late afternoon we were in blue-green shade, while the Wisconsin side was bathed in gold. That was when we sped off by boat across the River to swim in the glow at the Shearers' Island. A deep channel ran so close there that we could dive right off the shore, or swing out and plunge in from a long rope that hung from a high maple branch. Some afternoons we zoomed up-river to the Stutzes' golden sandbar, but that was different, a shallow beach where you had to wade out before it was deep enough to swim.

It made sense to go upstream in the boat. Then if your motor failed to start, if you ran out of gas or sheared a pin, the current would float you home.

"Let's go up to the Cave," I said one day. After many pulls on the starter rope, Piers, Eddie, and I took off in the bulky green outboard. Piers was running the motor, while I perched on the bow, toes dangling, keeping a lookout.

"Watch out, Piers! There's a deadhead." We had to yell to be heard over the motor.

I knew every house above ours on the Minnesota shore, the Harpers' log house, the big yellow house belonging to Mrs. Stutz, Otisville's grande dame, Mrs. Grant's where we had our art class, and three or four more. And then none.

Above the small stretch that was Otisville, the river split into two channels that came together by the Soo Line railroad bridge. A white wooden X on a tree marked the deeper channel, which was McLoud Slough.

"Head closer to shore, Piers, near the X," called Eddie. "It's shallow here." The water was a lighter color, the tan of a sandbar. We hugged the wooded Minnesota shore, with its fringe of pale blue forget-me-nots, through McLoud's until the river widened and we saw the bridge.

We made slow progress through the swift, roiling water in the shadow beneath that big, black, iron structure as we approached Cedar Bend. A tall tree at Cedar Bend, Auntie Georgie had told us, once marked the boundary between the lands of the Dakotas and the terrain claimed by their rivals, the Ojibwa. There, halfway up the steep bank on the Minnesota side, was the Cave. We looked up, framing our eyes, trying to spot the black opening. This was new to the three of us, a place we'd heard about from our mothers.

"There's Harp Falls, so we must be getting close," I said. Slender rivulets, the harp strings, plinked onto the black rocks at the river's edge, but we could not hear a sound over our motor.

"I see the Cave!" hollered Piers. He cut the motor, and we lugged the boat a little way up a gravel spit. Eddie tossed our mushroom anchor onto the shore. We began climbing through the woods, pushing our way through the underbrush, clambering over fallen branches. A pileated woodpecker hammered at a dead tree somewhere above us.

Panting from the climb and, in my case, from nervous excitement, we finally reached the yawning mouth of the Cave. It was high enough to stand in, and deep, like a vast, dark room in an old cellar. It had the dank smell of a cellar, too. Low tunnels appeared to penetrate further into the blackness.

"Aagh!" Piers snarled, just behind me. He knew I was scared.

"Can you see any markings on the walls?" Eddie asked. "Mother and Auntie Georgie said there were marks and pictures made by the Indians."

"They used to come here all the time with Uncle Archie," I said. Standing outside the opening, I shivered even though it wasn't cold. I was glad that no one had brought a flashlight, relieved that neither of the boys seemed tempted to explore the tunnels.

"Mother told me they carved their initials." Piers scanned the rock walls, but it was too dark to see. I didn't want to linger. "It's just a plain old cave," I said. "Let's go."

"You kids should go to Iron Springs," Auntie Georgie said one morning. "I can't believe you've never been there; we used to go all the time. You don't know what you're missing." It often seemed that our mothers and Uncle Archie had had more adventures than we did, explored the River more, knew more.

But after we discovered Iron Springs, we explored it until it was ours. You had to go up to the hard road and walk until you saw a little brook that ran through a culvert beneath the pavement. Then you followed the brook through the woods to the edge of the bluff.

That small brook was really determined to reach the river. It was hard to believe what that quiet-looking trickle of water had accomplished over time. How much time? Probably since long before the lumbermen, before the Indians, even, we decided. Maybe since the days of the woolly mammoths, before there were any people in the world.

At the edge of the bluff, a narrow crevasse was chiseled into the sandstone. There was a way to climb down. We learned where to put one foot, which edges to grab with our hands, and then the narrow ledge where the other foot could fit. The chasm was so narrow at the top that we could cling to its sides with both arms. There was no beautiful waterfall here, only a stingy, dropping stream that didn't even wet us. We descended slowly, one foot down and then the other, making use of every tiny niche, carefully clinging to rough angles in the rock or clutching at protruding roots Sometimes a bit of sandstone broke off in our hands.

When we finally reached the foot of the crevasse, the stream dropped more slowly across a gentle slope of rock. We stopped there to look up, proud of ourselves. The sheer cliffs on either side rose straight up, high up, higher than— what? Than a three-story house, anyway.

Iron had stained the cliffs rusty-orange, the color deepest near the top. These were old castle walls, we decided, marked with "The Blood of a Thousand Men." That was my name for this place. "No," says Eddie, "The Blood of a Thousand Indians." There were five of us that day—Piers, Mike Pettee, Pat Shearer, Eddie and I. Pat, a year older than me, was also addicted to making mental maps of our River world.

The rocky chasm dwindled down to nothing as we followed the trickle of water through the woods toward the wide, smooth river. Then we walked home along the rocky shore.

"Let's explore the Slough. It must go somewhere."

One day, my best friend Monnie and Margaret Harper and I dragged the old green Mueller canoe into the water, and paddled across to the opening of the slough, the winding, murky backwater that ran behind the Shearers' Island. The slough was narrow, green, and shady, after the wide, sparkling River. Its grassy banks were lined with willows, arching swamp maples, broken tree limbs, and now and then a patch of rare and brilliant cardinal flowers. Gently, we paddled and floated; even Margaret fell silent. I watched glistening drops of water fall one by one from my paddle. A thrush warbled from a treetop, and some creature—a beaver? a muskrat?— plopped into the murky water ahead of us. Around a bend we encountered a fallen tree that blocked our way.

"Oh-oh."

"Maybe I can get us around it," said Margaret, who was paddling in the stern. She was the sort of person who always seemed sure she could do anything, a trait that began to irritate Monnie and me.

But we had to get out and pull the canoe. "Ick!" called Monnie. "It's muddy . . . and weedy."

We had kept our sneakers on. That was the worst place. We followed the sluggish, meandering channel, ducking under overhanging branches, some of them laden with basking turtles. Suddenly the slough opened out onto a lake.

"It's a real lake!"

"Look at all the water lilies."

"Do you think anyone knows about this?"

"I bet Pat's been here. Even though he never said . . ." A heron flapped up into the air at the far end.

"We should call it 'Lily Lake,'" I said. I liked places to have names.

"Let's pick some lilies," said Margaret.

Monnie and I leaned over and pulled in a few of the yellow blossoms, their stems long and slippery.

When we got home we proudly showed our lilies to my mother. "They're lovely," she said. "Here, you can float them in this green bowl. You've been to Lily Lake."

"You mean, you knew about it?"

"Oh, yes, we used to go in there every summer, when the water was high, Auntie Georgie, Uncle Archie, our friends . . ."

That night in bed on my porch I heard the repeated cry of the whippoorwill from far across the River, on and on, over and over. The call came from deep in the slough. Of course they knew Lily Lake, my mother, the aunts and Uncle Archie.

Pat, it turned out, knew Lily Lake, too, but he'd never tried to climb the Wisconsin Hills that rose above the lake to form the eastern horizon of our River view. "Let's do it," I said one day. "Let's see if we can get to the top and see our houses." My mother and the aunts and Uncle Archie had made the climb long before us; I'd seen the hazy snapshots taken with their Kodak, views that showed the Ingersoll house, tiny in the distance, and little trees that I knew as giants.

Pat and I, and two of the others, paddled and pushed through the twisting slough to Lily Lake. There seemed to be no solid shore. We poled into the marsh grass and willows till we could go no further.

"Let's get out, " Pat said.

"I hope we can find the canoes when we come back down," I worried. We squelched through muck up to our ankles, until at last we began climbing into the woods.

There were no paths; this felt like an undiscovered Eden. We climbed and climbed, pausing now and then to catch our breath. At last we emerged onto a grassy clearing. I turned, and there, far below, I saw the River's silvery thread and the long roof of our old house. We flopped down on the grass.

"I'm going to come back here and hang a big red blanket in one of these trees," Pat said. "Then from your lawn we'll be able to see exactly where we've been."

One day Piers and Eddie and I discovered a place I never wanted to see again. We'd decided to explore the woods beyond Auntie Harriet and Uncle Bill's house. It was just plain woods, pine trees and oaks, so carpeted with pine needles that the walking was easy.

"Remember the day you almost set the woods on fire?" I asked. They'd been little boys then, playing with matches when they were supposed to be having their naps. "And you tried to put it out by filling pie tins with water from the River?"

We laughed. "Pie tins." It had become a joke. But I remembered Auntie Georgie's face, tight with fear and fury.

"Uncle Archie hitched up a hose," Piers said. "It could have been bad."

We trudged on, each of us silent with our own thoughts.

Ahead of us, the woods opened up. We found ourselves in an amphitheater, shaped by a sheer cliff of pink rock that curved around the space where we stood.

Piers had something to tell us: "Mother says if you whisper on one side it gets magnified so you can hear it at the other side."

We tried that; it was true. But I wanted to go home. "Our mothers used to call this Deadman's Gulch. Do you think someone fell off the cliff back in those early days?"

Piers and Eddie knew no more than I did about those long-ago days. But we did know about the fatal fall of Mabel Ulrich. It had happened one dark night just last summer. Her little cottage, empty now, stood on top, near the edge of the precipice. A long flight of wooden steps descended the cliff, but there was no fence, nothing, up by her house. Thinking about the accident kept me awake at night. She'd lived alone, no husband, no children. What was she doing there, wandering around in the darkness? And who discovered her body? I shivered.

Piers was at the foot of the steps, perhaps about to climb up. "Hey, Piers!" I called. "Eddie, come on, let's go."

Bossy Margaret Harper was a year older than I. She came over every day, as inevitable as the weather, apparently preferring my house, my family, my life to hers. There was no escaping her. "Oh-oh, here comes Mar-r-r-garet," we'd say, grinding our R's the way they did in Minnesota.

Occasionally I went to Margaret's house. The Harpers lived in the old Log House at the Landing, a short walk upstream from us. Any time spent at Margaret's house was a trial, because of her peculiar mother.

You never saw Mrs. Harper outside. She was always sitting on their screen porch, white-haired, with skin the blue-white of skim milk, dressed in white with white dress-up shoes, sitting idle, waiting, it seemed, for a captive listener. Her blue eyes pierced and held me while she talked, a monologue that seemed to have begun before I arrived, and that continued after I finally broke away. I heard about her children's infancy, their teachers, other people who meant nothing to me: ". . . Margaret was in kindergarten, and one day her teacher, Mrs. Pettigrew, kept Margaret after school because she'd been mean to Lenny Hayes, but Lenny's a dentist now, in Forest Lake, and they say he's very good . . . Margaret was so quick at fractions, she could measure out two-thirds of a cup of flour, and then . . ." Mrs. Harper seemed old, more the age of a grandmother than someone's mother. Margaret, abandoning me to her mother, was off-stage in the kitchen, making Tom Thumb Bars. Gentle Mr. Harper mostly stayed clear, out in his flowery refuge, half hidden by the bright dahlias, snapdragons, and cosmos he was quietly feeding or trimming.

As Mrs. Harper's flat voice droned on, I wondered how she'd become the way she was. I remembered the day she had uncharacteristically started to drive their long black LaSalle down our perilous dirt road, skirting the edge of our deep ravine, that sheer cliff that dropped down to the brook. Not a road to fall from. We'd all walked up that day and saw Mrs. Harper's LaSalle half off the road, supported only by two wispy pine saplings. Ed Wahlquist had come with his tow truck and ropes to winch the car to safety. Perhaps that had been Mrs. Harper's final outing.

Margaret Harper always knew a better way to do everything, and she didn't hesitate to instruct us all, adults included. "Watch this," she said to me once. With a flick of her wrist she swirled her sky-blue comforter into a special fan shape, something that only she knew how to do, she said. She tried to prove to Eddie and me that her one-horse outboard motor, the size of an eggbeater, was far superior to my family's minimally speedier six-horsepower Evinrude. "See, I can start mine with just my little finger." And sure enough she did that.

My mother, who scrupulously avoided making negative remarks about anyone, at least in front of Eddie and me, said that Margaret Harper's perpetual boasting showed that she had an Inferiority Complex. I thought to myself that what she had was a Superiority Complex. After I learned that none of my aunts and uncles could stand her, I felt better. Auntie Georgie might say, on occasion, "Let's get going before Miss Tiresome shows up."

Auntie Harriet and Uncle Bill helped me scheme to escape the constant Margaret Harper. "Hide!" Auntie Harriet once hissed when we heard her approaching. I dashed into their closet, crouching beside Uncle Bill's brown-and-white perforated wingtips. "No, haven't seen Alan lately," they lied. (Thirty years later, Auntie Harriet remembered Margaret and said, "I wonder who she's boring now?")

Margaret Harper's final appearance in my life was captured in a candid photograph of guests at my wedding. She is seen dangling her legs from a porch railing, teeth bared in a confident grin.

Auntie Harriet and Uncle Bill – 1944

– T H I R T E E N –

AUNTIE HARRIET AND UNCLE BILL always seemed much younger than my parents or Auntie Georgie and Uncle Herb, younger even than Uncle Archie. And they were, of course. My mother was already ten years old when Auntie Harriet was born.

She and Uncle Bill were not like parents, even after they had Janey. Genna and Janey were the same age, always "the little girls." They stuck together. Janey was pink and white like her father, with his blue eyes and a crown of tight blonde ringlets. In the summer she, like Eddie and me, was usually under Auntie Georgie's purview. This left Auntie Harriet and Uncle Bill quite free from the boring aspects of being parents. They whirled around in snappy cars to parties and clubs with Uncle Archie and their dashing young unmarried friends. Like Archie, they were avid fly fishermen, and often took off for a day or a week of trout fishing. "They are so silly," complained Auntie Georgie. "leading such careless, frivolous lives."

I found their seemingly carefree existence magically alluring. Auntie Harriet and Uncle Bill laughed more, and appeared to have more fun than anyone else in the family. They teased me; they flattered me. By the time I was thirteen I was spending more and more time with them, and their black Scottie, Hamish, who had a small, brittle bark.

Auburn-haired Auntie Harriet had softer features than Georgie or my mother. But of course she was younger than they were by a decade. Uncle Bill's high-domed head was half-bald, pink like his face from the sun, with a fringe of the blond curls that Janey inherited.

The tiny Guest House, Auntie Harriet's inheritance, was nestled in a grove of tall pines on a knoll over the water. She and Uncle Bill gradually expanded it in every direction, making an eccentric, patchwork house. Their new high-ceilinged living room was lined in pale pine boards. In their kitchen a ledge over the sink held an array of all the lotions and potions produced by Uncle Bill's family company. Maybe that was why he and Auntie Harriet seemed so blithe, why they lived more lavishly than anyone else in the family: they had more money.

Uncle Bill's family business bore what seems the unfortunate name: "Krank." During all the summers of my childhood we used Krank shampoo, Krank mosquito repellent, Krank everything you could think of—and most successfully the Krank hand lotion, "Balm Argenta." The labels on all these products bore the jagged Krank symbol. My mother and Auntie Georgie swore by Balm Argenta. I can see now its glass bottle with a pink cap, and a pump that squirted the milky lotion onto my hand.

Little sister Harriet is the star of my mother's first photo album. There she is in her white coat, hatted and muffed in white bunny fur, tucked up under a blanket in a white sleigh or her black wicker stroller. Beside her stands Agusta, the new young nursemaid, a capacious white apron covering most of her plain black dress. From season to season, Harriet is captured in black-and-white snapshots. At three she sits on the grass stroking Topsey, the family's brown dachshund, or ignoring Topsey, who rolls with her paws in the air.

The three sisters were old ladies, even Auntie Harriet, by the time I learned that Harriet's life was never as rosy and carefree as it had appeared to me. At eight, nine, ten she even looks worried in photos from those years in my mother's album, eyes downcast, squinting, frowning at their beloved little Topsey. I was already grown up when Auntie Harriet told me how scared she'd been as a child, mostly about money.

"We were the poor relations," she said. "We had to make do with untrained servant girls fresh off the farm because our parents couldn't pay the going wage. As soon as Mother had taught a new maid how to wait on the table, she'd up and leave for more money in a fancier household. I remember once we had a snooty English housemaid named Gertie. When I told her I didn't want butter and jam on my bread, Gertie said I only felt that way because Faddie couldn't afford both anyhow."

"Faddie took the streetcar to work, when all the other fathers were driven. But then our MacLaren cousins sent Harry, their chauffeur, to pick up Faddie and take him to his office in their big black motorcar because they were embarrassed to have him ride the trolley. It reflected badly on them. But it made Faddie cross to be patronized by his wife's rich relatives; he refused to ride in their car. And then, in the kitchen, Gertie said wasn't it lucky there was a nice warm drugstore near the trolley stop where my papa could wait on cold mornings."

Harriet picked up on Faddie's fury at those MacLaren relatives who gave the Ingersolls large household objects as Christmas gifts, a floor lamp once, and an overstuffed armchair. "Even as a little girl I knew people don't give each other 'useful' Christmas presents like that," fumed Auntie Harriet.

She'd worried that in his attempts to keep up, Faddie was spending too much on luxuries, his children's music lessons, their private schools. "It was all because he was a rich man's son. Our family would have been rich, too, he thought, except old Grandfather D. W. had lived till he was senile, and did queer things with his money—gave it away, threw it away, no one really knew. There was a story that he'd buried it under the house. I used to walk by and stare and wonder."

"Faddie was so proud. One time Mother was invited by a friend to go with them to Florida, all expenses paid, but Faddie said it was out of the question. Charity. He wouldn't think of allowing it."

Despite having been pampered and petted all through her bunny-furred babyhood, Auntie Harriet was still fretting as her big sisters grew up. During World War I, she told me, she watched from the stairs with jaundiced eye when Georgie and my mother entertained officers from Fort Snelling at Sunday afternoon teas. "I worried how much it was costing Faddie."

Worse yet was my mother's coming-out party. "Your mother had an expensive-looking white tulle dress, little silver bows all over it. There were bunches of pink tea roses and long-stemmed American beauties all over the house. Fancy food, and the silver candelabra tied with pink ribbon. And we had a black doorman in a dark blue coat and a megaphone calling the cars. There was a striped awning all the way to the curb. I didn't know how we could ever pay for all this."

"Oh, and two days later Aunt Katharine's snobby chauffeur came to say he'd go out to cut us a Christmas tree if we weren't able to afford one so soon after Jeannie's debut."

Poor little Auntie Harriet. I just listened. She'd had other worries, too. Archie sometimes teased and bullied her. Even though he'd taught her to swim, she so dreaded going into the water with him that she'd hide in the closet, holding her breath and praying he wouldn't find her.

Georgie bossed her, too. "She made me play the piano when her University friends came to our house. I hated it. Georgie always had to be in control. She used to quarrel with Faddie, shout, slam doors. I cried; I was always scared."

This was the first time I'd heard that Auntie Harriet sometimes resented Georgie. "She used to make me read Swinburne out loud . . . can you imagine? And when my eyes went bad, like all of ours, I came home wearing my new glasses, pleased as punch. Then I heard Georgie saying, "What a terrible, terrible sight! Now all her looks are gone.""

Every evening at the River Auntie Harriet and Uncle Bill played records. I went over to their house whenever I heard the strains of Cesar Franck's Symphony drifting out across the water, or Stokowski's bombastic rendering of Bach's D-minor Toccata and Fugue. My parents had brought me up with music, but the music Auntie Harriet and Uncle Bill played was louder, for one thing. And they listened to jazz. My parents never listened to jazz, or any popular music, except when they danced to it at a New Year's Eve party. My carefree young aunt and uncle had stacks of 78s by jazz greats with strange first names, like Muggsy and Peewee. Uncle Bill put a Bix Beiderbecke record on their late-model Magnavox player—and there was Auntie Harriet, laughing, hair pinned up, shoulders bare, twirling the ice cubes in her glass. I see her sleek white dress, bracelets of hammered Mexican silver, and those laced espadrilles with high wedge heels. At thirty, she looked the way I (at thirteen) yearned to look one day soon.

They laughed at my naiveté, but I didn't mind. It became a joke between us. One night, after they'd taken me with them to a movie in Stillwater, Uncle Bill pulled in at Huff's in Marine, and parked their car, a car like no other. It was a Mercury, a sporty new Ford product at the time, a long, eight-cylinder convertible, the color of heavy cream, with black fenders, shiny-spoked wheels, and red plaid seats.

I was quite used to Huff's; we often went in there for treats. But Huff's had a split personality, matched by a split in its architecture: two front doors, and a solid dividing wall down the middle. The right-hand door—the only one I knew—opened into the ice cream parlor, with rickety chairs, a marble counter, and four flavors. I'd slurped fizzy, frosty chocolate sodas there, and dripped strawberry cones on the hot sidewalk out front. But the other side of Huff's reeked of beer, truck drivers, and sweaty farm hands.

"This is the wrong side!" I said. But Auntie Harriet and Uncle Bill just laughed. We squeezed into a booth, where I sipped a coke and they drank 3.2 beer, Hamm's or Schmidt's. I was a quick convert to evil, if this was it. They teased me ever after about the "wrong side of Huff's." I would smile, and look demurely down. I never told my mother.

Cars, it seems to me now, played leading roles in the drama of my River family life. Our father's staunch adherence to boring black Chevrolet sedans and stately brown, wood-sided station wagons was an everlasting disappointment to Eddie and me. Uncle Archie and the Lewises were classier, I thought, with their powerful Lincoln Zephyrs. What was it about that word—Zephyr? It implied speed, I suppose, the speed of the wind, as a name for a car, or for the silvery modern streamliner we rode from Chicago, the Burlington

Zephyr. Uncle Herb drove in and out from St. Paul in a shiny dark blue Zephyr with four doors. Uncle Archie's was dark green, with tires that were white on the side. It had only one seat, just room for him and some pretty, laughing lady. My aunts and uncles all opted for the offspring of Henry Ford. Far racier, I thought, and more to my taste than dull General Motors. Auntie Harriet and Uncle Bill's eye-popping Mercury was still the best.

"Remember, Jeannie, how we were always dying for a car? The MacLarens were the first, but then the Fosters got a car. Everyone but us, it seemed."

"I remember wishing you and Archie and I could pool our money," my mother said. "But Faddie never trusted automobiles."

"He always used to say, 'horses are safer.'" The two sisters laughed.

Later, when World War II began, Uncle Bill Washburn was the only one of the uncles young enough to be drafted. He avoided the draft, however, by what seemed a perfectly legitimate maneuver. He and Auntie Harriet sold their big, beautiful house in St. Paul, rented out their River house, and took off for California with seven-year-old Janey, Janey's nurse Mrs. Brine, Hamish the Scottie, and most of their 78 records. Uncle Bill went to work helping turn out fighter planes at Lockheed.

Auntie Georgie and Uncle Herb were incensed. "It's so shocking, so cowardly," she fumed. "Evading his patriotic duty. Now they'll just go on in their same merry way in California, exactly as if the War wasn't even happening. I can't bear it." She said the same thing to Auntie Harriet and Uncle Bill, over and over. My mother took a more moderate stand. "But Georgie, it is a defense industry, after all, and Jack says it's just as important as the Army."

Nobody told me there was any friction between my aunts and uncles. I didn't find out until much later. The split was never truly healed. Auntie Harriet had always resented big sister Georgie's bossy ways. As she told me, "I was almost like one of her children; she raised me much more than Mother and Faddie." But now she was no longer a child; Georgie's fierce criticism was devastating.

She and Uncle Bill didn't leave St. Paul entirely right then. When the war ended, they bought a small house in St. Paul, and again spent summers at the River. Ten years later, they moved to California for good, severing all ties to Minnesota.

Archie and Helen on their wedding day,
with Piers, Genna, and Janey – 1940

– F O U R T E E N –

ONE AFTERNOON IN OCTOBER the Western Union boy brought a telegram for my mother. I watched her rip it open. It was from Auntie Georgie. "Uh-oh," she breathed. "Uncle Archie and Helen are going to be married in St. Paul on Saturday. They want me to come." As soon as my father got home, she told him. "You have to go," he said. "Of course."

"What'll I wear?" That was almost the first question. She rushed into Saks the next day, and came home with a little black hat that had a polka-dotted veil, to go with her red dress. The day after that, my father put her on the train in Newark.

She called us long-distance from St. Paul. "Aunt Katharine is giving a cocktail party for them, and Harriet's having a ladies' tea for Helen. Everyone's trying to do the right thing," she said.

She called us again after the wedding. "It was all just perfect," she said. "The same church, Alan, where Daddy and I were married. Aunt Helen had on a gold brocade dress, and she looked quite stunning. Archie had ordered white gardenias for us, so we three Ingersoll sisters did look pretty flossy walking down the aisle on the arms of the ushers—I wish you could have come, too."

Last season for the old Taylor house – 1940

My mother, Eddie, and I had spent one summer in the Taylor House, with my father there for his two weeks. Eddie and I were perfectly content, not minding all the frolicking mice that kept our mother awake and drove her wild. The house was perched right on the edge of the steep bank, about thirty feet above the river. The living room felt like a ship's cabin, with small windows through which you could see only water. "There's no bathroom," my mother told her friends; "only a hand pump in the kitchen sink." We brushed our teeth at the sink. The outhouse smelled sweet, like the pine trees from which it was built. If you wanted hot water to wash dishes or yourself, you had to heat it on the two-burner gas stove. In the evening, when we lit the oil lamps with their painted china bases, the room felt cozy. My mother hated it. A frustrated architect, she was already plotting to tear down the Taylors' cabin and replace it with a dream house of her own design.

My mother had already started having brush and small trees cleared from the land around the Taylor cabin where our new house was to be built. She paid Harlan Gabrielson forty cents an hour for sawing and stacking firewood. He burned the brush in the meadow into a great blazing, smoking pyre. My mother had an atavistic reverence for white pine, despite its being the most common species in the valley. She insisted that Harlan preserve each white pine he came upon, no matter how small. "We've discovered pines no one knew were there!" She was ecstatic.

She'd found a builder, Mr. Steffand, and told him about the house she wanted. They walked around; they talked. A week later she got his estimate: $3000. Too much! She cut out one bedroom. She wired my father. Still too much; they couldn't afford it. But she refused to give up. In St. Paul she negotiated a $2000 bank loan. They decided to go ahead.

"I wouldn't wait too long if I were you," said wise Uncle Herb. "This war in Europe: you never know. There may be shortages."

My mother stayed in Minnesota for a long time after Uncle Archie's wedding, three whole weeks. In New Jersey, Evelyn Lindgren was looking after Eddie and me, and doing the cooking. She was young and homesick, fresh from her job at Lorraine's Beauty Parlor in far-off Scandia, Minnesota. My father and I went grocery shopping at King's Market on Saturdays, when he didn't have to go to the office.

Even if Uncle Archie had not been getting married, my mother would have been at the River. She was supervising the construction of her new River house. She stayed all by herself in Gangie's old room at the Big House, with Georgie's dogs, Baloo and Lottie, for company.

We got letters from her almost every day. "Two days after the wedding, the Taylor house was gone—only a pile of junk." She and Mr. Steffand, the contractor, marked the perimeter of the new house with stakes. "I wanted to make sure we'd get the most sun and the best views up and down the River."

"The color is beautiful," she wrote. "The maples are pure gold, & such green, green pines—I haven't seen a fall here for years, since 1928."

Every few days the mailman would bring us a little packet of snapshots from her, black-and-white views of autumn foliage, piles of debris, stacks of lumber, men pouring concrete for the foundation. They had to blast out stumps and boulders with dynamite. "I never heard such a roar," she wrote, "and up went a great shower of earth. The dogs have gone into hiding."

She spent $50.00 on electric wiring for the new house. We did not yet have electricity at the River, but it was coming closer. A man from the power company came down to talk to my mother. "Harriet & I want it," she wrote, "if Georgie can be talked into it. It will cost us each $100.00." Since that still lay in the future, my mother ordered a shiny, white "Coolerator" ice box that would be filled with an enormous block of ice each week, in the same old way, by swarthy Mr. Bruett the Ice Man, with his big iron tongs.

When she telephoned us, my father let me listen on the upstairs phone. "You'll love the big Anderson windows . . . they frame our River view. And the cute built-in beds in our bedroom. Georgie went with me to the auction at the Ekdahls' farm. I bought a sweet pine bureau, six thumb-back chairs, and an old wooden trunk for blankets." The roof was on the new house when she took the train home to us in the east, just in time to vote for Wendell Willkie for president.

Auntie Georgie and Uncle Herb probably went with FDR.

The next summer we moved right into the new house. My mother plunged into unpacking and arranging things. She stood by Willard the Painter while he mixed pale translucent stains for the pine board walls in each room. I'd never seen her so happy as she was that year. No sick headaches, ever. Maybe, in everyday life, I thought, even though she was always busy, she didn't have enough to do. It wasn't the same as this, anyhow.

That first summer in the new house, my mother sighed and complained sometimes, especially after a grueling, hot day in St. Paul, checking off things like measuring cups or curtain rods from her shopping list. But once she got back to the River, changed out of her city clothes, and sank onto a long canvas deck chair on the lawn, she said, "It's so satisfying to have a project." That was her word: satisfying. She was proud of her work, especially when her snooty Aunt Katharine admired those clever built-in beds and the charming geranium wallpaper, or when Auntie Georgie said, "Our house seems so old and dark and cluttered."

Our new house had a spacious, airy living room with a table at one end where we had our meals. But it was not a big house. There was my mother's room (my father's also, of course, during his too-short visits), my porch, a modern bathroom, and next to the kitchen a hot, claustrophobic "maid's room" half-filled by the water heater. On the shiny painted floors throughout the house were narrow rag rugs woven on her big loom by Mrs. Edquist, the wife of the farmer who brought us milk, butter, and eggs.

I had the best room in the house, I still think. It was screened on one side, overlooking the ravine. Lying in my bed at night, I could hear the barred owl and the whippoorwill—

monotonous and soothing—far off across the water. From below my porch the clear, cold, water of the stream bubbled ceaselessly over the stones on its way to meet the wide, silent River. The stream was always cold, even during the worst heat waves. Water flowed around the spring box, an extra place to keep food when we ran low on ice. Cool piney air rose up toward the house and through the screen to where I lay beneath old striped blankets.

Over the bed on my porch my mother had hung a framed Currier and Ives print. She hung more of those iconic American images against the whitewashed wall of the narrow bedroom hall. They'd come out of a calendar sent to us by the insurance company. "They cost me nothing," she crowed to anyone who came to see our new River house. "The frames I got at Woolworths.'" She was always proud of being thrifty—"Scotch," she called it, implying that such habits as re-using gift-wrappings and saving chicken bones for soup were the result of her MacLaren heritage.

Most of our Currier and Ives prints featured cozy domestic scenes: the well-turned out little family walking to church, a Christmas-card sleigh pulling up at the old farmstead, curly-haired lads rolling hoops, sleek trotting horses leaving the barn. The one above my bed was different, dramatic, and alarming: the whole, endless western prairie was on fire. The flames in the distance seemed to touch the sky, smoke rose into high-piled clouds that reflected the orange of the blaze. In the foreground, three or four Indian braves in feathers and fringed leather rode bareback on rearing, plunging, panicked horses, and struggled to maintain their seats while soothing the frantic beasts. I knew there would be no fire department to rescue them and no happy ending that I could envision. When I switched off the light at night, I listened to the cool watery sounds from the stream below.

The flute-like notes of the rolling stream still floated up when I awoke in the morning. I sat up. A beaver somewhere down the River slapped the water hard with its tail. My porch had its own door to the outside. I walked out onto the stone terrace and the grass. Every morning the mist rose off the River, but this day was different. The air and the sky were white. Dense fog shut out the world: the Wisconsin shore and the hills, the tops of the pine trees, the dock, the boats, and even the River had disappeared. There was nothing now but me on our little promontory. If I walked to the edge I would fall off into infinity.

We didn't go for our early swim that fog-bound morning, but Auntie Georgie walked over as usual in her yellow terrycloth robe. She and my mother sat in the living room with their turquoise cups of coffee.

The sisters all agreed, finally, to allow the Northern States Power Company to bring its poles and wires down the hill to their three houses. Our new house already had the wires in its walls. Eddie and I fought like steers against the prospect of electricity. We begged to keep the kerosene lamps that smoked and smelled and singed your eyebrows if you leaned too close. We loved the extra-bright Aladdin lamps, bright enough for even the tiny print in *David Copperfield*. I was adept at filling the glass lamp bowls with oil, trimming the wicks, replacing the mantles. I knew how to adjust the flame so the lamp didn't smoke. I was good at cleaning the fragile glass chimneys, with just the one required drop of ammonia.

I was almost fourteen, and popular music and my own records were important. But we could play all our 78s on the wind-up portable. Why did we need electricity? Eddie and I were tigers: "No, Mommy. No! Please!" We cherished the soft glow of the oil lamps, the music we cranked up, the ritual it all involved. This was our life at the River, our summer.

We lost the battle. Auntie Georgie had been on our side, but even she finally gave in. When the electricity came on, our mother was ecstatic. "It's just dazzling!" Eddie and I weren't delighted by dazzle, but she was less conservative than we, less romantic. She had all our old oil lamps wired for the bright new era.

Our phone, however, was still the old-fashioned kind you cranked, just like the one in the Big House. All of Otisville shared a party line. Each house had its distinctive ring. Ours was two short and a long. If you called from away you'd ask for 46Q. We could eavesdrop if we wanted, but other people's conversations were usually boring. Mrs. Benson, who did the laundry: "Ja, so, well . . . so I said to him, 'Olaf, I guess you better go,' and then he says, 'Ja, guess so.'"

We lit a fire in the fireplace for the first time near the end of August. The living room filled with smoke. "Oh dear," said my mother. One fly in the ointment.

Eddie's Grouch House – 1947

Eddie was often bad-tempered that summer, especially when he had to spend a boring hour at the table every morning with his gray arithmetic workbook. I didn't blame him. Our mother had to hover to make him stick to it, those long columns of addition, the word problems involving trains traveling at different speeds. She got cross, too. When they reached an angry impasse, she'd send Eddie to the "Grouch House," i.e. the screen house, to simmer down. He had a secret stash of comic books out there. The Grouch House soon became Eddie's own cabin. He kept it neat as a pin, fishing rods in the corner, tennis balls on a high ledge, pajamas hung on a nail, and his own oil lamp.

My mother had our new house that year, and Uncle Archie and Helen had new twin babies, blond Bruce and Laura. They didn't look much alike. Laura's face was narrow and delicate; Bruce had a round head, and looked as if he might grow up to be a football player.

Uncle Archie and Helen often came out to the River that summer, staying at the Big House. I didn't call Helen "Aunt Helen;" she was just Helen, and she was always kind to me. She had suggestions on my clothes, and advised me on my hair: "You should try it up." Her suggestions were almost diametrically opposed to my mother's. "Yellow's not your best color," Helen said. "Black would be good on you." Black. Whoa.

She gave me a dress of hers once, one of those two-piece ones she favored that left your midriff bare. It's hard to believe I could wear something of hers, since she was pudgy, and I was so skinny that my mother still congratulated me whenever I gained a pound. Helen gave me expensive presents for Christmas and my birthday: a lacy negligee, once, that looked sort of strange with my flannel pajamas. Another year it was an enormous, velvet-lined, blue leather box with a tiny key for all my (non-existent) jewelry. Nothing educational, nothing I needed. Her gifts made me feel like someone else.

I do not know what Uncle Archie was doing then, or if he had a job. Little hints of trouble cropped up. "Archie's coming out to talk business with us tonight. A conference; just the grownups." My mother was depressed after these sessions; Auntie Georgie was, too. "Oh, Jeannie, what'll we do? Poor Arch . . ." Uncle Archie's and Helen's marriage, their lives, even, began turning sour very soon.

One summer Helen invited my mother and Georgie and me to visit her at Devil's Lake, a resort in Wisconsin, where she'd rented a cottage for a week or two. "Come on up," she'd said. "Your kids would love it."

"Oh Lord, I suppose we should," my mother said to Georgie. "I guess we can stand it for one night."

They took me with them, only me. The three of us set off one August afternoon in the Lewises' Lincoln Zephyr for the two-hour drive to Devil's Lake. The closer we got, the smaller the trees. We knew Uncle Archie would not be there; was he off fishing? Apparently those dear little twins would not be around, either. I can't recall where they were, or who was looking after them. Our trip was just to see Helen.

When we finally found her cabin, it was already late. The sun had set, and the lake was gray. She suggested a swim, but I was the only one who plunged into the weedy water. When I came back, Helen and Auntie Georgie and my mother were already having their highballs.

Helen was a good cook, which was one thing for sure. We had spaghetti and coleslaw and blueberry muffins on the screen porch of her cabin. The wind blew our paper napkins, and I was cold, and it didn't seem like summer any more. After supper I started reading *The Five Little Peppers* on the bed I was to share with my mother. Moths flapped around the bare light bulb overhead. Then my mother came in and said Helen wanted her and Auntie Georgie to go off with her for a little while to meet some of her new friends. "She says it's not far, and we'll be back very soon. You'll be okay, and Aunt Helen says the people in the next cabin are awfully nice."

I was fourteen, and it was dark. I watched the car lights waver and disappear down the bumpy dirt road. It was cold, and the blankets were thin. I tried to go to sleep, but I was scared, so I read some more. Once I heard some men laughing, but it was far away. I heard a car rev its engine; I heard a bang, like a firecracker, or maybe a gun. I fell asleep finally, because I did not hear my mother and my aunts come back.

The next morning we left. I'd poured myself a glass of milk. Helen didn't fix breakfast, but she came out in her pink housecoat and messy hair to wave goodbye.

"Thank God we're out of there. Lordy!" my mother said, as soon as we were on the hard road.

"What a nightmare! Ye gods." Auntie Georgie gave a long exhale. "The most god-awful place."

It came out bit by bit that Helen had taken them to a rustic bar, off in the middle of nowhere, far from Devil's Lake. I heard everything; maybe they forgot I was right there in the back seat.

"Have you ever been so cold? Out there on those logs . . ." Auntie Georgie said.

"Even inside, by that bar, it wasn't much warmer."

"Helen really is a drinker, isn't she . . . oh, poor, poor Arch!"

"And the way she chatted up those god-awful men; I couldn't stand her flirting. I thought we'd never get her out of there . . . it must have been three in the morning." They had been cold, tired, and longing for home, longing even, for Devil's Lake.

"Well, I guess now we know the worst."

"Maybe."

"Devil's Lake—I have to admit that sounds about right for Helen," my mother said.

The new house, with a Mexican chair and an oil lamp,
overlooked the River – 1941

– FIFTEEN –

MY MOTHER AND EDDIE and I made too many trips
to town. Our mother believed—probably even before we'd
gone to Arizona—that the only good doctors and dentists
in all the world were those we saw in St. Paul. (Eddie and
I spent too many summer days in Dr. Owen's dental chair
or Dr. Birnberg's spartan office.) If she didn't take us in the
Green Car, we might ride in early with Uncle Herb in their
Zephyr. Or Mrs. Edquist at the Copas station flagged down
the Soo Line train for us.

My mother was as organized as a Marine Corps colonel
in charge of a battalion. She kept track of everything in our
house. She made lists; she had a special technique for each
homely household task. Her insistence that we all do things
her exact way drove me crazy. The older I got the more I
minded. But nonetheless, I followed her rules. "A place for
everything, and everything in its place," she'd say. She had no
patience with anyone, including her children, when she was

searching frantically for something that had been misplaced.

She'd always been the opposite of her own sweet, vague mother. In one of my mother's old diaries I discovered a list she'd made when she was seventeen of everything she decided the River cottage needed, ordinary objects like more waste-paper baskets, a straw rug for the porch, and spring-closers for the screen doors.

Her instructions for closing up our new River house for the winter included a typed list of at least forty essential tasks. "Do not leave ink in the house," she ruled. "It will freeze and break.

"Leave oven doors open to discourage mice.

"Close damper in chimney to keep out squirrels.

"Roll up Portuguese rug with mothballs. Tie. Stuff newspapers in open ends."

She knew the way to wash dishes. You had to wash the dishes before you really washed them in Ivory flakes. Glasses first, then the old plated forks and spoons, the rooster-patterned plates, pots last of all, everything rinsed, dried with a linen towel, and put back where it belonged. Usually there was a maid to do this, but Eddie and I put in our time at the sink.

Every Thursday when our current Minna or Violet had her day off, my mother inspected the aluminum saucepans in the cupboard. With a steel wool Brillo pad in her thin white fingers, she etched a silvery X across the murky-gray bottom of each pan, an unsubtle hint that the entire pot should be scoured to a blinding gleam only to be obliterated that same afternoon when the unfortunate young woman used it to boil the potatoes for our evening meal.

My mother filled our new River house with antique Swedish pine chests and tables, old Swedish oil lamps (wired for electricity), and those rag rugs woven by Mrs. Edquist. Scattered through the rooms were artifacts that my mother had picked up in Mexico during our disastrous Arizona interlude. We had a settee and some armchairs made of pigskin stretched over the back, arms, and seat, and fastened to a lattice frame of wooden splints. They creaked when you sat on them, but were not uncomfortable, unlike the colorful painted chairs with rush seats that were too stiff and straight to be used as anything other than a place to leave a towel or your clothes. On the walls, interspersed with the Currier & Ives, my mother hung two or three strands of dried Mexican chilies. She'd brought back candlesticks and a pair of sconces made of hammered Mexican silver. Over her pine bureau she hung a mirror with a pierced and scalloped silver frame. I wasn't sure I liked these mementoes of our alien Arizona hiatus. Swedish Minnesota, on the other hand, felt safe and dependable.

Everyone who worked in my family's kitchens, cleaned or repaired our houses, washed our clothes, kept our lawns cut—every shopkeeper, everyone we depended on was Swedish: Swensons, Lundgrens, Edquists, Rosengrens. Everyone except my River family. My cousins and I had adopted a few Swedish words. "Ja" was the one that drove our mothers crazy.

"Alan, before you take off in the boat, I want you to sweep up the pine needles on the terrace. Have you made your bed?"

"Ja."

"Say yes, for heaven's sake. Not this ghastly 'yah,' as if you don't know any better. Cut it out."

At the same time my mother and my aunts, besides filling their houses with Swedish furnishings, bought Limpa every day, that dark, sweet Swedish rye bread that we all gobbled up. But my link to the Swedish immigrant culture became a bit more intimate for a day or two each August. Piers and Eddie and I were taken to the Edquists' farm, supposedly to help with the threshing. I cannot think of any possible help we provided; for us, it was a special summer treat.

Threshing Day was always clear and dry, the late summer sky a dome of deep blue. By the time Auntie Georgie dropped us off at the farm, the giant threshing machine was already noisily at work, so loud that you had to yell to be heard. A tractor with a steam engine provided the power to separate the wheat from the chaff. The machine was towed from one Scandia farm to another: All the neighboring farmers traveled with it, sharing the work, depending on each other.

Dressed alike in denim overalls, long sleeved shirts, and straw hats, some with a red bandana knotted at their necks to keep out the itchy chaff, each man had a certain task. Someone drove the team of horses that brought the fresh loads of mown wheat to the high threshing rig, while others forked the wheat into the whirling hopper. A fountain of golden wheat grains arced up against the cobalt sky. A shower of chaff fanned out below. The air was filled with dust, the shouts of the men, the din of the machine, the stink of gasoline, the sweet fragrance of the wheat. The men would spell each other for a turn at the pump, to guzzle water from the tin cup.

The morning was only half over when the women and the boys too young to work on the threshing rig moved sawhorses onto the flat ground near the house and laid planks across them to form long tables. We kids carried chairs, stools, and benches and set them in place, and then forks, mugs, and tumblers. The women brought out pitchers of lemonade and cold milk.

The big, airy kitchen was crowded with women busily stirring hot pots on the black iron range, and heaping mashed potatoes, meatballs, beans, rye bread, cucumber salad, and cabbage salad onto platters and bowls. Steam floated up to the ceiling.

"Watch out, kids. This is real hot."

"Outta the way now, before you get burnt."

The engine noise stopped while the men splashed their sweaty faces under the pump, then sat down to eat. They didn't talk much while they passed the bowls of food and stabbed slices of bread with their forks.

We kids were allowed to carry out berry pies, jam tarts, and the cookies that were twisted like pretzels. We never sat down, but somehow we were fed. In bed that night I coughed and itched all over from the dust and the chaff. "Tomorrow you can wash your hair in the River," my mother said.

Our station wagon loaded for the drive to the River – 1941

At the end of every August Uncle Archie helped my mother load our wood-sided Chevy station wagon for the drive home to New Jersey. On our first long day, aiming east across Wisconsin, we encountered an endless convoy of olive-green Army jeeps and troop trucks, heading in the opposite direction along the winding two-lane road. We passed each other for hours, open trucks carrying uniformed soldiers who waved to us. Eddie and I waved back. "Let's hope this doesn't mean we'll be dragged into this war," my mother said.

I looked at her. "Well, these soldiers don't look old enough to be in a real war, anyway." Eddie made the sound of a machine gun.

Frances, our cook, at the new River house – 1941

– S I X T E E N –

IN THOSE DAYS my father didn't seem to belong to the River. Back in New Jersey he was more of his real self, the strong, funny, kind father who took us to the Museum of Natural History and F.A.O. Schwarz, taught us to pitch and catch a softball, played his mandolin and the piano, showed us how to use the hammer and saws in his workshop, who could put a penny in one ear and pull it out the other or add more switches and signals to the Lionel train layout. But at the River for his two-week vacation, he seemed like a foreigner. So pale compared to the uncles, his long thin legs as white as milk, his shoulders turning pink like ice cream. He never went barefoot as they did, never wore shorts with no shirt. Of course Uncle Herbert wasn't like the other uncles, either, but he belonged there, in his usual chair on the porch or on the bench at the tennis court.

The first morning of my father's vacation I stood on the shore, about to plunge into the water with him. Suddenly he exclaimed, "Ow." You'd never hear him complain, or even raise his voice. But now he turned, and came hobbling out of the water. Sitting down on one of those black boulders dropped by the glacier, he raised a foot onto the other knee. Blood and water dripped onto the sand from a v-shaped gash.

"Daddy, you're bleeding!"

"Get your mother."

This was his first day. My mother and I helped him up to the house, leaving a trail of red drops across the grass.

"Keep it up, Jack." She rinsed the wound and tied it with gauze that turned pink.

"A bottle, it must have been. Imagine throwing a bottle into the River. Probably someone from the Public Landing."

Later Uncle Archie, in sneakers, poked around in the water until he picked up the jagged half of a brown Hamm's Beer bottle.

Nothing like this had happened before, not at the River. My father spent his entire two weeks with his foot elevated.

One summer day we all squeezed into the two outboards for a picnic on the Stutzes' sandbar. Piers and Eddie and I made drip castles in the sand while the grownups drank beer and ate sandwiches stuffed with tomatoes and salami. My father kept his shirt on, even when he swam.

"Ick," said Piers. "Tomatoes in the sandwiches; ugh. Isn't there anything for us?" Eddie and I didn't say anything, but we three ate just the bread, no tomatoes, no salami, no crusts. But we all slurped watermelon slices, spitting seeds into the water. When it was time to head home one of the boat motors wouldn't start. My father and Uncle Bill took turns pulling the starter rope, but nothing happened. By the time they gave up the current had floated us most of the way home. My father's face was pink, his chest still as white as the underbelly of a fish.

Later I heard him ask my mother, "Does Piers always fuss like that about the food?"

"Georgie never says a thing. She spoils him rotten."

Our mother was stricter with us than he was. "No dessert unless you try the creamed celery," she'd say. Or, "Do I hear a please? The magic word."

Always on one of the days our father was at the River, he took Eddie fishing in the ravine. Eddie was still too young to fly cast, so together they cut a pole, tied a piece of line and a hook to the tip. They dug worms and put them in a coffee can.

The stream came across Mr. Abrahamson's pasture, through a culvert under the Otisville road, and down through our wooded ravine, over the waterfalls, winding over rocks, until joining the river right below our new house. The stream was so cold it made your feet ache; the stream made the River feel almost warm.

I watched the two "men" start out. I liked seeing them go off together, away from our mother, not even thinking about Eddie's gray arithmetic workbook. Most mornings all that summer our mother kept him at the table after breakfast, scratching away with his pencil. "You have to finish this page, Eddie, before you can go out. It's the only way you'll ever get to third grade."

Now, starting out with our father, Eddie looked so small, with his pale hair angled across his forehead and his mouth half open so he could breathe better. They were both wearing sneakers with no socks, pant legs rolled up to their knees.

"Good luck," I called. "Oh, don't forget your worms!"

An hour and a half later they were back, sneakers muddy. Our father held the fishing pole. "Look what I caught!" Eddie held out a forked stick from which two tiny trout dangled. "They're brookies."

The trout were beautiful, gleaming, their colors still bright.

"Did you really catch them, Eddie?" I looked up at our father.

"Indeed he did. And now we're going to clean them, so Violet can cook them for Ed's breakfast tomorrow."

The next morning, following my mother's instructions, Violet started bacon in the black skillet, tossed the trout in cornmeal, and fried them in the drippings until they were brown and crisp. Eddie was pretty fussy about food then.

"You have to take a taste, Eddie, at least," said our mother.

"Don't worry," our father said. "They'll be eaten."

But Eddie was hooked on fishing. He told Uncle Archie about his catch.

"I bet you it was really your father who hooked them," said Piers.

"You weren't even there, Piers!" I was furious. "What a dumb thing to say."

Once Piers caught a catfish. Harlan, who worked around the place, showed Piers how to bait a hook with hamburger stuck together with soap. Night after night Piers stood on the rocky shore flinging his lure out over the dark water.

We heard him shout. "Hey, I got one." In the pale moonlight he came running up the bank. The screen door banged behind him, and there he was holding out a net with his still-flopping trophy inside.

"Not in the house, Piers," my mother said. "It's dripping." Piers was flushed, and dripping, too. He pulled the big, ugly fish out of the net, and, with a smirk, held it up to my face. The catfish was almost two feet long, its fierce mouth surrounded by spiny whiskers. I screamed, and ran down the hall. Piers followed, thrusting the fish at me.

"Arch says catfish are good eating," Auntie Georgie said the next day. But no one ate Piers's catch.

Reading in the living room one evening, I could hear my parents talking out on the lawn. My father's white shirt blazed in the dusk. Ice tinkled in their glasses.

"Oh, Jack, I miss you when you're not here. Georgie can be so bossy. She always knows best. Poor H came over in tears the other day—Georgie has no use for Bill, and says Janey is way behind Genna, who's already starting to read."

"But Georgie's always been like that, you know. She doesn't mean half of what she says; some of it's just a pose."

"And Piers is way ahead of Eddie . . ."

"Now Jeannie, you know that's not true. Eddie is wonderful, so good at making things, building things; he has entirely different skills than Piers."

I had a costume closet in the attic of our house in New Jersey, stuffed with the more glamorous remnants of my mother's outmoded wardrobe. My friends and I used them for dress-up. My mother's spangled party dresses from the 1920s, with their once-shocking short skirts, just cleared the floor for me at nine. The dress in which my mother had first charmed my father was one of these. Of lettuce-green chiffon, its skirt was composed of triangular bias panels that had hung—or floated, when she danced—in points somewhere around her knees.

My father had been introduced to her at a party, after which he had written home to his family, "I have met the girl I am going to marry." The year was 1920; he was fresh out of the Army, and new to St. Paul. He'd been sent there to manage a branch office of the large manufacturing company for which he would work until he retired at sixty-five. Through his new job he met Faddie, who invited him to come for dinner. There he saw my mother again. And again.

He asked Georgie to help him pick out a ring for my mother. They went to Bullard's and selected the little square-cut emerald that was always on her thin white finger.

My father had always gotten on with my mother's family. He'd admired Faddie: "A gentleman of the old school." Faddie put on his dinner jacket and black tie for dinner every evening. Even at the River, I wondered? "He was a great reader; never without a book." Although Faddie's business ventures never quite panned out, he was "a model of probity," said my father. "Not a trace of snobbery in him."

Auntie Georgie and Mother, their early morning swim – 1959

– SEVENTEEN –

NEARLY EVERY MORNING, after we were in the new house, Auntie Georgie walked over from next door at about eight with Rigo, her German Shepherd. Out on our lawn she and my mother, in their familiar frayed and faded terry-cloth coats over flowery bathing suits, drank coffee out of those turquoise-blue cups. I joined them, while Rigo and Lottie, our Sealyham, wagged their tails and sniffed each other. Then we walked down the six mossy steps to the shore, where the clear, freezing cold stream ran into the warmer, quieter River, water the color of iced tea. "It's from the iron," my mother always said.

Mist was rising over the water. The shore across the River was still dim and shadowed, but from over the Wisconsin hills the morning sun felt warm on my shoulders. The cry of a pileated woodpecker burst through the silence, followed by its rat-tat-tat hammering on a tree in the ravine. My mother and Auntie Georgie spread their coats over a boulder, and plunged in. The skirts of their bathing suits floated out around them like petals. Uttering little cries of exhilaration, they kicked furiously to get warm. Soon they settled into slow breaststrokes, their heads in white bathing caps held well above the water. And then they talked.

"Arch wants me to take the twins for a week or two," said Auntie Georgie. "To give Helen a break, he said."

"Oh Lordy," my mother said. "You've got to say no. H and Bill want you to take Janey, too! Why do they all think they can just dump their kids on you? They know better than to ask me." She began kicking furiously.

"I don't know, Jeannie, I just feel so sorry for Bruce and Laura—and for Archie, too."

I swam fast against the current. I couldn't help remembering how often our mother had left Eddie and me with Auntie Georgie. When I turned back, the two sisters were still talking about everybody and everything under the sun, settling nothing. I circled around them, listening. I loved to hear them talk. From them, I thought, I'd finally learn what life was all about. Sometimes they looked at me, and Auntie Georgie would say something about my "marvelous Sterbé eyes," a reference to some long ago Polish princess. I never knew what she meant, and I knew it meant nothing except to them, since my eyes were usually hidden behind my glasses. But I liked her saying it.

One morning Auntie Georgie was sitting on the big front lawn, feet up, an open book on her lap, as always. I sat on the grass beside her, hugging my bare knees. She looked at me, intense brown eyes framing her narrow nose. She sees right into me, I thought.

"Listen to this," she said, "from Christina Rossetti:
> *"Raise me a dais of silk and down;*
> *Hang it with vair and purple dyes;*
> *Carve it in doves and pomegranates,*

> *And peacocks with a hundred eyes;*
> *Work it in gold and silver grapes*
> *In leaves and silver fleur-de-lys;*
> *Because the birthday of my life*
> *Is come, my love is come to me."*

Another day it was the dark and haunting poems of Rupert Brooke and Wildred Owen, two bright voices lost amid the horror of the First World War:

> *What passing bells for these who die as cattle?*
> *Only the monstrous anger of the guns.*
> *Only the stuttering rifles' rapid rattle . . .*

Auntie Georgie lent me books. "You must read this," she said, handing me Oscar Wilde, *The Happy Prince*. Then came Aldous Huxley's, *Crome Yellow*. "Huxley's marvelous; try it; let me know what you think." I didn't always "get" the books she offered me. But I tried. All I understood of *To The Lighthouse* was that Mrs. Ramsay—so intense about the people she cared for—reminded me of Auntie Georgie herself. Now in pictures of Auntie Georgie, with her sharp, narrow features, I see Virginia Woolf.

Auntie Georgie was among the early subscribers to Mr. Rodale's *Organic Gardening*. "He's obviously a crank," my mother sniffed. But Georgie, undeterred, fed us wheat germ, and forbade Fred Rosengren to sprinkle any more "Vigoro" on her lettuce and Swiss chard.

My mother was a reader, too, but her tastes were different. She loved books of adventure: polar exploration and mountain climbing, two pursuits guaranteed never to be part of her actual life. During World War II she was reading about espionage and intrigue, in *Paris Underground*, and George Millar's *Watching in the Night*.

Five years after I'd recovered from my great illness, my mother was still urging me to nap for two hours every afternoon all summer long. "You may read, dearie, if you'll first be perfectly flat and quiet for 10 minutes—you know how—and then read quietly on your porch bed with the door shut so you won't be disturbed." I'm not sure whether she was more anxious about my health or my required school reading.

A year or two later, stretched out on the striped cushion of one of those old metal lawn chaises, I read *War and Peace*. My mother's copy seemed especially timely; one endpaper in her edition had a map of Napoleon's fatal Russian campaign, while the other depicted Hitler's disastrous march to Stalingrad. The sun beat down on my bare legs; the sweet, warm fragrance of pine needles rose around me. An outboard started up now and then on the River; I heard my mother's voice in the house, probably reminding Evelyn to be sure to save all the chicken bones for soup. The soft thunk of tennis balls roused me out of Russia, and I ambled along the path to the court, wanting to miss nothing of the precious River summer.

My mother and her old friend, Lib Clark, were out on our lawn. I heard Mrs. Clark's shrill voice: "So there I was, naked as a jaybird, just standing there, stark naked, when . . ." Her voice dropped then; I couldn't hear the rest.

I always tried to listen when my mother and Auntie Georgie talked together or with their friends. My mother's ordinary River days were pretty much taken up with calling Roy Strand with her grocery order, collecting our dirty laundry for Mrs. Benson, reminding Eddie to rinse his feet when we came up from swimming. But listening to her conversations, especially with Auntie Georgie, I knew that real, grown-up lives were sometimes as strange and romantic as stories in books.

Anna Quinn—Mrs. Quinn to me, of course—was a source of wonder to my mother and Auntie Georgie, as well as to me. She and Mr. Quinn and their two children spent their summers in an old white farmhouse halfway to Marine. Mrs. Quinn was Italian, beautiful, immaculate, and exotic. Her voice was musical, her accent soft and sweet compared to all the Minnesotans. "Deeck-ie! Sa-andra!" When she came over to see us, she called to her two children, trying vainly to round them up to go home. They usually ignored their mother, responding finally in the harsh, sharp voices that I suppose we all had.

My mother and Auntie Georgie talked together about Mrs. Quinn. "She told me she sleeps on a stone pillow to keep from getting wrinkles." Auntie Georgie winced. My mother examined her nails. The emerald flashed in the sun. "It protects her hair, too, she says."

"Anyhow, it doesn't sound very pleasant for Frank."

Frank was Mr. Quinn, a dull, innocuous man, it seemed to me. He had once been a naval officer, stationed, according to my mother and Auntie Georgie, in Italy, where he and the lovely Anna had fallen in love. I supposed he might have been handsome then, in his officer's whites. Both sisters agreed that her life now was more or less tragic.

"She grew up in Florence," Auntie Georgie was saying, "in one of those enormous old stone palazzos . . . the ones that appear to have no windows, but then there's a huge courtyard inside."

"Her father was a Count," my mother said. "So does that make her a Countess?"

On another day I was startled to hear my mother talking about her old flame, Don Bigelow, who'd come home on a brief leave from the Foreign Service. His wife Honor and their boys had remained in Geneva. Don had just left

My best friend Monnie at our tennis court – 1943

the River after spending the weekend at Auntie Georgie and Uncle Herb's. Now, discussing him with Georgie, my mother sounded both elated and wistful. I could tell that she was captivated still.

"After twenty years . . ." she murmured.

One day a thick catalog from something called "Johnson & Smith" arrived. Piers and Eddie and I pored over its black-and-white illustrations. After we each pondered over our choices, we sent in coins to order amazing gimmicks and gadgets: 10 cents for a scary-looking fake spider, for 15 cents a tiny buzzer designed to startle someone if you held it while shaking their hand. Or a Whoopee Cushion for a quarter. Monnie and I pooled our resources to send 50 cents for a book entitled *How to Love and Be Loved*. "That should be really good," said Monnie. "I can't wait."

"Put your address," I said. "If it comes to my house, my mother will find it."

Finally the book arrived, a discouragingly thin pamphlet. We studied it behind closed doors. Very disappointing, not whatever we'd hoped for. "Flirting with your Handkerchief: if you drop it, that says 'come closer.' The Language of

Flowers: violets mean 'maybe.'" Monnie stuffed the booklet into her bottom drawer.

Two days later my mother told me she wanted to talk to me. She shut the door into her room. There it was, on her bedside table: *How to Love and Be Loved*. Oh, no.

"When you are a little older, dearie, I'm sure you'll find some nice boy who will like you for the fine person that you are." I felt more like a criminal. "This little book won't really help," my mother went on. (I already knew that.) "Boys like a girl who is interested in them, who asks questions, and listens to what they have to say. Be a good listener!"

But the boys at dancing school in New Jersey barely spoke, so how could I be a good listener? And at the River the boys I knew just talked the way we always did.

My mother and I had already had the birds-and-the-bees talk, and The Wonderful Story of How You Were Born. That was old hat. Now *How to Love and Be Loved* had given her the idea I wanted to know more. She was right, of course.

My father, Uncle Herb, and Auntie Georgie at the court – 1959

– EIGHTEEN –

AUNTIE GEORGIE WAS VISITING US in New Jersey on December 7, 1941, the day the Japanese attacked Pearl Harbor. We were sitting by the fire, listening to the Philharmonic, when we heard the news on the radio. The first air raid warning sounded the next day.

The war already seemed very close to us in New Jersey. Refugee children were coming to my school, and my parents' friends now included people who'd fled Europe. My father became a Civil Defense policeman, and my mother, a Red Cross Nurse's Aide.

After Pearl Harbor, there was talk of gas rationing. "Four gallons a week! That's all?" My mother couldn't believe it at first.

"You can figure it out, Alan." My father liked to encourage my math skills. "How far would one gallon of gas take you?"

Each gallon took our Chevy station wagon twelve miles. We could never make the 1300-mile journey to the River by car. That was an easy arithmetic problem.

At the River that summer the war felt so remote to me it might as well have been happening on Mars.

"I managed to buy eleven pairs of silk stockings, " gloated my mother. "That ought to carry me for the duration. I had to go to three different stores."

She and Auntie Georgie were talking during their early morning swim. I was listening, as usual.

"Oh, Jeannie, that's so selfish! We're not supposed to be thinking how we look; people are dying."

Auntie Georgie was right, I thought. I didn't like feeling disloyal to my mother. Of course I said nothing.

With Faddie's old spade, Fred Rosengren had turned over the vegetable garden for Auntie Georgie. He was the only man left to do any work for our family; all the younger men, including Harlan and Arthur, had been drafted.

I watched Auntie Georgie plant a row of beans. It was hot, and she was wearing just her bathing suit, the one with the faded blue roses on it.

"This is a Victory Garden," I said.

"No, Allie, it's just our same old vegetable garden." That was just another fashion she didn't bother about.

When the tomatoes finally turned red at the end of August, she and my mother spent a long day canning them in the kitchen at the Big House. This was the first time either of them had ever done such a thing. Since Auntie Georgie had done most of the work in the garden, my mother drove up to the Scandia Merc to get a big aluminum canning kettle and cartons of glass quart jars.

Dena was off on her vacation, so the sisters had the kitchen to themselves. Fred Rosengren had filled three bushel baskets with plump red tomatoes.

The Fannie Farmer cookbook was on the table, open to the canning page. My mother turned on the gas under a pot of water. "George, can you remember Mother doing this? I know she taught us how to skin tomatoes in boiling water."

"Well, yes, that was almost the only thing she knew how to do in the kitchen."

"I still think they should be peeled for salads. But, truthfully, I'm not sure we're much better than Mother. Of course you're so lucky to have Dena; she'll never leave. But I don't think I'll be able to get anybody in New Jersey—they're all getting more money now in the defense plants, even the colored. But to me the idea of cooking dinner every night . . . oh, dear."

"Here's a little knife, Allie; you can help," Auntie Georgie said.

The kitchen filled with steam. Piers stood at the kitchen door. "Hey, what's going on? Aren't we going to have lunch?"

"Go on over to our house, Piers," my mother said. "Where's Eddie? Tell Evelyn I said she should make sandwiches for you."

When Uncle Herb got home we all had to admire the beautiful jars of red tomatoes.

"Thirty-six quarts," Auntie Georgie said.

"I'm glad I have our station wagon. If I weren't driving home to New Jersey, what would I do?"

"Just leave them all for us," Uncle Herb said, with his gentle low chortle.

"Well, next year I probably won't have any choice." My mother sounded serious. "With the gasoline rationing, we'll have to start taking the train again, the way we used to."

The next day the sisters undertook another kitchen project, unfamiliar and time-consuming. They turned a basket of not-quite-ripe produce into jars of Gangie's "Green Tomato Pickle."

"I'm so glad I had her cookbook re-bound," my mother said. "All Mother's receipts, in her dear, old-fashioned handwriting; it makes me cry." My mother began reading through the book. "They all traded with each other, the St. Paul ladies . . ."

"For their cooks, Jeannie; none of them actually made these things themselves."

"But don't you remember, Mother always made the strawberry jam, and the crabapple jelly. Look, 'Mrs. Lightner's Sugar Cookies, Mrs. Clark's Pudding Sauce, Emma's Sponge Cake.'"

"Jeannie, we've got to get started on this."

"Oh, Lordy; this is going to take two days! 'One peck of green tomatoes, six large onions. Chop fine. Sprinkle with half-a-cup of salt and stand overnight.'"

"I hope we have enough tomatoes. What is a peck, anyway? Allie, go look it up in the big dictionary."

I scampered off, happy to have a task. "It's one-fourth of a bushel," I announced when I came back.

"Oh, we have plenty. And the onions." My mother trimmed the vegetables, while Auntie Georgie went to work with the crescent-bladed chopper and the old wooden chopping bowl.

"This is awful! I'm crying." The sisters took turns, each chopping until her eyes became too painful.

"That's it till tomorrow. Come on, Alan, I've got to get in the water." We all went swimming.

The next morning Auntie Georgie had me read through the recipe. "'Drain through colander. Add five green peppers, chopped.'"

"Aagh, more chopping," my mother said.

"Oh, this won't be half bad. Get me that big kettle from under there, Allie."

I looked behind the blue-checked curtain that hung over the shelves down next to the sink. I read them the rest of the instructions. "Pour into 1 quart vinegar and 1 quart water. Put 2 lbs. brown sugar; 1 Table spoon ground cloves; 1 Table spoon ground ginger; 1 Table spoon ground cinnamon. Cook until tender.' Someone else wrote in '1 1/2 hours.'"

"Thank heaven we have enough brown sugar. And the spices."

"We'll have a lot," my mother said.

They each ended up with six glass jars of Green Tomato Pickle. I wrote the labels, and stuck them on.

"We're pretty hotsy-totsy, aren't we?" Auntie Georgie sounded triumphant. She flung an arm around my mother. "Herb, I think we've both earned a highball." It was getting dark then. Moths flapped around the bare light bulb that hung from the wooden ceiling.

Auntie Georgie's head was down when she came across the meadow to our house one morning. "Herb's been rejected by the Marine Corps," she sighed. "He really wanted to do it. 'Too old,' they said."

"Oh, I bet he didn't like that," said my mother. "But Georgie, really, he couldn't have done it. The paper needs him. And you need him."

"Partly I'd hoped if Herb went in, it would show up H and Bill for the way he's weaseled out of it. Lockheed . . ." she sniffed, "California. But Herb's not as petty as I am. And he's practically running the paper now. Almost half the staff has been drafted. Or volunteered; all the young ones, anyway."

"And he has to send stuff to the *Times*," added my mother. Uncle Herb was the *New York Times* correspondent for the upper-Midwest. We were all proud of Uncle Herb. Newspapers were the source of news; everyone read the papers.

One Sunday Uncle Herb and I were battling Monnie and my father at doubles when Piers came running out to the court. "Father," he hollered. "Telephone—it's important."

That was the end of that tennis game. Mussolini had resigned. Herb had to leave for town immediately to write an editorial for a special extra edition of the paper.

I worshipped Uncle Herb. Through him I felt close to the heart of what was really going on in the world. A year later he moved closer to the war when he flew off to report from London, while the Germans' new "buzz-bombs" whistled eerily overhead, and silent V-2 rockets rained ruin. He was in London for almost a year. I missed him; we all did.

One night after dinner I walked out across the dewy grass, blind at first from the house lights. Down at the landing, in the mosquito whine, I could see perfectly. No moon, just a heaven spangled with stars—the Dipper, Cassiopeia, the Milky Way. The water lapped gently against the wooden boats. From the wooded islands across the River I heard a barred owl, its repeated hoots falling off each time in a descending moan.

The path up toward the old house runs close to the River bank. The grass was cool on my bare feet. A faint light came from a lamp in the big living room, where Auntie Georgie would, I knew, be sitting with a book.

The screen door clicked behind me. "'Tyger! Tyger! burning bright,'" I called. "'In the forests of the night . . .'"

"'What immortal hand or eye dare frame thy fearful symmetry?' Come on in, dearie." She put her book down. Baloo gave a soft grunt of welcome; old Lottie barely opened her eyes; her stumpy tail twitched once.

"Sit down, Allie, and listen to this. Tell me what you think:
My candle burns at both the ends.
It sheds a lovely light.
But oh, my friends
And oh, my foes
It will not last the night."

"Mother quotes that, when she thinks I'm up too late with my homework. Edna St. Vincent Millay—is that what you're reading?"

She read me another verse, but I had a question, something I'd wanted to ask. "How did you get to know Uncle Herbert?"

"He and I were at the University at the same time," she said, "But unlike me, he was much too busy to have a social life. He was already working part-time at the paper to pay for his college tuition, and for graduate school. He won a fellowship to Harvard, thinking he would go into teaching, but then his father got sick, and he had to give it up. He worked on Al Smith's campaign for the presidency, and he had an offer from Bernard Baruch. But he wanted to be a journalist, so when the *St. Paul Dispatch* invited him to join the editorial page that settled it."

"Good for them," I said. I'd always looked up to him. He made newspapering seem the most glamorous, eminent sort of work I could imagine.

"Herb and I knew each other for a long time. I was traveling, having a lovely time, not at all sure I wanted to settle down—with him or anybody. Then I started working at the paper, too. Faddie would have hated that. Of course the only job there for me was on the Women's Page, but it was better than nothing! And my boss, Amy Birdsall, was wonderful, a really smart lady."

The lamp on the table shed a pool of light; the rest of that high-ceilinged room was dark.

"Keep telling," I said when she paused.

"So I worked for the paper till Uncle Herb and I got married in 1930. If Faddie had still been alive then he would have probably had a fit at the idea of his daughter marrying a Jewish newspaperman, a descendant of immigrants from Eastern Europe. But Herb's parents were well educated, prominent and respected in Marshall, Minnesota, where his father started the general store. Herb and his sister were the star pupils in their school." She took a deep breath. "We had a tiny wedding, but very proper, very conventional. Archie 'gave me away,' and I wore Gangie's satin gown. It was at House of Hope Church, and Cousin Margie played the organ. But it was very small."

My mother arranging wildflowers

– NINETEEN –

"DO YOU KIDS have any idea what time it is?"

In her yellow bathrobe, with a few metal curlers in her hair, my mother appeared suddenly at the door into our living room. Standing there, without her glasses, she looked befuddled, as well as cross. "It's two o'clock in the morning!"

I was embarrassed to have her burst in on us like that, embarrassed to have my friends see how she looked at night when she went to bed.

Thorne clutched her Coke; beneath her bell of dark hair the pink circles on her cheeks turned pinker. The ash of Jim Gray's cigarette was about to fall. Silent Ricky slumped in his chair. Monnie stopped shuffling the cards from our last game of "Oh Hell." Pat stood at our record player holding his favorite Jo Stafford, "Sunny Side of the Street." And Margaret was there, of course, Margaret Harper, in the big armchair, facing the vase of flowers from their garden that she'd brought earlier to my mother. None of us said anything.

As soon as my mother went out, everyone got up to leave. Margaret set out on foot, the others in Jim's father's Chevy. I heard the rhythmic creak of Pat's oars as he rowed home across the moon-flooded River.

In the morning I heard my mother and Auntie Georgie talking as they walked down the bank for their swim. I pulled on a bathing suit and followed. My mother said nothing about how late my friends had stayed; she didn't even seem upset. All she talked about with Auntie Georgie was Monnie's mother, Mrs. Russell, Margie to them.

"Margie sets no limits for her girls, no rules at all. She'd let them stay out all night if they felt like it; she's just so anxious for them to be popular."

"Aagh," sneered Auntie Georgie. "Her standards are so low. You'd think she'd want to encourage their minds. Or their musical talent; Monnie has a real gift."

"I hope you're listening, Alan," my mother said. "Always remember this, darling: It cheapens a girl if no one sets limits for her. Boys will get the wrong idea; they won't respect her."

I swam fast away from them without saying anything. Respect was not exactly what I was looking for then, not from boys, anyhow.

Later that day, Auntie Georgie was on the porch with her feet up on the wicker stool. I walked over to her, and she put her book down. "Hello, my Allie, best beloved. What's up?"

"Nothing special. Ma thinks we all stay up too late. She gets cross. But she says she wants me to have fun."

"Oh, we mothers. We want our kids to grow up and be happy, but then we can't face it that they're not children any more."

"I'll be fourteen next week."

"Pretty old . . . old enough for me to tell you about the book I'm reading." She held it up. "Don't tell your ma. She'll probably want to read it, too, but she wouldn't like me telling you about it."

"*Lady Chatterley's Lover*," I read. "What's it about?"

"It's a sad story, very sad, about an unhappy woman and a man who's had a hard time. But for a little while they're happy. Together."

"Well, isn't that okay?"

"Yes. It is. For Lady Chatterley and the gamekeeper it was. But it caused a scandal. And the book is still considered scandalous by a lot of stuffy people." She waved it in the air. "This book was even against the law in the U.S.A. People had to sneak it in. It's still a very puritan country, Allie. Terrified of sex."

"Well, Ma's reading that thick book with the orange cover: *An American Tragedy*. It's supposedly about a woman who was having a baby, and she wasn't even married. Isn't that a scandal? "

"Oh, yes—and she had to die because of it. The wages of sin. Huh." Her long gold earrings made a tinkling sound when she shook her head.

Just then Piers and Eddie came running up from the river, followed by Uncle Archie. "Look what I caught," Piers called.

"Next time, Allie, I want to hear what you think about the boys out here: Ricky and Jim, Pat Shearer, Roddy, Mike . . ." Auntie Georgie stood up to greet the fishermen.

"I hate my frizzy hair," Monnie said. "It's like steel wool." The ideal was long, sleek hair with a ripple here and there, like Lauren Bacall's. Monnie and I fretted over our looks while we worked on our tans, talked about boys, and waited for love.

Auntie Georgie had dropped me off at Monnie's house in the afternoon. The Russells lived high on the hill above the River. Monnie and I sat at the long table on her porch with our magazines. We'd collected a bunch: *Western Romance, Hollywood Love, Secrets of the Silver Screen.* We kept them hidden behind her bed. In my house I knew my mother would have spotted them pretty quickly.

Monnie and I read stories aloud to each other, laughing at every ridiculous detail. Our plan was to write our own stories, equally trite, equally cliché-infested, and submit them to the magazines. We had no doubt we would succeed. It was so simple. Looking out into the treetops and chewing on our pencils, we waited for inspiration. A warm, chocolate-y smell reached us from the kitchen, where Mrs. Russell, as usual, had something sweet in the oven.

Amber, our titian-tressed heroine, wore a snug blue-and-white checked dress that was perpetually, sort of accidentally, slipping off one shoulder. And then into town rode the Unknown Cowboy, "brawny, broad-shouldered, and bronzed from weeks in the saddle." In the next paragraph, "Hal suddenly clutched her to his manly chest, gazing down into eyes that were limpid, liquid lakes of lilac. 'Amber,' he breathed hoarsely, 'this is bigger than we are.' She uttered a faint mellifluous moan, and then . . ."

But Monnie and I, laughing nervously, could write no further.

"Let's go see what my mother's making; it smells good."

The Russells' living room was furnished with a curvy Victorian sofa and chairs, contrasting with pine board walls and a row of Quimper plates on the mantelpiece. I always paused to examine the Swiss music box, which sat on a wooden post that had been carved to look like the trunk of a tree. Three carved wooden bears climbed up its branches as if they, too, wanted to look into that music box.

Ours was the only tennis court on the River at Otisville. It was an old court, installed in 1913 by Faddie, only a year after the Big House was built. In my mother's album are snapshots of girls reaching up to serve in skirts almost to their ankles, of Archie, in long pants, white shirt, and tie, swatting at the ball. By the time I was thirteen the court had become the hangout for all of us cousins and our River friends.

Except on Sundays. The uncles usually took over the court then, in their white shorts. Pat's older brother Roddy and Margaret's big sister Libby were invited to play with them. Both of them were eighteen, and much better at tennis than any of us. "Good shot, Libby," yelled Uncle Bill. "Boy, what a terrific gal. Got it all."

Uncle Herb shook out his pipe. "Yeah, she has great form. A strong serve, too."

It seemed as if they admired more than her tennis. Long-legged, laughing Libby: I couldn't wait to be eighteen and good at tennis, returning the hard serves of a tall, strong, lean Roddy, having the uncles admire me.

We spent much time searching for lost balls, combing through the leaves and grass with our wooden racquets. Was it white, the one you'd found? Or some old dead ball that had lain there for weeks? Once Roddy brought a can of red balls, the latest thing. "Maybe they'll be easier to find," someone said. They weren't.

The court was clay, carved into the hillside, and fenced with peeled logs and chicken wire. A spectators' bench had been built into the up-hill side. There was not quite enough space behind the service lines: if you ran back to return a high lob you might find yourself backed up against grapevines. During frenzied rallies, the ball sometimes disappeared into the matted greenery. Moss grew in the shady back corner. After a rainstorm it took days to dry.

"You'll have to roll it before you play," said Uncle Herb, overseer of the court. We pushed the heavy old roller back and forth, and swept the tapes with the broom that had been there forever.

I got a new racquet for my fourteenth birthday, a Wilson, strung with pinging catgut. I kept it in a blue rubberized cover, and a wooden press tightened with thumbscrews. Our chief coach, Uncle Herb, had a Slazenger racquet. Once I found Piers's racquet on the bench, twisted into a pretzel after a night of rain.

"Don't look for the ball now," called Mike as I poked through the long grass. "Come on, let's finish this game."

"It's brand new," I muttered as I ambled back to my place at the net.

"Your serve, Mike," called Jim.

Pat's cousin Miles was there that day. He came up from Des Moines every summer to visit the Shearers on their island for a week or two. Neither he nor Pat was especially good at tennis, but they were so much fun to listen to. I was glad to finish our set so I could join them on the bench. They teased me. "Look at Alan's feet, Pat," said Miles. "They're tiny! I don't know how you can even walk with such little feet. Let alone play tennis."

"What do mean? My feet are huge," I exclaimed.

None of us had shoes on. We never did, even for tennis. "Let's measure," Pat said.

I put my foot against Miles's slim tan one. "See," he said.

"Well, of course yours is longer. You're a boy, and you're taller."

"Measure it with mine," said Pat. He put his foot up, and I pressed mine against his, our soles touching.

They both sat back then, laughing. "Look Alan's turning pink."

"Doesn't she remind you of Chickie in Des Moines?" asked Miles. "We picked her up to go somewhere, and she said she forgot something. So she went back in her house, and we heard her yelling at her mother." Miles's voice rose to a squeak. "'Why must you always embarrass me in front of my friends?'"

He and Pat laughed. "And then she came out, cool as a cucumber."

I admired their gesturing hands and long fingers. They seemed so sophisticated, so wise to the ways of a world I yearned to belong to. Sitting and laughing with Miles and Pat on the bench by the court, half watching the others play doubles, I felt part of their world. But I envied that unknown girl, Chickie from Des Moines.

Fancy dress party at the dancing school in St. Paul. Scott Fitzgerald, top right, in a clown costume; in front of him, my mother wearing a big hat – 1910

– T W E N T Y –

SUMMER, AT THE RIVER. That was almost the only time I even saw any boys, let alone talked and walked with them as if they were regular people. All winter in New Jersey boys seemed like creatures from another planet, barely human, encountered only briefly in the stiff formality of dancing school, where from behind a partner's back they made hand signals to other boys that said "Please cut in, please rescue me from this ugly clunk of a girl I'm stuck with."

There were no boys at my school. No men, either. The entire faculty was female. None of them were encumbered with husbands: Miss Hunt, Miss Day, Miss Mixner, Miss Sampson, Mlle. Avizou. We all wore uniforms, were penalized for any vestige of weak femininity, a leftover trace of lipstick, or a scrap of old nail polish, even the colorless kind. The only dance held at school during my four years there was the Father-Daughter Dance. Some of the fathers may have enjoyed it. But men in general were frowned upon, best left to the pages of Muzzey's American History textbook. Mary Jane, who sat next to me, had a letter from a boy at Choate. "He signed it with X's," she murmured. "I'll see him at Christmas time." If only Pat or Ricky would write to me. The signed photograph of Cary Grant that I'd sent for stayed upside down in the bottom of my desk in study hall.

"I look as if I were wearing a nightcap," Auntie Georgie said. She and my mother were on the screen porch at the Big House, looking at old pictures. My mother was the one who'd hung onto family photos from their growing-up years. I hung over their shoulders. Their early lives seemed far more exciting than mine.

The focus of their attention was a battered studio photograph of about forty children in attendance at the "Fancy Dress German" of Professor Baker's dancing class in April, 1910. The sisters took turns holding the picture up to their myopic eyes, and commenting on how they each looked. Auntie Georgie, age thirteen, stares straight ahead, unsmiling, in a Bo-Peep mob-cap, her long hair falling over her shoulders. My mother, too, looks solemn, though somehow happier, dwarfed beneath a vast picture hat with an enormous bow on it.

"You're so clever, Jeannie, to write all the names on the back."

"I'd never remember half of them if I hadn't. Look at Larry Boardman, next to you; doesn't he look absurd in that cap like a hotel bellboy."

There were little Dutch girls, an Uncle Sam, shepherdesses with long ringlets, a cowboy, boys in tartan kilts or colonial powdered wigs, a clown or two, and, at one side, rotund Professor Baker himself in white gloves, white tie and tails. "I heard later that Professor Baker was moonlighting all that time as the bartender at the White Bear Yacht Club."

"Scott's right behind me," my mother said. "I don't know why he's in the back row; he wasn't very tall." Scott Fitzgerald is dressed in velvet, with a white ruff around his neck, and a crown with a zig-zag edge on his head. The sisters loved to talk about Scott Fitzgerald.

"They always needed more boys in the dancing school, so Mother invited Scott, even though his family was not quite up to the social mark . . ." My grandmother was the one who had organized the dancing school.

"Argh, Mother was such a snob, "Auntie Georgie said

"Well, so were we. Remember how we used to make fun of Scott's mother? Everyone did. She was so untidy, and had no idea how to dress, her skirts always trailing in the dirt . . ."

"Yes, and the pins kept dropping out of her hair, so it was always falling down. And she had an odd way of talking, sort of a lisp, so it was hard to understand her."

"Scott's father was a complete failure; no one seemed to know what he did. And the St. Paul ladies were all so snooty to Mrs. Fitzgerald . . . including Mother."

"Oh, I know." Auntie Georgie sighed. "I bet they never even spoke to her."

Side by side on the green glider, my mother and Auntie Georgie began looking at my mother's "Memory Book," a scrapbook from her early teens. I was entranced by this book, which I was sometimes allowed to examine. It lay for the most part on a high closet shelf in New Jersey, behind her sweaters. Now she'd brought it especially to the River, to share with her sister.

My mother's younger life always seemed as far removed as the Land of Oz from the braces, glasses, acne, chewed nails, and frozen shyness of my own. The evidence lay between the frayed black covers of this thick Memory Book, as she'd titled it. For four years—1910, when she was thirteen, to 1914—she pasted every invitation she'd received, every place card, pressed flower, or scrap of dress fabric, souvenirs of all the parties or performances she'd attended, each with neatly-inked dates and comments.

"You went to so many concerts," I exclaimed. I was leaning over my mother's shoulders, as she and Auntie Georgie went page by page through the book. This was my first chance to hear them talk about it.

"What on earth was this? I have no memory of 'Jappyland: An Oriental Musical Carnival . . .'"

"I can't remember it either. But I'm sure we both went." My mother read aloud: "'An Operatic Spectacular Extravaganza—400 in Cast 400—including 60 Geisha Maids.'" The two sisters laughed.

"Oh, the bobbing parties were the best," said Auntie Georgie. The book was filled with quaint, charming, hand-made invitations, to sledding parties, sleigh rides, teas, luncheon parties, dances.

"What's a bobbing party?" I asked.

"St. Paul is cold in the winter, dearie, much colder than New Jersey, and snowier, too," Auntie Georgie said. "But we had fun in the winter. Faddie built a big wooden toboggan slide outside our house on Ashland Avenue. Every night he'd pour water down the slide, so it made a slick, icy track. All our neighborhood gang gathered at our house to coast down . . ."

My mother chimed in, "We'd slide all the way across to the next block; of course there weren't any cars then. But a bobbing party was special. A bunch of us would be invited to someone's house when it was just dusk, and then we'd pile onto a long bobsled they'd hired especially."

Auntie Georgie interrupted, "A team of horses would pull us around the snowy streets for a couple of hours, and finally we'd end up back at the house."

"Oh, yes," my mother said. "And we'd all peel off our scarves and our heavy coats and have hot chocolate and delicious buttered toast by the fire . . . that was my favorite part. Scott wrote about it, do you remember, Georgie? In *This Side of Paradise*, Amory kisses a girl at one of our bobbing parties."

"I don't remember any kissing," Auntie Georgie snorted.

Scott Fitzgerald was just a name to me then, the childhood friend my mother and Auntie Georgie talked about the most.

The girls they remembered were different from those I knew; I imagined them all as rich, beautiful, daring, and slightly decadent.

"Remember Nana French?" My mother couldn't get over Nana's arrival at the Schultz's big fancy house at one of those parties after bobsledding. "She was lovely-looking, with that cloud of dark hair, very chic. And then still wearing her raccoon coat and snowy galoshes, she just flung herself right into the middle of Mr. and Mrs. Schultz's huge, creamy, satin-covered bed, and sprawled there, laughing."

"Yeah, well," Auntie Georgie said. "And a couple of divorces, we heard, and who knows what else."

All the really pretty, really popular girls had come to sad ends, meaning chiefly to divorce—that was the message I got.

Better than all my mother's other pasted-in mementos, as far as I was concerned, were the dance cards, relics of a custom now lost in the misty past. These cards survive from dances held at the Country Club, or at someone's house, like "Arthur Foley's dancing party." Dangling from each card is a tasseled miniscule pencil. The card lists a dozen or more different dances, with initials penciled-in by the boys who'd asked my mother for certain long-ago dance numbers. Scott Fitzgerald scrawled his "S.F." beside two-steps or waltzes at most of their parties.

"All your numbers were taken, Jeannie," Auntie Georgie said now. "I'll bet my cards were half empty."

What about the girls whose dance cards were left with blanks? That would be me, I thought, a wallflower.

Auntie Georgie turned another page. "Look at this, probably Scott's first play. *The Captured Shadow*. 1912, just before he went off to Princeton."

"Alice Drake got a part in his Civil War play," my mother said. "*The Coward*, at the Yacht Club. We all went. There was a hop afterward, and we danced." She sighed. I wasn't sure whether her sigh was for the play, the hop, her youth, or all of it together.

Cousin Joan poses next to Eddie – 1942

– T W E N T Y - O N E –

THE TWO WEEKS my father was able to spend with us at the River went by too fast. Even before the first of August he had to go back to New Jersey and his job. My mother didn't want to leave him alone for the rest of the summer, so she left us instead.

Now that we were in our own new River house, she thought she was conferring a favor by offering it for a few weeks to friends, in exchange for the (minor) responsibility of looking after Eddie and me. For us, these interludes were a mixed blessing. Of course we wanted to be at the River, but we really preferred our own house with our own mother in it.

I was not a child anymore. My mother still recorded my weight, and was happy whenever I gained a pound. But she no longer expected me to rest on my bed every afternoon. "You'll be fine, dearie," she said as she was leaving.

The person to whom she offered the house—and us— was Auntie Georgie's old friend, Mrs. Pettee. She and her two children stayed with Eddie and me for the month of August. Mrs. Pettee talked a lot, and taught us the rudiments of bridge.

Our father's sister, Aunt Bess, came the next summer, from St. Louis. She was our "maiden aunt," back when there were such people. Not being used to children, she was anxious lest we catch a chill or became overtired or drowned. She brought our second cousin Joan with her, a perfectly nice, though precocious, girl of eleven, Eddie's age then. I won't say Joan flirted with Eddie and Piers and their friends, but she knew how to strike a pose; my black-and-white snapshots survive as evidence. There is Joan, reclining against a boulder, hugging one knee, toes pointed and chin uplifted. Or leaning back with one arm behind her head, the other angled at her waist like a model or a movie star. She'd done her homework, having surely devoted her idle hours to movie magazines, maybe *Screen Teens* or *Hollywood Love*. No one I knew posed like that. I was older, but Joan made me feel old-fashioned, and I didn't like it.

One hot afternoon the blue sky turned dark like tarnished silver. The first raindrops made silent circles on the water, spreading and crowding each other over the whole surface. Mountainous black storm clouds blew up the River. The wind picked up, turning leaves inside out on the trees, and fanning the water into white-capped waves. Piers and Eddie and I dashed out in the rain, down to the motorboat, and out into the wild torrent. I saw tall, thin Aunt Bess come out onto the lawn, waving frantically, her pale linen dress flapping about her shins as the rain came down. We couldn't hear her frantic calls over the motor. We thudded and bounced over the waves. A sword of lightning plunged through the sky, followed by a crash of thunder. Then came the heavy downpour. We headed into shore, and ran dripping and laughing up to the house.

Aunt Bess looked wan, her hair damp and untidy. Smug Cousin Joan was perched across an armchair, swinging her ankles. "You almost gave Aunt Bessie a heart attack," she said.

The last time our mother palmed Eddie and me off onto others was the worst. Mrs. Power took over our house and us with her own two boys. She had been almost our mother's only friend during the winter we'd spent in Tucson. I can't remember which of her sons had the health problem that had driven them to Arizona. Richie was about my age. Jim was Eddie's contemporary, subject to screaming tantrums when crossed. Eddie and I used to look at him in amazement as he lay on the floor, kicking and howling.

I had never liked Mrs. Power. She talked incessantly in a nasal whine. She never smiled.

At the River that summer, Mrs. Power didn't care how long we stayed out on the tennis court. Or how late in the afternoon we remained on the sandbar up the River. Surely she hated being in our house as much as we loathed having her, for after a couple of weeks she took herself back to town, sending her twenty-something stepdaughter to fill in for the final few days. The stepdaughter was angrier even than Mrs. Power. I can't say I blame her.

Each morning, after I'd made my bed and cleared the breakfast table, I escaped to Auntie Georgie's where I knew she'd be sitting on the porch with her coffee and a book.

"Come on in, dearie. How's it going over there with Mrs. P?"

"Oh, she's awful. . . ."

"Allie, you can come over here anytime; you know that. Now there are lots of nicer things to think about." She held her book out so I could see it: *Medieval Latin Lyrics*.

"Do you know about Petrarch? He was an Italian poet who was madly in love with Laura. He wrote hundreds of sonnets to Laura, even after she died in the Plague. His only solace was a beautiful wooded valley in France, where a spring bubbled out of the rock. Vaucluse—that was his refuge. '. . . and from those boughs the wind shook down upon her bosom flower upon flower.' And oh, there's so much more."

"Sounds pretty romantic," I said.

"Sometime I'll tell you about Heloise and Abelard. That was another great love affair. He was a philosopher, a thousand years ago, and she was his niece. Then she had a baby, and that was so shocking that he had to go into a monastery, and Heloise became a nun. But he wrote her many, many, many love letters."

"Things like that don't happen nowadays."

"But they might, Allie. You never know."

The old River house – 1944

– T W E N T Y - T W O –

UNCLE ARCHIE AND HELEN had a new baby. Brenda had dark eyes, dark hair, the opposite of those blond, blue-eyed twins. Bruce and Laura were three years old. Helen, in a professional photograph, looks like the perfect mother, arms around her three adorable little ones, all clean and shiny.

We were on the porch at the Big House one day. The twins were running through the house on their sturdy little legs. "Hey, kids, cut it out. I mean it." Uncle Archie was not smiling. "Outta here. Scram!" He held up his hand in a threatening gesture. Bruce and Laura scurried away.

"Arch, Arch, slow down," said Auntie Georgie. "They're just acting like kids."

Things were starting to come undone. Uncle Archie seemed different, often angry. Helen was drinking too much. The sisters caught her in lies. I overheard them talking. "You mean she told you her father was the president of the company? Arch said he was a salesman," my mother said.

"I don't know, Jeannie. I just don't believe all that stuff about her family. It doesn't hang together."

"Maybe it's lucky for her that they're all dead now. But no one has no family." Uncle Archie was preoccupied. He didn't smile. He didn't seem to have a real job. And now Helen wanted, needed more money, always more. My mother and Auntie Georgie were on the porch, talking. "Jeannie, it's unbelievable what she's doing . . ."

"Oh, Lord, what do you mean?"

"This was only one example, I'm sure. Apparently Helen marched into Schunemans'—Miss Freely told me this— you remember her, she's worked there for years. Anyway, she called me and said, 'I hate to tell you, Mrs. Lewis, but I thought you should know, I mean your family and all. . . .'"

"I can just picture it," my mother said. "Helen in all our old St. Paul shops, with that low, smoker's voice of hers, 'Oh, charge it, please.' I can hear her." My mother gave an airy toss of her wrist, imagining Helen.

"She's been passing checks when she's had zero bank balance." Auntie Georgie took a gulp of air and blew it out. "And she's borrowed from old friends of the family, Mother's friends even. Herb and I paid Mrs. Foster back, but how many others are there that we don't even know about? It's worse than embarrassing. And we paid her huge bill at Ramaleys, but we can't do it all; you and Jack should pay some, too."

"I don't know, Georgie, whether we should be covering for her—I'll see what Jack thinks. But H and Bill ought to do their share, too."

My parents paid some of the bills. My mother wrote Archie a long letter about what he owed them. The two sisters could hardly talk about anything else.

"Oh, lordy, this is absolutely ghastly."

"What would Faddie say? I hate to think. Thank heaven he isn't here."

"Jeannie, what are we going to do about poor Arch? Think of what this is doing to him."

"I know, George, but we have to think of what's best for

all of them. It's his family now. Jack agrees; we have to try to be practical . . ."

"Practical! How can you say that? It sounds so cold . . ."

And this was just the beginning.

Auntie Harriet and Uncle Bill's contribution was to lend their River house to Archie and Helen for a month. Helen tried to win over my mother and Auntie Georgie. She invited us for dinner a few times. The food was much fancier than we had at home. Helen passed delicate hors d'oeuvres like asparagus wrapped in thin, thin bread, or perfect toast points around a bubbling hot cheese dip. One night we had Chicken a la King flecked with red pimento, and individual salads of tomato aspic, each a perfect circle shape, turned from its mold and frilled with cucumber. Helen had learned to cook Uncle Archie's rainbow trout—perfectly brown, crisp on the outside, pale pink within, trimmed with a lemon twist and one green sprig of parsley. Ladyfingers were featured frequently in Helen's desserts. But not one of her special recipes, the delicious treats that I still remember, is included in my mother's collection of handwritten recipes from friends and friends' cooks.

Meanwhile Uncle Archie couldn't seem to hold a job. He couldn't land a job. He came over to talk to my mother sometimes in the evening. One night from my porch I heard their voices, low and solemn, until long after midnight.

"Archie came to talk to me last night," she told Auntie Georgie the next morning as they were going down for their swim. "He and Helen had had a bad evening. It must have been after one when he left our house. Oh, George, Helen is draining him dry. Poor Arch." Helen was always the one they blamed.

Cousins in the green canoe – 1942

– T W E N T Y - T H R E E –

MY MOTHER WAS SMALLER than her sisters, smaller than Uncle Archie. Harriet may have been the tallest, but none of them were what you'd think of as tall. I passed my mother in height by the time I was thirteen. "You're so lucky to have those long legs," she said. She and Auntie Georgie both wore glasses, and both wore the same sort of clothes each day at the River: wide soft pants of thin, faded blue denim, cotton shirts, striped or plaid, with round collars, cardigan sweaters. Auntie Georgie was often barefoot; my mother wore navy blue Keds. She didn't like people to see her in pants; she knew she didn't have the long, photogenic limbs of Marlene Dietrich or Katherine Hepburn.

Auntie Georgie's reddish hair was not "set" like my mother's into neat waves. Once a week my mother drove to Lorraine's Beauty Shop in Scandia to have her brown hair rolled up in metal curlers. She had to sit for forty minutes or so under the hot, roaring helmet until she was dry. When she swam she always held her head well above water, so as not to spoil Lorraine's handiwork.

"You are so lucky, Alan, to turn that lovely brown," my mother said. No matter how long she sat in the sun, her legs and shoulders remained pasty white and puffy, with a fresh sprinkling of freckles. I can still picture her reclined on a canvas lawn chair, in her halter top (fashioned from a red bandana), hoping her skin would tan.

Having fought a losing battle against the enforced sunbaths of my childhood, now, in my teens, I did it all on my own. I worked on my tan. For hours in the afternoon, I baked on the sandbar, or on a chaise on the lawn. I read. Aware that my school had taught me no history, I plowed earnestly through a thick textbook that covered the twists and turns of western civilization. That took a lot of sun time.

I finally read Fitzgerald. One image that haunted me from *Tender is the Night* was Nicole on a Riviera beach: " . . . a young woman lay under a roof of umbrellas making out a list of things from a book open on the sand. Her bathing suit was pulled off her shoulders and her back, a ruddy, orange brown, set off by a string of creamy pearls, shone in the sun." Pure glamour. Someday, I thought, I'll wear pearls like that.

Each summer we'd talk a parent into carting two or three of us and the green canoe up the River to Taylors' Falls, where we'd launch our craft into the swift current. There, the River rushes along between steep cliffs of dark, volcanic rock: "Basalt," someone said. Long, long ago the River was wide and fierce; its swirling water gouged a deep, narrow channel through that hard rock from far inside the earth. Water had carved the rock into curious forms, leaving deep round holes and sharp pinnacles. The current swept past a rough pillar of rock that rose eighty feet in the air. It was called The Devil's Chair.

Just below Taylors' Falls the basalt gives way to softer sandstone, the valley broadens out, the River becomes shallower and more placid, until at last, way south of Otisville, beyond Marine, below Stillwater, it joins the mighty Mississippi.

Half-paddling, half-floating along in our canoe beyond Taylors' Falls, we always stopped to swim and have our picnic on the half-rocky, half-sandy island near Franconia. When I made that day-long trip with Monnie, she and I mostly floated, smeared with baby oil and iodine, our paddles resting on the gunwales, both of us face up to the sun's rays and their reflection off the water. When our friend Jacquie once joined us, Monnie and I thought she was ridiculous to insist on her picturesque straw hat. "Mummy's French, you know, and she says I mustn't ruin my charming complexion." Jacquie laughed as she told us, but the hat stayed on.

All of us washed our hair in the River, suds floating off with the current. Behind a rock near the swimming dock we stashed a cake of Ivory soap (It Floats! was its slogan). I can still envision Uncle Archie lathering his armpits, his furry chest, then taking a running dive into a fast crawl upstream. Sending our soapsuds off down the River seemed perfectly reasonable; who could complain?

Even more unsavory, in hindsight, was the catch-and-release method of sewage disposal. The old outhouses had been built over self-contained pits, but now that our houses had fancy new indoor plumbing, the system changed for the worse. Everything ran into an underground cesspool. Each invisible catch-all had an outlet pipe that trickled directly into the River, slightly downstream from each house. We knew where these little pipes opened near the water's edge, an evil smell, a patch of too-green moss. "Don't be so silly, Alan," said my mother when once I had the temerity to complain. "Flowing water purifies itself."

That was one of her regular pronouncements; there were others. She had abiding faith in certain old proverbs. "Never put off till tomorrow what you can do today;" "A stitch in time . . ." and out came her sewing basket at the first sign of a dangling thread or a loose button. "A rolling stone gathers no moss:" her moral judgment on people who didn't settle down. Like Uncle Archie. But why was it good to gather moss, I wondered.

She believed devoutly in the wisdom of Polonius's advice to his children in Hamlet: "Neither borrower nor lender be / For loan oft loses both itself and friend—"

She often invoked this sentiment with respect to Archie, too, justifying her frequent refusal to lend him more money. But Hamlet, I learned when I read Shakespeare myself, considered Polonius an interfering busybody, a "tedious old fool."

All of a sudden Cousin Hick appeared at the River. It seemed sudden to me, although I suppose she and Auntie Georgie had been planning her visit for some time.

Cousin Hick Richards was Auntie Georgie's and my mother's second cousin, a decade older than they were. She lived in New York City. She'd come occasionally to see us in New Jersey, so she was not exactly a stranger to me. But it was strange to have her here among us, in summer at the River, for an entire week.

I was embarrassed by her appearance, although she certainly wasn't. When I'd seen her before, fully dressed, she'd looked more ordinary than now, at the River in the heat of July. Cousin Hick was tiny, lean, and wizened. She wore flared shorts of faded tan, a miniscule halter top, and an odd old canvas hat over her thin, colorless hair. "Cousin Hick is deaf," Auntie Georgie reminded us. "She can't hear you unless you speak directly at her."

"What are you trying to say, Alan? Speak up, child." Cousin Hick had hearing aids in both ears, with wires spooling out of them to the battery that hung in the hollow of her flat chest. That was what I found most embarrassing: the wires, her near-nakedness, her knobby little knees, the gnarled, brownish hand that clutched her walking stick. She did not swim, or climb into a boat, but she walked for an hour or more every morning, striding up the hill and along the Otisville road where everyone could see her. As a self-centered teenager, I felt personally affronted by her oddness, as if her unusual appearance reflected poorly on me.

"Sat in the sun with Hick who talked more of her esoteric nonsense," noted my mother in her diary.

Cousin Hick had strong convictions, and they were unconventional. She felt vibrations. "This house has good vibrations," she said, "Can't you feel them?" We all went to lunch one day at Great-Aunt Katharine's house on White Bear Lake. She and Cousin Hick were cousins, too. Lunch at Aunt Katharine's was fancy and perfect, as usual. Afterwards she gestured across the porch.

"Do come see my garden," she said, in her dulcet contralto. "My phloxes are just at their best this minute, such heavenly shades of pink and salmon. And, oh, my darling lilies . . ."

Cousin Hick was not looking at the garden. In her brisk, clipped little voice she said to Aunt Katharine, "What you need, my dear, is a coat of paint." We all turned to look at the peeling clapboards.

Cousin Hick's family, the Richards, had had money. She'd grown up in a spacious Park Avenue apartment, and a country house in Connecticut. Hick—her given name was Harriet—had never married. Her inherited wealth had become a burden she couldn't wait to shed. She began giving us her "things," starting with her mother's jewelry. But money—Cousin Hick's share of it—all went to a figure she referred to as "The Tibetan."

I never heard Cousin Hick described as a Buddhist; it's possible my mother might have accepted that. "The

Tibetan!" expostulated my mother, although not in Cousin Hick's hearing. "Who is this Tibetan? Hick has these crackpot ideas. But they're just milking her dry—she's their cash cow! They know they're onto something good. What a racket. But Hick doesn't see it. They've pulled the wool over her eyes."

Maybe my mother was right; perhaps Cousin Hick was being preyed upon by thieves. But it was her choice, after all. She tried to convince my mother and Auntie Georgie of the rightness of her ideas. She could talk forever, it seemed. She questioned us. She asked me why I spent time in front of the mirror, why I lay in the sun, read "frivolous" books. And as for twelve-year-old Eddie, tooling up and down the River in the tiny motorboat he'd built for himself, she asked him, "What's the use of it?" To little Genna, standing to watch as Cousin Hick topped the four-minute egg she ate each morning for breakfast, she said, "Go on now, child. Get on with your day."

Auntie Georgie was less judgmental than my mother. "Oh, Jeannie, she's harmless. She just needs an audience. Why do you mind so much what she does with her money?"

Cousin Hick looked up to Uncle Herbert. He was amused by her, and chuckled over her bizarre rants. "How well do you know this Tibetan, Hick? Does he live in New York?"

"He is the Way," she said.

After Cousin Hick's mother and then her only sister had died, the Tibetan and his cronies moved into the Richards family's elegant duplex apartment. Cousin Hick gave away everything she'd inherited, and moved into one tiny room in lower Manhattan, where she lived on next to nothing a year. My cousin Genna has the Richards flat silver, Eddie got a complete set of Dickens, and I have her set of Italian painted bedroom furniture.

My mother's long-ago beau, Don Bigelow, came home to St. Paul on leave from the Foreign Service. He spent a weekend at the River, bringing with him some things of Aunt Anna's. My great-aunt Anna Ingersoll, the last of Faddie's many siblings, had lived and died as an expatriate in Florence almost forever. The three Ingersoll sisters—Auntie Georgie, Auntie Harriet, and my mother—were her only heirs.

There wasn't much: some jewelry, and a stack of lovely little Florentine notebooks, filled with Aunt Anna's spidery Spenserian script.

"Jeannie, this is rubbish," said Auntie Georgie. "It's too boring for words. I vote we just toss it into the fire."

"Wait a sec, George; not so fast. She wanted us to have this published."

But after my mother had struggled through some of Aunt Anna's writings, she agreed. They burned it all one evening in the fireplace at the Big House. I later wished they'd saved some of it, at least. Whatever it was. Now we'll never know.

Aunt Anna's will specified an equal division of the jewelry between her three nieces. Auntie Georgie and my mother sat themselves down at the end of the porch at the Big House. They didn't seem to mind that I was there, sitting on the floor, watching them and stroking Lottie's furry head. Auntie Georgie loosened the crimson cord on a small blue brocade bag, and held it upside down over the wicker table. The jewelry all tumbled out with a tinkling rush into a glistening pile. A ring rolled onto the floor; I scrambled under my mother's chair to retrieve it.

"Good Lord, Jeannie. How do we do this?"

"We should make three piles. You go first."

"Well, what about H's share? Wouldn't you know she'd be in California when she ought to be here."

"I guess we just take turns choosing for her."

"Well, we have no way of knowing what's really valuable, so we might as well pick out what we like."

"Yeah, some of it looks like junk."

I watched Auntie Georgie dangle a strand of gold beads from her fingers. From the pile my mother plucked a small gold watch suspended from a fleur-de-lys lapel pin. Auntie Georgie chose the pendant earrings because she was one who'd dared to have her ears pierced. My mother thought pierced ears were vulgar.

Soon they'd made three neat piles. To Auntie Harriet they assigned some bracelets, a necklace of tiny pearls, and a garnet ring. Besides the watch, my mother's pile included three pieces that have now come down to me. I love to look at them, although I do not wear them: an amethyst pin that I imagine fastened at the neck of Aunt Anna's black bombazine jacket; a bracelet of thin gold links; and a necklace with golden teardrops dripping from loops of fine chain. There was another bracelet, too, a delicate mesh of gold, inscribed, "Etta 1868." Etta was Aunt Anna's and Faddie's sister, who died of consumption at twenty, a year after she'd been given that bracelet. I've lost it.

I spent hours reading in the afternoon, in the sun or on my porch, those endless, solitary afternoons. I escaped into novels from the 'thirties: *The Grapes of Wrath, Main Street,* and *The Good Earth. Gone With the Wind* I spurned simply because it was popular. (That did not keep me from seeing the movie with Margaret Harper, one long, steamy hot afternoon, on the worn plush seats of bleak Osceola's un-air-conditioned theater.)

Auntie Georgie urged me to read the nineteenth-century poets: "No, not Tennyson, but oh, the Pre-Raphaelites!" I came under Uncle Herbert's literary influence, too. He talked about books to me or to anyone else who might be there. He knew so much. I hung around listening to Uncle Herbert, his talk interspersed with his rumbling, merry laugh, and pauses to re-light his pipe.

One of his favorite writers was Max Beerbohm. He pulled out his pipe, and chortled, a real belly laugh, talking about *Zuleika Dobson*, Beerbohm's 1911 Oxford novel. "Marvelous satire," Uncle Herbert said. After working my way through it, I made the mistake of trying to impress Pat Shearer, my hero from across the River, with my sophistication. "It's a satire," I said of Zuleika.

"Of what?" asked Pat, "A satire of what?" I couldn't say. What did I know? I was mortified.

To Uncle Herbert I was always "Allie," which made me feel special. From his chair on the porch, between puffs at his pipe, he talked about Sidney Fay's book on the origins of the First World War. "Fay's the only one who really gives the whole picture."

Uncle Herbert lent me his copy, with its torn orange paper jacket. I struggled through it, out on our lawn, consulting the atlas to find Ypres and the Straits of the Dardanelles.

I loved it when his newspaper friends from far-off cities visited the Lewises at the River: Russ Wiggins, who edited a paper in Maine, a dashing editor from Toronto, and another from the Winnipeg paper. A handsome blond foreign correspondent from Chicago talked to me at the tennis court: "What does a pretty girl like you do out here for fun? Besides walking around in bare feet all the time. Doesn't it hurt?" He put his arm around my shoulders as we walked back to the porch. Uncle Herb fixed their highballs. Nursing my coke, I leaned back against the cushions in what I hoped was a sophisticated way, laughing softly at their stories of deadlines and newsrooms, gossip from Washington, the latest from London, pretending I understood.

The rope swing over the water at the Shearers' island – 1944

– T W E N T Y - F O U R –

"OH LORD, it's going to be one of those nights." My mother and Auntie Georgie groaned when they saw drinks, ice, and whooping guests being ferried across the River to the island. I was stricken with envy, watching the Shearers gear up for one of their parties.

"Yoo-hoo!" Friends arriving from the city called across from the Landing, just upstream from our house. The Shearers spent summers on the low-slung island on the Wisconsin side of the River. From our lawn or the living room windows I watched and listened to the Shearers. They had to lug everything across the River: food, drinking water, tubs of pink geraniums, a wind-up record player, once even a piano, as well as all their visiting friends. They had a telephone on our side of the River, in a box affixed to a tree near the Landing. I longed to be part of their island lives.

From my porch I could hear them arrive at the Landing in one of their Fords. I knew their voices. I saw Pat hop nimbly into a loaded rowboat, heard the rapid clunk and creak of oars, the splash of each stroke, as he rowed across to the island. I watched and listened one day as handsome Roddy, attended by a lovely, long-limbed girlfriend, painted the wooden steps at the Landing. "Beat Me Daddy, Eight to the Bar" shrilled from his portable Victrola. Then another record, "Green Eyes." Its plaintive whine was almost more than I could bear.

Sometimes you could hear what they said from across the River. You could watch Roddy do a neat jackknife off the end of their floating boathouse and swim twenty fast strokes upstream and back. You could see Pat weeding the nasturtiums and portulaca he'd planted in front of the main cabin. I watched Roddy chopping wood. I heard no sound as the axe struck the log. The solid "k'chunks" of impact didn't reach my ears until Roddy's tan arms held the axe up in front of him, ready for the next stroke.

Their main cabin was made of logs. Pat, my contemporary, and Roddy, a few years older, each had his own sleeping cabin. Even Josephine, their pretty young cook, had her own cabin. We all had cooks then, so it didn't seem odd to see Josephine tripping around in her pink uniform and snowy apron on a small damp island without plumbing, electricity, or phone, and no one to talk to.

Unlike my family, the Shearers seemed not to observe a distinction between generations. Pat and Roddy called their parents Henny and Dave. They even called their parents' friends by their first names.

It was years before I was included in the Shearers' parties, before I was one of the lucky ones lolling lazily on their decadent lawn chaise, a chaise as wide as a king-size bed. At last, I was among the revelers laughing at everything anyone said, while the moon struck a path of light across the water, and the sky was sprinkled with stars. I was in love with the

Shearers, their island, and their idle, carefree friends.

It came as a shock to learn that my mother and Auntie Georgie disliked the Shearer parents, two people I considered enviably sophisticated and fascinating. "Oh, that David; he thinks he's so funny," I heard Auntie Georgie say one day. "What a stuffy guy he is; I can't stand him."

She and my mother both complained about Henny, the mother: "That whiny voice, going on and on; I can hear her all the way across the River. She's the most boring creature."

Sometimes on Sundays the Shearers and their friends took over the tennis court. Roddy was our local star, and David, the father, was an ace at the net. Glamorous, long-legged friends—all female, it seemed—hollered and hooted with laughter as they raced around the court. Enviably tan in their brief white tennis dresses, they all had exotic, unfamiliar names—Arlette, Gabrielle, Clelia, Sybil—and shaggy, dark, Shetland-pony bangs. I watched from afar.

Monnie and I had long been enamored of Pat Shearer. Our perceived rival for his affection was Margaret Harper, whose blatant ploys for his attention drove us wild. When a group of us went off to the movies in the old Green Car, Margaret made an undignified dash to sit beside Pat. She wooed him with little bunches of flowers or fresh ice cubes for his Coke. Pat seemed oblivious to the frenzy he caused.

On Monnie's porch she and I drew comic strips with Margaret Harper as the victim. We portrayed her crude flirtation, her unseemly attempts to win Pat's affection. In our cartoons, naturally, all her efforts won only Pat's scorn. In real life, Pat paid almost no attention to Margaret. It was to my house that he often came; we were friends. Nonetheless, whenever Monnie and I saw Pat coming, we'd roll our shorts up another notch, tie our shirts a little tighter over our bare middles, and toss our hair back. Not until all of us were grown did we learn that Pat hadn't really been interested in girls after all.

One morning Pat asked me to come with him while he

released some tropical fish he'd bought. We rowed across to the island, where he showed me a pool left from the spring high water. Pat had three Mason jars with little fish swirling around inside: guppies, gold fish, tiny angelfish. He held out a packet of fish food. "I don't know what they'll eat here, but just in case."

We opened the jars, one after another. The fish darted around the pool. "They look happy," he said. "They're free." We stood up. "Sprinkle in a little food," he added. "Not too much." We watched for a few minutes.

"I think they like it here," I said.

When we looked the next day, we couldn't see any fish. "Birds, maybe," Pat said.

Uncle Archie's '32 Ford V-8 convertible, the Green Car, was the first car we cousins were allowed to drive. You had to be fifteen to get a license in Minnesota. That was the only requirement, no tiresome test or anything.

The Green Car had its peculiarities. Long ago, the gearshift had been twisted into a spiral by Uncle Archie, perhaps to make more room for his bare knees. The canvas top was permanently open. There was a rumble seat at the back, where the trunk would be on an ordinary car. The rumble seat had no handle, so it, too, was always open.

Pat Shearer, designated by my mother as the most trustworthy, was the driver when a bunch of us went to the movies in Stillwater. One night, after we'd laughed our way through one of those "road" movies—The Road to Singapore, perhaps, with hapless Bob Hope, and Dorothy Lamour in her sarong—we ran out of gas. It was no one's fault, really; the gas gauge hadn't worked in years. Ricky Gray and I were delegated to hitch a ride to Marine for gas. It was late, and we waited a long time near the Arcola Bridge for a car to come by. Finally we got a lift from a farm couple in their venerable black Chevy, out inexplicably late themselves. We jounced along in their back seat as far as Ed Wahlquist's house. Mr. Wahlquist was the man who ran the Shell station

in Marine. Ricky and I threw pebbles up at his window until
he woke up, dressed, took us to his gas station, filled up a
can, and then drove us in the wrecker back to Arcola and the
Green Car. "Thanks, Mr. Wahlquist," we all said, not feeling
as if we'd asked him for a special favor. It was probably four
in the morning before he climbed back into bed.

According to Auntie Georgie, Ricky Gray was incredibly
brilliant. I watched for signs of his intellectual prowess, but
he hardly ever spoke. At my house in the evening, he lurked
in the background with a supercilious smile, sniffing as he
thumbed some currently popular novel that lay on the coffee
table. I can't remember why I spent most of one summer
feverishly attracted him. "Why on earth do you like him?"
asked Monnie. "He's so odd, and he never says anything."

"I know, but I just keep wondering what he's thinking
about. He's so smart, and I keep hoping maybe he'll talk to
me about books or something. I'd be a good listener."

His brother Jim was older, taller, cynical. I chanced to
be walking through the woods with him on the day I turned
seventeen. Jim Gray looked down at me: "So, were you sweet
sixteen and never been kissed?"

"Well, and then did he kiss you?" breathed Monnie when
I told her.

"No," I said. "We just kept on walking."

That same summer, dark-eyed Karen landed among us while
on a visit to her grandmother. None of us had ever seen her
before. The grandmother, Mrs. Taylor, lived up the River
from us. She'd prevailed on fifteen-year-old Karen to stay on
at the River longer than planned. It seemed like weeks to me,
consumed as I was by jealousy. Poor little Karen apparently
had no clothes other than the dress she'd travelled in—
plus her purple polka-dot bikini. With her flowing mane
of dark hair, Karen looked so appealing, so waifish in the

baggy brown cardigan borrowed from her grandmother, the garment she appeared in day after day. When the sweater came off, as it frequently did, to reveal the bikini, I felt a murderous fury. My modest two-piece cotton bathing suit was suddenly dowdy, my bosom hopelessly flat. It didn't help to have Uncle Bill roll his eyes: "Whoa! Who's that?" I'd been pretty well knocked off my perch in Otisville.

From our living room window, I watched as handsome Roddy Shearer (who never had time for me) cruised all afternoon up and down the River in his outboard, with Karen in her teeny-weeny bikini, perched seductively in the bow. She assumed a smooth pin-up pose, leaning back on her arms, one tanned leg slightly raised, the other trailing over the gunwale, cleavage and chin angled skyward, hair streaming back over her shoulders. I seethed. That was a long week.

The Shearers' careless island summers came to an end, finally. During the drought years of the 1930s, the River had been shallow, the Shearers' island high and dry. In the late 'forties, however, the rains came, and the Shearers' luck changed. The spring high water washed through their little cabins. Mud caked the floors. Pat worked harder than any of them, trying to clean up their flooded island home. They learned to take preventive steps each fall, hoping to forestall major flood damage. Mattresses were raised to the ceiling; they even heisted up the piano. But the end was inevitable. In 1950 Auntie Georgie noted in the Log Book: "the highest water in 50 years. Two Shearer cabins carried to Stillwater." It got worse after that, and finally they gave up.

My mother and Auntie Georgie didn't miss the Shearers. The sisters' River peace and quiet was restored. "Now we just look across at green and trees the way we always used to," my mother said, once the last relics of the Shearers' heyday had drifted away.

Eddie on the aquaplane he built – 1948

– T W E N T Y - F I V E –

THE SUMMER OF 1945—the war was ending at last. Already in June it was half over, the half in Europe. Now we just had to take care of the Japs, on all those faraway islands in the Pacific, places with names we'd never heard before.

Uncle Herbert, in his usual chair on the porch, talked about Churchill, Yalta, Stalin, our new President Truman, the evil that had blanketed Europe, hopes for the future, as well as the risks.

His months in wartime London had not been entirely grim: "Sometimes Russ and I had lunch at White's, a marvelously stuffy men's club. The waiters were ancient. They'd wheel the huge trolley over to our table, and whip off an enormous silver cover." With a swoop of his hand, Uncle Herbert showed us the size of that silver dome. He puffed on his pipe and gave a roar of laughter; "And there on a vast silver platter was the tiniest scrap of sausage or kidney. . . ."

Pat Shearer was in the Navy V-12 program, at St. Thomas College in St. Paul. Every weekend he came out to the River. I'd see him in his spotless white sailor's suit, rowing across to the island. Roddy, older than Pat, was far away, an Air Force pilot. The jaunty, smiling face on the big Camel cigarette billboard was Roddy to me, tanned and handsome in his uniform, puffing away.

Twice that summer I went with some of Monnie's and my friends to the Saturday night dance in the plain, whitewashed hall over the fire station in Marine. Arthur Ostrand played the fiddle, and Mr. Gabrielson, the accordion. Harlan, who sometimes came to scythe our meadow, invited me to waltz. He showed me how to dance the schottische, a slowed-down Swedish version of the polka. My skirt with the red roses printed on it floated out in a bell. Even when Harlan's size 13 farm boot landed on the toe of my black ballet slipper I felt light and free.

Charlie Ekdahl's store on the hill at Otisville was empty and abandoned. We had the idea of turning it into our own nightclub. Of course we could use it, said Bud Stutz, who now owned the old eyesore. Monnie dreamed up what seemed the perfect name: the Store-Klub, after the eponymous Stork Club in Manhattan, tabloid-famous at the time as a glittering cafe society hangout.

We worked all week scrubbing out the place, and festooning it with crepe paper, as if for a high school prom. Margaret and Monnie and I scoured the back streets of Stillwater one day, trying to buy enough Coca-Cola and Royal Crown, then still in wartime-short supply.

All the aunts and uncles, all the parents were invited to our grand opening, the grownups having had cocktails first at Auntie Georgie and Uncle Herbert's. We played our best records at the store, "Sentimental Journey," "One O'Clock Jump," our Harry James, and Jo Stafford singing "Sunny Side of the Street." I wore my dress with the cherries on it.

Silent Ricky Gray asked me to dance, but I didn't care about him any more.

We'd thought we'd keep the Store-Klub going, but that one evening turned out to be enough. A week later twenty-four of us roared in our motorboats up to the big sandbar for a picnic. Everyone came back to my house afterward. The next day my mother complained to Auntie Georgie, "They were all still here at 3 AM! You and Herb must have heard them. I hardly closed an eye. . . ." But I could tell she didn't really mind. For some reason, my social life was gratifying to her.

Archie, Helen, and the children were often at the River. They stayed sometimes in the Washburn's house. Helen whipped up fancy dinners for the family or for parties. One night, Uncle Archie's birthday, my mother took him two Currier and Ives railroad prints, and a bottle of Scotch. Another time Helen organized a party for a bunch of her friends—including my mother—at the Riverdale Club, a slightly sleazy nightspot in the looser precincts of Somerset, Wisconsin. The next day I overheard my mother telling Auntie Georgie about the evening: "Oh, George, Helen got so tight. We were all drinking Stingers, and she got absolutely plastered. No, no, Arch didn't come; he probably knew how it would end up. I felt lousy this morning . . . Jack won't like hearing that I went along. . . ."

"Come on, kids, get in the boat." Uncle Archie was rounding up Bruce and Laura.

"They should have their life jackets on, Arch," my mother called.

"Nah, they can swim." Then he yelled at the children, "Hurry up, kiddos, let's get going. Move! I'm not gonna wait all day."

"You don't need to be so hard on them, Arch," Auntie Georgie said. "They want your approval. A little praise goes a long way."

It was early in August when the war was finally over. On my birthday we heard the news that the first atomic bomb had been dropped on Japan. My mother and I were having breakfast out on the terrace after our usual early morning swim, when Uncle Archie came walking over. I picture him in his brown sweater and shorts, barefoot as usual, striding across the lawn. He was jubilant.

"This means the end of the war! Do you realize? Now it's over. No more fighting, no land war in Asia."

But it meant more than that to him. "It was so small; no bigger than a grapefruit." He cupped his hands. "And with this unbelievable power! Can you imagine what that means? It's a whole new source of energy! Everything's going to change—everything. Soon—in our lifetimes, probably—everything'll be powered by atoms: refrigerators, light bulbs, our cars, even. . . ."

From the papers and the radio that August day no one had any idea of the extent of the fallout from the bomb that the U.S. had dropped on Hiroshima, fallout that still continues. But for Uncle Archie it was a glorious day, the last time I saw the uncle of my childhood, his optimism and his sense of adventure and possibility temporarily restored.

Xandra Kalman – 1970

– T W E N T Y - S I X –

"IN PARIS I ALWAYS STAY at the France-et-Choiseul," said Xandra Kalman in her cigarette voice. "It's small, and of course they know me."

If I ever went to Paris, I thought, the France-et-Choiseul would be my hotel, too. If it suited Mrs. Kalman surely it would have the same allure that she had.

Xandra Kalman was my mother's and Auntie Georgie's old friend. She was older than they were, probably almost sixty. I'd never paid much attention to her before that day, when she came out from St. Paul for lunch.

"Darling Jeannie, how are you?" She clasped my mother's hands in hers. "Alfred did not like coming down your steep driveway." Alfred was her driver. He had on a dark uniform and cap, even at the River.

"Oh, your little house is so sweet," she said in that husky voice. She didn't know how hard my mother had worked that morning to have everything perfect—artful arrangements of ferns and wildflowers on the tables, and herself in pale blue linen and pearls. I'd swept the pine needles off the terrace, and helped set the table for four ladies. Cousin Margaret had come, too, and Auntie Georgie, who'd put on her gray-striped dress and dangly earrings. Eddie and I were going off with our sandwiches, but I lingered, listening.

Before lunch the ladies gravitated to the old iron lawn chairs with the springy seats. "Charming view," said Mrs. Kalman. "So rustic . . ."

"What may I bring you, Xandra?" my mother asked. "Dubonnet? Or sherry? I have both."

"Dubonnet, please, my usual—with a twist." The others wanted the same. Evelyn, our cook that summer, passed cheese straws.

I studied Xandra Kalman's tiny, plump feet, encased in perfectly white shoes that looked like expensive antiques, with little bows on the instep and curved heels. I decided that her shoes, like her ivory bracelets, her chain-handled purse, and her long black car, were actually very old, but perfectly preserved. I imagined a maid whitening her shoes after every wearing, just as Alfred was now dusting off that car.

Mrs. Kalman seemed ageless to me; I couldn't picture her young. My mother had told me she'd been a famous beauty. Now the white skin of her arms and neck was as smooth as if it were inflated. Her unwrinkled hands were always in motion, lifting her glass, flicking the ash from her cigarette; her stubby fingers danced, her crimson nails and diamond rings twinkling in the sunlight.

Xandra Kalman's taut round contours were encased in a red flowered dress that gave no hint of a human body inside. Her crimson lips had left their imprint on her glass, her cigarette, and almost, I thought, on her words. Her dark brown hair was waved close to her head, with a twirl in front of each ear; surely in her glory days her hair had looked the same.

She did all the talking; even Auntie Georgie was just listening and laughing. Xandra Kalman's stream of talk was what drew people to her. ". . . I was sick as a cat that entire day . . . I'd thought at the time that Madeline's mayonnaise was a bit off—or was it the crabmeat? Madeline has never been able to keep a decent cook . . ."

"I felt a bit queer after that party, too," my mother said. "The crabmeat . . ."

But Xandra Kalman was already off on another tack. Gradually, inevitably, her anecdotes slipped back in time, to the famous people, those glamorous days and nights in Paris in the 'twenties. She and her husband knew Scott Fitzgerald from St. Paul.

"We'd just arrived at the hotel, when adorable Scott came running in, crazy as ever. We said 'How did you know we were here?' 'Only the Kalmans would have four Oshkosh trunks,' he said, 'and then I saw your initials.'"

I couldn't bear to miss a word. "That little Zelda was a madcap, just like Scott. We found them a house at White Bear that fall when they came back—1921, and then they ruined it. Zelda was pregnant. They had a party, and left all the doors open so everything froze, all the pipes burst, and the whole place was ruined. Then they were kicked out of the Yacht Club, and they had to check into the Commodore Hotel. I was the one who had to get all the clothes, everything for that baby—and Oscar kept trying to make Scott cut down on the drinking."

Mrs. Kalman went on in her throaty voice. "I'll never forget that night at the University Club. We were all there, and Scott was absolutely plastered. He kept saying he was going to dive into the pool from that balcony. Crazy; he would've killed himself. Finally Teddy Mudge just swept the glass out of his hand . . ." She swept her own be-ringed white hand into the air. "Scott was furious, never could stand Teddy—but Teddy'd saved his life. Oh, Scott couldn't wait to shake off the dust of St. Paul."

"Zelda loathed St. Paul," said my mother.

"I don't blame her," murmured Auntie Georgie.

Mrs. Kalman was still holding forth. "In Paris he used to get furious at Ernest, always—he just stormed out, dragging Zelda. I'll never forget that day we all motored out to Senlis. Scott had insisted he'd bring the picnic. When we opened the hamper there was nothing in it but Bombay gin and a shaker! We laughed . . ."

Someone said, "Xandra, tell about the day Lindbergh landed."

"You wouldn't believe the crowd; everyone was there. He was as close to me as I am to you, Georgie. He was so good-looking, so young—we were all young then . . ."

Evelyn, in her pale blue uniform and white apron, came out to announce lunch. I walked away, down to the water, surfeited, as if from a great feast.

Xandra and Oscar Kalman had been married in 1917, my mother told me later. He was a rich banker, at least twenty-five years older than she was. "The Kalmans were lunching with Scott and Zelda in Paris when Zelda had her first breakdown. Xandra told me that years ago, and I think it's true."

"I remember when Scott had a summer job hammering nails at the Northern Pacific freight yards," Auntie Georgie added. "And then *This Side of Paradise* came out, and suddenly he was famous. Remember, Jeannie? We couldn't believe it."

"I'll never forget the Christmas Eve scandal." My mother exhaled.

"What happened?" I asked. "Tell."

"Scott was drunk," she said. "He and Slunky Norton, that little chimney sweep who used to clean all our chimneys, burst into St. John's Church right in the middle of the solemn midnight service. The church was packed, everyone in their best, and in came Scott and Slunky, blowing on these shrill toy trumpets. They staggered up one aisle and down the other. Can you imagine? It was chaos."

I saw Xandra Kalman again three years later at a dinner party in St. Paul, on the wide terrace of the University Club. The sky above us was full of stars; we looked down on the pool, glowing blue from underwater lights, with the whole sparkling city spread out beyond.

She dominated the talk as usual. "Oh, we all had such fun in the old days. The stories I could tell! Dear Scott was always the life of the party." She paused. "Years later, when Scott was broke, Oscar lent him money. 'Just to tide me over, Kallie,' Scott would say each time. He had nicknames for all his friends."

She rambled on about Paris: ". . . that absolutely divine little café on the Rue de l'Odeon where we always went. . . ." And then in that low voice, "I remember one day at Deauville. . . ." Xandra paused, and her face seemed to droop. She's old, I realized. "Scott's dead, of course. Poor Scott. And now Zelda, too."

Zelda had perished that spring in a blaze at the asylum where she was incarcerated.

I'd always imagined Zelda as Nicole—in *Tender is the Night*—on the beach, her back brown and bare, her string of creamy pearls inappropriate yet alluring. And Dick Diver, Nicole's husband? To me he was Scott, as his wife's illness worsened, and life was not so much fun: "He stayed in the big room a long time listening to the buzz of the electric clock, listening to time."

Alan in her new fur coat, ready for college – 1945

– T W E N T Y - S E V E N –

MY MOTHER DROVE ME into town in the Green Car. She was taking me to Hope Furs, St. Paul's best furrier, to look for a fur coat for me.

"Everyone shops at Hope Furs," she told me. "Aunt Katharine, Cousin Gerry, everyone. Nothing keeps you as warm as fur. And you'll be going to all those football games."

But warmth was only part of it. Getting my first fur coat was a symbol of growing up, a rite of passage before I went off to college.

"How are you, Miss Lillian?" inquired my mother. "We're here to look for a fur coat for Alan—something not too expensive. She's going East to college this fall."

"Oh, isn't that lovely. We have some charming new styles for the younger set." Miss Lillian, seasoned saleswoman, nodded sagely, then vanished into the back room, returning moments later with three possibilities.

"This one's beaver," she said. "Very warm." She twirled me in front of the three-way mirrors.

Another saleswoman came over to admire. "It just suits you, dear."

"She's going out East to college," Miss Lillian told her. That was how they said it in Minnesota.

The next coat was muskrat. "I love that color on her," said my mother.

"This one has a scarf at the neck; nice and cozy. And very flattering." Miss Lillian looped the scarf beneath my chin, one end nonchalantly flipped over my shoulder.

"And that one's how much?" my mother asked.

"This one? It's only $324." Far more than the price of anything I'd ever owned, more, probably, than my clothes allowance for the entire year. But this was a new life I was headed toward. I could hardly wait.

Out at the River that afternoon in my bare feet, I modeled the coat for the aunts, and posed under the pine trees for a photograph. Except for that coat, I've never heard of a gray muskrat. Perhaps he was a very old muskrat.

"We must try to get that dress, dearie," my mother said, tilting her head to one side. "It's so you."

She had brought Monnie and me one summer day to a fashion show aimed straight at girls like us. While we ate chicken salad on the terrace of the University Club, teenage models—some of whom we knew, all of whom we envied—flounced around on the deck of the swimming pool below us. Monnie and I had studied the pages of *Mademoiselle* magazine's "Off to College" issue, so we knew how we wanted to look. I'd put myself in those photos. That might be me, I imagined, off to a football game in saddle shoes and pleated plaid, my blonde hair only a tiny bit windblown, a young man in a thick white sweater with a P on it smiling down at me, as a few red and yellow leaves came sifting down. Or me in a full-skirted dress of gleaming blue, heading out for an evening of pure delight, the same merry young man or his twin leading the way.

"I just adore that black one, don't you?" Monnie sighed with longing at the fashion show.

"Oh, yes," I said. I pictured it more for me.

My ordinarily parsimonious mother was splurging on an entire trousseau of new clothes for the start of my college career. She was more excited than I was about an experience she'd never had. The very day after the fashion show we made another trip to town. Auntie Georgie came with us.

"I really want to get to Frank Murphy's before other people snag all the best things. We don't want to lose out!" My mother drove a little faster.

"You must have that one, darling," my mother said. "It's adorable on you."

I stood before them in emerald green velveteen that fanned out in back from a bow at my waist, a modified bustle.

"You look like what's-her-name in the Huxley novel," Auntie Georgie said. "You remember, Jeannie—*Antic Hay.*"

"I think she looks like one of those Gibson Girls." My mother pushed at my hair. "Except that girls don't wear their hair up nowadays."

Next I paraded in a dress with a bare black top and a ballerina skirt of iridescent stripes. "What do you think, Jeannie? Anna Karenina? Except for the short skirt."

My new dresses put Auntie Georgie in mind of certain literary heroines, but that was as close as any of us came to thinking what college might really be about for me.

"Oh, Georgie, I'm gripped by this new book; you've got to read it: *Modern Woman: The Lost Sex*." My mother didn't often allow herself to read in the middle of the morning, but there she was, out on the lawn with an open book in her lap.

"Jeannie, it's a horrible book. Marg lent it to me last winter, and I couldn't bear it. How stupid to say all the problems in the world are caused because we're such lousy mothers."

"But she's a psychiatrist, Georgie. She knows how we're damaging our kids: we're either too protective, or too bossy, or not loving enough. And she knows how frustrated we all are."

"Oh, sure. And if Mom's too intelligent, or too educated, or even thinks of having a career, it'll emasculate our husbands, and we know what that means. Penis-envy: that's her favorite word."

"Ahem! Ssh." Piers and Eddie were walking out onto the lawn.

"You look like a medieval saint, Piers," his mother said. "With the sun shining like gold through your hair."

Richard and Alan at the River – 1948

– TWENTY-EIGHT –

"NATURALLY WE ALL SAY you're too young for the BIG STEP. But we think it's nice anyway."

I was deep in the middle of exams, halfway through my junior year at Radcliffe, when Auntie Harriet's letter arrived at Cabot Hall. Both of my St. Paul aunts were wildly excited by the news that I was engaged to be married.

"And will you give our best to Mr. Emmet?" Auntie Harriet went on. "But, dear niece, what is Mr. Emmet's first name? You were so Jane Eyreish in your letter that WE DON'T KNOW."

"I wish I could see you right now in your own particular starshine," wrote Auntie Georgie from St. Paul. "The deep north where it is only 37 below zero and a cup of hot coffee poured on the snow freezes in a straight line going down."

She then struck a different note: "It delights us that you are coming out here to be married—it is after all your proper home, and your birthplace . . . I can hardly wait to see the Stirbé eyes in her grandmere's wedding dress."

Those Stirbé eyes again, still a mystery to me. My proper home? Well, I had told them that the River was where I wanted to be married. Gangie's wedding dress? I hadn't thought of that. But since I was "too young," anyhow. . . .

That was how it began.

Wedding plans were already being taken out of my hands.

Another letter came from Auntie Georgie. "I want to hear how you met Mr. Wonderful, whom I haven't even yet laid eyes on. Your old auntie has to know all about it before she gives her blessing."

I wrote back. "Are you sure you want to hear? Well, here goes. It was exactly a year ago, after exams. Seven of us went skiing at Stowe: four boys I didn't even know, and two girls besides me. Ann was engaged to Elsie's brother Paul, and I guess the rest of us were supposed to be chaperones.

"Nick and Bill had cars, and somehow I ended up riding with two complete strangers. Nick drove, and I was squeezed in the middle between him and Richard, whose legs were so long. It was late when we left Cambridge, and pretty soon it was dark, and it was snowing, and we drove and drove for hours through New Hampshire and Vermont.

"The snow was falling and the wipers creaked back and forth and his arm was around me and I could have said un-unh or pushed him away, but the snowflakes fell and the wipers creaked and my head was on his shoulder. I breathed the wool smell of his thick white crew sweater.

"We might not have survived that trip. Really. Paul decided we should all meet at the end of the day when the lifts shut down, and then ski cross-country to the Ranch

Camp, this horrible place where we were staying. It got dark in the woods, and you couldn't see the trail. Paul and Bill were zooming ahead, and then Elsie fell, and she wouldn't get up. Richard leaned down, talked to her, and helped her. He was just so kind. . . ."

Auntie Georgie wrote back: "I can see the stars in your eyes all the way from Minnesota."

Yes, I thought, but she didn't know that after that ski trip things hadn't all been so starry. Back in Cambridge, I kept waiting, hoping he'd call. And then he didn't, and I hardly saw him, and it was awful. Our friends kept telling me that he was so busy—crew practice every day, races every weekend, and writing his thesis.

Over Labor Day we were both in Bill and Elsie's wedding in Cincinnati. It was about ninety-nine degrees every day, and there were parties every night. We all sat around someone's pool, and it was heaven. Then I was seated next to him at the dinner the night before the wedding. His glasses and his white shirtfront sparkled in the light from the candles, and I breathed the spicy smell of what I later learned was his Bay Rum. That was the first time I'd heard him sing: "Taking a Chance on Love. . . ." I looked up at him, and then I knew.

My family had met Richard at Christmastime. Soon after that he'd solemnly asked my father for my hand in marriage. That, he thought, was the proper procedure. He assured my father that even before finishing law school he could provide adequately for us both. This was a delicate allusion to something my father already knew: Richard's great-grandfather had been a founding Standard Oil partner.

"You ought to be very careful, Alan," said Ann, a stuffy, self-righteous senior, "before you get yourself mixed up with a rich Long Island playboy whose parents are divorced." But I knew Ann didn't know what she was talking about. She didn't know Richard. I told her so. Before long I was struggling to hold my own against my mother and the aunts, a losing battle. Unlike Ann, they knew exactly what they were talking about.

Auntie Harriet, as was typical of her relationship to me, expressed a merry irreverence toward what I thought was my serious new maturity. ". . . I wanna be Matron of Honor," she wrote, "and Janey wants to be a bridesmaid, and Johnnie, he wants to be a ring bearer and Dinah the Poodle wants to be Flower Girl. We'll just leave out Henry the Scottie. What he wants is out of all reason. He wants to be the minister. Can you imagine?"

On paper half covered with my cousin Janey's typing practice—"fox fox fox jog jog sob sob"—she and Uncle Bill offered us their beach house at La Jolla for our honeymoon. "All you have to do is leave it CLEAN. But knowing your rigid upbringing I am sure I need say NO MORE." My mother was not amused.

The wedding would take place during the coming summer. By February, my mother was already in a tizzy. The actual date had to be left open, raising her anxiety another notch. Richard was on the Harvard varsity crew. If Harvard prevailed in the Olympic tryouts our wedding could not occur until after the Games. If Harvard lost, we might be married sooner.

By the middle of June my mother was in a fever of anxiety. The minute Eddie finished school, she and he drove to Minnesota so she could get to work on this wedding, already more hers than mine.

I stayed in New Jersey with my father. He and I and our neighbor, Major Bates, rode in the major's big Cadillac to Princeton to watch the Olympic rowing tryouts on Lake Carnegie. With all Richard's family, we sat through three days of steamy, hundred-degree heat. The University of California nosed out Harvard by inches in the finals.

My mother met my train in St. Paul. "We're going to stop in at the House of Hope, dear, just for a few minutes. I want you to see it." This was the majestic church where she and my father had been married, and where I had never set foot. My plan was that Richard and I would be married on the lawn at the River. A small wedding, just close family, and our favorite friends. It was all arranged in my head, under the pines with the River as a backdrop. I was happy about my grandmother's Paris bridal gown, since worn by my mother at her wedding, and by her two sisters at theirs. I pictured my bridesmaids in summery white with blue sashes, carrying bunches of field daisies, wreaths of daisies in their hair. The tall handsome groom in one of those pale summer suits.

Once I'd arrived at the River, my mother talked and talked for the next three days to me and to everyone else about all the difficulties involved in arranging a River wedding. "We just can't do it, darling. We've all decided against it."

The "all" did not include me. I was only the bride. I never stood a chance against the powerful matriarchy of my mother, the aunts, my Great-Aunt Katharine, and—a potent new figure in the equation—my mother's Cousin Gerry.

What they said was, "How would all the guests from the East ever get down our hill? And where would they park? Where would they stay? And what if it rained?"

"Really, Alan," said my mother, "Think of those New Yorkers in their high heels. It would just be impossible."

"Impossible," echoed strong Cousin Gerry in her faint, little girl's voice. Cousin Gerry was an older cousin of my mother and the aunts. I scarcely knew her. She'd seldom even come to the River, in my memory. But now she was bossing my bossy mother. To my astonishment my mother not only tolerated Cousin Gerry's stern edicts, she welcomed them. After all, the family honor was at stake: St. Paul honor; mid-western honor.

My mother, Cousin Gerry, the aunts—all the women of my family were on the defensive. It was up to them to show the fancy easterners—Richard's family—that they knew— that St. Paul knew—How Things Ought to be Done.

The guest list kept growing. Wedding plans multiplied like fruit flies. I had a lonely status as a minority of one.

In July Richard arrived at the River in his dark green Plymouth to meet all the relatives. I didn't find out until later that Eddie was disappointed by his brother-in-law-to-be's car, so dull, so conservative. Why not a Lincoln Continental convertible, he wondered, or an MG?

For the next four days Richard was paraded around like a blue-ribbon pig at the Washington County Fair. One day we all went to White Bear Lake for the obligatory lunch with Great-Aunt Katharine. "Do I have to?" wailed Eddie. Our mother let him off.

Aunt Katharine's ancient little uniformed maid served us sherry and tiny cheese wafers on the screen porch overlooking the water. "Show me your ring, Alan darling." I held out my left hand to Aunt Katharine.

"Oh lovely, my dear," she trilled. "So unconventional."

The ruby in my new ring had belonged to Richard's grandmother. He'd had the stone re-set for me, wrapped by interlocking bands of platinum so it looked almost like two rings. A new work of art, we thought. I wished Richard and I were in one of the little sailboats we could see on the lake below us.

Aunt Katharine's wispy old chauffeur rolled us in her long black Cadillac a couple of hundred yards to the Yacht

Club for lunch. For years after that, Richard could reel off that entire lunch menu:

Thick crabmeat bisque with buttered biscuits
Sweetbreads in heavy cream sauce
Strawberry shortcake with clotted cream

"Oh, do have another biscuit," urged Aunt Katharine in her plumiest voice. "The food here is . . . simple. But good." Richard and I looked at each other, trying not to laugh, swallowing as much rich food as we could.

Finally back at the River, Richard said he still felt like one of those force-fed geese. We peeled off our White Bear clothes, went for a swim, and two hours later ambled over to the Lewises' for another meal, a family party in Richard's honor. Nothing was fancy there, of course. No one was dressed up; I was in shorts, but still the food kept coming. I passed Dena's hot cheese biscuits to go with the highballs. Dena and Mrs. Wooding brought dish after dish from the steamy kitchen—baked ham stuck with cloves, potato salad, the summer's first corn, little homemade rolls. We ate on our laps.

Again we ended up with strawberries and thick cream. Auntie Georgie came around waving the coffee pot. I was afraid she'd spill it.

"Do have another cup of coffee," she warbled, sounding unlike her usual self. "There are pots and pots of it in the kitchen." Richard never forgot the nightmare vision of all those pots.

"Why drive all the way back to New York?" Auntie Harriet asked Richard. "Why not just stay, and we'll have the wedding right here. Tomorrow!" She sounded a little giddy.

"Yeah! Great idea," echoed Uncle Bill.

"Oh, H, don't be silly," my mother said. "You know we

can't do that." The highballs had all the grownups chattering in their party voices.

"I'll be back," Richard said. "My family wants to come, too." He left the next day.

"So dearie, I want to hear how he proposed? Did he go down on one knee, while you waved your fan and fluttered those long eyelashes?" Auntie Harriet and I were sitting on the dock, with our toes in the water, thinking about swimming.

I laughed. "It wasn't quite like that. Do you really want to hear?"

"Yes!"

"It was after New Years, and we'd been visiting my family and his. I was heading back to Cambridge before Richard, and he was putting me on the train at Grand Central. Anyhow, we were walking down that great marble staircase, and we got to the landing halfway down, and he stopped me. He said, 'Wait a minute.' He put my suitcase down, and pulled out a pack of the Beechnut gum he likes—he doesn't smoke because of rowing—and he offered me a stick. So we just stood there in the corner, while people kept going past us up and down, but no one was paying any attention. I looked up at his face, but he seemed to be looking at one of those lights that hang from the ceiling. Then his eyes were on me, and he said 'I want to ask you—um—will you marry me?' "

"So you said yes?" Auntie Harriet asked.

"No. I said, 'I'll think about it.' Then I got on the train—it was a sleeper, the Owl—but I didn't sleep much."

I was in awe of Richard's tall, beautifully-dressed mother. She'd been sick that spring with what turned out to be an ulcer. Now she was better, but not quite herself. Richard called from New York. "She's hired a private railroad car to bring everyone out to St. Paul. Can you believe it? Our friends will love it."

"I've never heard of anyone doing that," I said.

My mother was elated when she heard that Richard's mother had arranged for a private railcar to bring our brides–maids, ushers, and the New York family out for the wedding. That was the way things ought to be, she said, the way her family's rich relatives had traveled in the old days of glory.

She and Auntie Georgie and I were sitting around one evening on the porch at Auntie Harriet and Uncle Bill's. They all had their highballs. The talk revolved as usual around my upcoming wedding. My mother was describing the mother-of-the bride dress she'd finally found for herself. "Very simple, pale gray, little cap sleeves, just to the floor . . . quite stylish, I think. Now I just have to find a little hat. . . ."

Auntie Harriet turned toward me. "Dearie, you still haven't told me how you finally told Richard yes." She turned to the others. "I'm sure you've all heard what our little Allie said when he proposed: 'I'll think about it.'" They all laughed, including my mother.

"Oh, must I tell? I was so dumb. It's embarrassing."

"Tell," said Auntie Georgie.

"Well, we were back in Cambridge, and we saw each other, and it seemed like weeks before he brought it up again. I was afraid he'd forgotten. Or changed his mind."

"I've never heard this part," my mother said.

"We were having dinner at the Bella Vista, a not very fancy place on Church Street, and he said, 'About that matter—that question I asked you. . . .' So anyway, I said yes, right there in the middle of dinner. And we were happy, and then we called everyone, and that's it."

Just then Uncle Herbert walked in, holding one of those yellow Western Union envelopes.

"This just came," he said, handing it to me. "Addressed to you, Allie."

"Who's it from?" My mother quizzed me. "What does it say?"

"It's from Richard's mother," I said, finally. "She says, um, 'Have found pretty short dress. Will that do, or shall I struggle further?'"

"Oh no!" cried my mother. "Now I have my dress, and it's long, and we've got to be the same. And long is much more formal. . . ."

"This is definitely a formal wedding, if you ask me," said Uncle Bill.

"Well, what shall I tell her?" I said.

Everyone had another drink or two, and Auntie Harriet brought out a chicken dish and the salad.

"It has to be long," my mother kept saying.

"What should I say?" I asked again.

"She's just got to go shopping again." Auntie Georgie wasn't taking this seriously. Neither were Uncle Bill or Auntie Harriet. For some reason they were laughing, then finally, even my mother laughed.

"But she's been sick. . . ." I murmured.

At last we were having dessert, and everyone was still talking and laughing. I said, "I really ought to send her a telegram tonight." I seemed to be the only one taking this seriously.

Uncle Bill said, "How about just 'Struggle further'? That oughtta do it."

Everyone thought that was hilarious. Finally I caught their mood. I walked out to their wall phone and called Western Union.

My telegram to my future mother-in-law consisted of two words: "Struggle further."

I'd had engagement presents from the aunts and some of my mother's cousins and friends, lace-trimmed slips, bureau scarves, sets of place mats. Auntie Georgie handed me a prettily-wrapped package on her porch one evening. The first thing I pulled out of the box made everyone laugh. I laughed, too, though secretly I was a little shocked. She'd given me a frilly black garter, trimmed with a small gilt dollar sign.

I loved my two unconventional aunties, Georgie and Harriet, different as they were from each other. Both were rebels, as my mother was not. I'd felt sure they'd back me up in my longing to be married at the River. But now they were siding with her.

"Don't be sad, Allie." Auntie Georgie patted my shoulder. "We'll get them all out here, maybe the day before. We'll have a big lunch on the lawn for all these fancy Emmets and all your friends from the East. They can swim in the River, and jump off the rope swing . . . what do you think?"

I thought that was a pathetic minimum of what I'd wanted. But now the invitations had been ordered, the House of Hope Church reserved, Ramaley the Caterer enlisted, and the tent people were measuring the Lewises' backyard for a canvas canopy over the reception.

"Don't worry, darling." My mother tried to comfort me. "They'll all get to see the River. And everything will be perfect in St. Paul."

"I hate St. Paul; I've always hated it. And the Lewises' backyard is so ugly!"

"It will look lovely, I promise. Cousin Gerry is working on the flowers with Mr. Johnson at Holm & Olssen. They're even painting the side of the garage to match the tent! Cousin Gerry's idea."

I tried on the old family wedding gown. Too loose around my middle; too short.

"Call Miss Stella, Jeannie," advised Auntie Georgie. "She can fix anything."

Soon Miss Stella was kneeling at my feet. "There's no

way to lengthen it," she muttered around her mouthful of pins. "I'll add an underskirt—tulle."

"Richard and Pa and the ushers—they can just wear summer suits, can't they? August twenty-first—it might still be hot."

"Oh, Alan, no." My mother looked horrified. "Not with that satin dress. They'll wear cutaways."

"Striped pants and all?" But it was already decided.

Months before I'd asked three friends and Richard's sister to be my bridesmaids. Richard's brother-in-law was to be his best man, with Eddie as one of the ushers. In July my mother told me I must have my twelve-year-old cousins, Genna and Janey, as bridesmaids.

"Oh, Mother! The little girls? But why?"

"Dearie, we must. Think of all Auntie Harriet and Auntie Georgie are doing for you—the parties, putting people up. The Lewises are turning their whole house in town over to us."

So that was decided upon.

My mother and I were going into town for a day or two every week, for fittings on my wedding dress and the veil and to buy the new wardrobe my mother insisted I must have. We picked out my "going away" costume, a navy blue, close-fitting jacket, with a long skirt that fanned out in soft pleats, the "New Look" according to that year's dictates from Paris. And of course a pile of fancy nightgowns and underwear: pink, white, lacy, threaded with ribbons. Sometimes Auntie Georgie came to the fancy shops with us. She and my mother were having a great time.

"Yes, Allie, you have to have that one," said Auntie Georgie on our fifth day of shopping.

"It's so hard to choose," I moaned.

"I think we should get both."

Another day we ordered stacks of monogrammed towels, and a pile of those linen guest towels that no guest ever uses.

My mother, it seemed, had abandoned all her old scruples about thrift. She said this was not the time for economy. She'd even Invaded Principal, a practice that led straight to ruin, or so she'd always said.

"You must ask Cousin Margaret to play the organ; she'd be really hurt if we didn't."

The first things Richard had ever given me were recordings of Handel's "Water Music" and "The Royal Fireworks." Back in the days when I'd dreamed of our River wedding, I'd imagined drifting off in the green canoe with Richard, down the River in the moonlight, while everyone waved and the "Water Music" floated out from our record player, from Auntie Harriet's, and from Pat Shearer's.

In Cambridge, I'd been singing with the college chorus and the Harvard Bach Choir; Bach was my favorite composer. I made a list of a few of his organ preludes and fugues. "Really, Alan, Cousin Margaret won't know these elaborate toccatas and so forth." My mother looked at my list. "You must let her decide what to play."

We met Cousin Margaret for lunch one hot day at the Women's City Club. I put my list down next to her salad plate. "Oh, but everyone loves the Lohengrin," she trilled. "So familiar . . ."

"You mean, 'Here comes the bride'?" To myself I hummed the fanciful lines: forty inches wide. As children we'd thought that was hilarious.

"And I was thinking at the end. . . ," I persisted despite feeling I'd met a stone wall—"some of Handel's 'Royal Fireworks.' It's so festive, maybe—maybe with a trumpet, too ('. . . and here comes the groom, thinner than a broom')."

"Oh, dear, Bach is so . . . tedious. Not really right for a wedding. Or Handel either. And everyone expects the Mendelssohn. It's the 'Wedding March,' after all!" Cousin Margaret said with a brave little smile. "Da-da-de-dum-de da." She fluttered her small white hands, keeping time with her frail soprano.

My mother nodded.

Cousin Gerry, a Garden Club stalwart, had already talked to the florist when she went with my mother and me to find the perfect dress for the bridesmaids. "We have to give Mr. Johnson enough time," she told us in her faint little voice. "So he'll be sure to have enough of everything we need. He says tuberous begonias and gladioli will hold up well. It may still be hot. . . ."

"But, but . . ." I murmured, my voice now as feeble as hers. "I've never liked gladiolas. . . ."

At Daytons' Bridal Department I approached the saleswoman. "Just something fresh and simple," I said. "Maybe white, with blue sashes. . . ."

I saw Cousin Gerry's pink-tipped hand reach out to fondle a sea-foam green satin the saleswoman had just brought out. "Jeannie, dear," she said. "Imagine this with pale, pale apricot begonias and glads."

"Oh, Gerry; heavenly!" my mother agreed. "Wonderful fabric, this heavy satin; it will go perfectly with the old wedding gown."

"One or two flowers in the girls' hair, too. Charming. I'll talk to Mr. J., the florist."

Auntie Harriet – 1944

– TWENTY-NINE –

THE WEDDING WAS TWO WEEKS AWAY. I'd had my early morning swim, as usual, and was pulling on my shorts, buttoning my shirt. Down the hall, my mother was on the phone, talking in her high-pitched long-distance voice to my father. "What day are you coming, Jack? I really need you; there's just too much. . . ."

The decisions had all been made, I thought, and the script was set to unfold on schedule. The pressure seemed to lift during this brief hiatus. I walked over to Auntie Harriet and Uncle Bill's that afternoon.

"Hi, Allie! Come on in. You're just in time to have a beer with us. How 'bout it? Hamms' or Schmidts'?"

"I'll take a Coke, if you have it."

"Oh, you're the same old Alan," Uncle Bill said. "Remember how shocked you were that time we took you into the bar at Huffs?"

"Yes," I said. "The wrong side." We laughed.

"Allie," Auntie Harriet said as she slumped back in her chair, "your ma's in a real swivet about Richard's family, the divorce, the stepmother, the stepfather, stepbrothers, half-brother, half-sister, etcetera; I can't keep it all straight. How 'bout you, sweetie? What do you think about all these fancy people you're getting mixed up with? Tell your old uncle and auntie."

"They're nice, I promise. His father is really cozy and funny. He and Jessie have these two cute little children."

"Are they all coming?" asked Uncle Bill.

"No, but Richard's two stepbrothers are coming with his father; Davy's ten, and Harry's about fifteen. Richard's grandmother, too, and his father's sister, Aunt Katsie. She's really funny, and she's Richard's mother's best friend."

"Whoa. Wait a sec. His father's sister?" Auntie Harriet knocked the ash off her cigarette. "So there was a divorce, but they don't all hate each other?"

"No, they seem to get along; I don't know." I shrugged. "That's just the way they are."

"Well, that's good. Tell your mama to cool it."

"You tell her," I said.

One morning I ambled over to the Lewises' house. Uncle Herbert was on the porch as usual. "Hi, Allie. Sit down, sit down." He laid his pipe down, and the thick red book he'd been reading.

"*The Gathering Storm*," he said. "Churchill. It's the first volume of a history of the whole war that he's planning to write. Now that he's out of government, he has time. That and his painting."

"Richard's reading that now, too! He wrote his thesis on Neville Chamberlain, and his trip to Munich in 1938, when he tried to appease Hitler and prevent war."

"Ugh, that was Chamberlain's 'peace with honour,'" Uncle Herb said. "Churchill called it 'a total defeat.' I'd love to talk to Richard about all that."

Auntie Georgie came out to the porch, in the soft, baggy, faded blue slacks that she wore every day at the River, her tortoiseshell glasses halfway down her narrow nose.

"Allie! How did you manage to escape from your ma? She has your life pretty well programmed right now."

"Yeah. The gathering storm," chortled Uncle Herb, with his deep belly laugh.

"Nothing much seems to be happening at the moment."

Auntie Georgie held a lighted cigarette. She sat down in one of the straw chairs, next to the blue Mexican ashtray. Unlike most people, she seldom smoked. "Your ma's quite terrified of Richard's mother; says she's so tall, so beautiful, so rich. How about you, Allie? What do you think?"

"Um, I don't know. She's his mother, but, yeah, she's kind of. . . ."

"What's the new husband like? What does Richard think of him?"

"Holly, they call him. He makes a big effort with Richard, but Jane, his sister, can't stand him. Some of them laugh at him, but he's nice to me."

"Your ma says they go to Martha's Vineyard in the summer. But don't you start turning up your aristocratic nose at the St. Croix River, Miss Alan, don't you dare." Auntie Georgie waggled her finger at me. Uncle Herbert laughed.

"That's just what Auntie Harriet said," I told them. "Uncle Bill said he'd give me a poke in the snoot if I get too big for my britches. But don't worry." Now I was serious. "I'll never give up the River. And Richard already loves it, too."

"So, give us the low-down, Allie. I hear his father's new wife is a lot younger; she must be about H's age. Herb, Carrie told me that her sister June was at school with this Jessie. And June is H's oldest friend."

"New wives, new husbands, all these steps—how do they get along? That's what I want to know." But Uncle Herb didn't seem to expect an answer.

"I think it'll be O.K.," I said. "I hope."

My mother and Auntie Georgie were bobbing around in the River the next morning, their two heads well above the water, talking, talking, as usual. Their furiously kicking feet churned the water.

"Kathleen Fitzpatrick called me last night, George, and guess what she's doing. She offered to turn over their whole house in town to the bridesmaids and ushers. Poor Phil, she never asked him; he wasn't even consulted."

"Typical Kathleen; the grand gesture."

"Well, it's pretty nice, all the same. She's even leaving their two maids to cook breakfast for the kids, iron the girls' dresses and so forth. Alan," my mother continued, "you and I will have to move into town on Monday, to the Lewises'. There's just too much to do." Then she turned to Eddie. "You can come in later with Auntie Harriet. You and Daddy have to go to Wyser's, the rental place, for your suit."

"Aagh." Eddie groaned. He and I exchanged a look, rolling our eyes.

"And, Eddie, I want you to finish painting the lawn chairs today. I mean it. And next week you'll have to sweep the terrace and rake the lawn. All Richard's family is coming out that Friday, so everything has to look nice. And I can't be two places at once." She couldn't stop talking.

Eddie took off in the little motorboat he'd built. I walked over to Auntie Harriet's house. She was sitting out under the pine trees with her feet up, the new John O'Hara novel open on her lap.

"Hello, little bride. Are you feeling like a princess? Or a prisoner?"

I sighed. "Well, both, sort of. Mother's all wound up. I can't wait till Dick gets here on Tuesday. It's going to be fun.

Our friends are coming on the train with Dick's mother and her husband, his sister, his grandmother, a lot of people. Two aunts. His father's driving out, with Jessie and her boys."

Every day at the River people were coming to our house for drinks, or we went to them for supper. I was included now with the grownups, my mother's old friends, and I scarcely saw my usual River pals. Monnie, whom I'd wanted to be a bridesmaid, was jaunting around Mexico. The others all seemed too young now; I'd entered a new phase.

"I don't imagine you'll want to go back to college, now that you're getting married." This was Mrs. Power, my least favorite of my mother's friends.

"Oh yes I will. Richard wants me to, and I promised Daddy. I'm going to take one term off, so I can learn how to cook."

"Hmm." Mrs. Power turned away.

"It's been another grueling day of errands," my mother sighed. "And it's so hot. I've hardly had time even to dunk into the River. Alan, hand me the list. . . ." She spent any spare moments addressing engraved announcements to people who hadn't been invited to the wedding.

Gifts had begun to arrive. My mother had bought a white album in which we recorded each wedding present. I put a check by the names of people I'd thanked. My mother put a small "R" for "return" next to the gifts she'd decided should be exchanged—a duplicate toaster, for instance, or a vase she thought was ugly.

"Jack, we'll have to pack all these up to go into town to the Lewises'."

In St. Paul, my mother, Auntie Georgie and I went up to the third floor of the Lewises' house, where a long table had been put up to hold the wedding presents.

"It'll be covered with white satin," my mother said. "And of course some flowers."

"No," I said. "No, that's so tacky."

"But, dearie, everyone will want to see what you've gotten. And they'll want to see what they gave you." The table remained. Of course.

Pretty soon that table was laden with Tiffany plates, candlesticks, and a flotilla of silver bonbon dishes. One end was anchored by Auntie Georgie and Uncle Herbert's gift, an old silver tureen with Richard's and my entwined initials engraved on the side.

"We didn't want to give you anything useful, Allie, my darling, not to such a high-minded pair as you and Mr. Emmet." Auntie Georgie hugged me.

Perhaps Auntie Harriet shared Auntie Georgie's sentiment. She and Uncle Bill gave us an equally large, equally useless present that weighed down the other end of the display table. Another covered tureen, another antique, this one of blue and white china. Secretly I liked it better than the silver one. I wondered why they'd given us rival tureens. Auntie Georgie had purchased hers first. Was Auntie Harriet trying to strike back at her bossy older sister? No one said anything, certainly not I.

My father arranged for a small fleet of hired cars to take the out-of-towners from one fancy event to the next during their three days in St. Paul. This was his particular contribution to the festivities. He had the schedule typed up, six pages: "Manson-Miller Car #5," for example; "Thursday, 5:30 PM, from St. Paul Hotel to Lewis residence, 657 Fairmount Avenue," with the names of those who were to ride in Car #5. He'd helped my mother think of everything. I, the ingrate, was dismayed by their thoroughness.

"What's the matter, Alan?" inquired my mother when she saw me frowning at the elaborate transportation memo.

"Oh, I don't know, it just seems so . . . organized." I had a mental image of Richard's and my friends casually hopping into someone's snappy car that simply happened to be there, that it should all just happen.

The River seemed far away once we'd moved into the Lewises' house in town. I was ensconced in Genna's small back room; I can't recall where she and Piers and little Finlay had been relocated. There are many things I cannot remember.

The out-of-town contingent was to arrive in St. Paul on Thursday. The night before, my parents, the aunts and uncles, and Richard and I gathered for supper at the Lewises'. My mother had walked into my room that afternoon as I brushed my hair in front of the little mirror over Genna's bureau.

"I have something for you, dear," my mother said. She held a glass quart bottle filled with pale pink liquid. "Have a spoonful of this." She poured some into the spoon and held it out.

"Why? What is it?" It tasted sweet. "Is this the same pink syrup you used to give us when we were little? Our 'trip medicine'?"

"Oh, Dr. Dorrity prescribed it. Just a little phenobarbital, so you won't get overtired. We want you to be fresh and pretty for your wedding, darling."

When I went downstairs I told Auntie Georgie my mother was dosing me with the pink syrup. "She thinks I'm still a child."

"Oh, Allie, you know your ma!" She laughed. "It won't do any harm, anyhow."

For three or four days I didn't worry about a thing. My mother fed me the syrup at regular intervals, and I didn't protest. "Just to take the edge off," she'd say. If anyone should have been imbibing that syrup, it was my mother. Maybe she was.

Auntie Harriet and two ushers at Alan and Richard's wedding in St. Paul – 1948

– THIRTY –

"JUST TO MAKE SURE," my mother said as she plied me with a spoonful of syrup and a tumbler of bubbling Alka Seltzer. She had me tucked into bed after I'd finally been dragged away from the festive dinner on the eve of our wedding.

Two days earlier, Richard's family and our friends had arrived in St. Paul. Most of them had ridden the private railroad car reserved by his mother. My bridesmaid Elsie couldn't stop laughing and talking about what fun they'd had on the train.

"Oh, I wish we'd been there," I said to Richard. "Why did we have to miss the best part?"

"Oh, silly; we didn't." He put his arm around me. "And some of our friends might not have been able to come if Moo hadn't done that."

"Why do you and Jane call her Moo?"

"After she and Dad were divorced, and he'd already married Jessie, Jane and I used to sing, 'She's nobody's Moo Cow now.' Pretty mean, we were."

"And now she has the ulcer," I said. He and I were in his green Plymouth, heading out to Wold-Chamberlain Field to meet his old friend Nicholas King. Then there was Nick walking from the plane, large and perspiring in the rumpled seersucker he'd worn since boarding his flight in Paris. We dropped him at the Fitzpatrick's house, where our friends in the wedding party were staying. He lugged his battered, brown leather suitcase out of the car.

"We'll see you around five-ish," Richard told him. "Someone will pick you all up to go to her aunt and uncle's for drinks. Alan's pa has it all worked out: who goes where, when, and with whom. He's incredible; the whole thing's incredible."

Nick laughed. I looked up at Richard, happy because I knew he liked my father.

"Here, Alan, dear." My mother slipped another spoonful of syrup into me. We were about to go downstairs at Auntie Georgie and Uncle Herb's for a cocktail party, the first encounter of the two clans.

"But why, Mother? I'm fine."

"I know, darling—but we don't want you to get overtired now, just when everything's finally about to happen. And with all these people here."

Auntie Georgie came into my room then, dressed in pale green and her dangly earrings. "Oh, Lord, Jeannie. Do you think we're ready for this?"

I could hear the caterers scurrying about downstairs. We three were all ready, I in a new blue silk dress, wearing the spray pin that Richard had just given me. "Turn it the other way, dear; this way, so it makes a smile." My mother reattached it, and, looking in the mirror, I decided she was right. She wasn't wearing her usual little wire-rimmed glasses.

This was her party look, but it made her seem different, and I knew she couldn't see very well.

"What do you think, Georgie, shall we have a little nip before we go down?" My mother pulled a medicine bottle filled with amber liquid out of her pink toiletry bag. They each took a swallow from a doll-sized glass.

"Fool's courage, Jeannie. Before we face the. . . ." I was afraid she was going to say "enemy."

"They're nice," I said. "Don't worry; they're just Richard's family."

Uncle Herb and my father were downstairs before us. Soon the out-of-town family flocked in. Richard's mother, tall and slim in red linen, had to bend over to talk to mine. "I was actually in St. Paul's once when I was a little girl," I heard her saying. "We were on our way out to Portland to see our grandparents, and sister Mac and I had been exposed to whooping cough. They made us get off the train, and into quarantine here, at Anker Hospital. For weeks!"

"Oh, I never knew you'd been here before! That's what they did then, quarantine. But not a happy memory of St. Paul." My mother barely came up to Richard's mother's shoulder. Her emerald ring, her pale fingertips seemed quaintly modest next to his mother's long scarlet nails and gold-looped wrists. We all turned then to talk to other people, but I felt a small burst of fury having heard my almost mother-in-law refer to the city as "St. Paul's," as if confusing it with the boarding school to which Richard and his brother had been sent.

Then I was having a lovely time. Richard put his arm around my shoulders. My favorite people were all here, in one place.

"Who's that on the sofa, Allie?" Auntie Harriet had her auburn hair pinned up; her shoulders were bare beneath her wide black hat. "You've gotta keep us old folks clued in."

"The one with the fan?" asked Richard. "That's Aunt Katsie, my father's sister."

"She's wonderful," I said. "She reminds me of you, Auntie H!"

As I turned to greet more people, I overheard Cousin Margaret talking to Cousin Gerry. "Poor little Alan. I don't envy her that mother-in-law."

"Formi-dable," Cousin Gerry replied in her faint little-girl voice, pronouncing the word as if in French. "But I must say, she doesn't look so bad, for someone who's divorced."

I noticed Helen, all in black, tight ringlets on top of her head, chatting away with Holly, Richard's stepfather. Her plump fingers were wrapped around a martini glass that tilted from side to side as she popped another asparagus canapé into her mouth. "May I bring you another cocktail?" asked courtly Holly. I couldn't see Uncle Archie; maybe he was out on the porch.

Soon we were all at the University Club, having dinner that first night on the wide terrace under the stars, overlooking the blue-lit pool.

Friday was the River day. The sun was shining, and it was hot, but not too hot. "You'll love the River," Richard had told his friends. They did. Bill and Elsie took our canoe out. "Hey," they yelled. "There's a current!" Richie was the first to jump into the water from the rope swing. "I'm next," called Polly. We all swam. Eddie offered rides in his motorboat.

The grownups milled about the lawn, glasses in hand. "This is charming," Richard's mother was saying. "I can see how you must love it, Jean. Your house is next door, Herb? Is that the old house? I want to see everything."

"Oh, Lord." I heard Auntie Harriet muttering to Georgie as the little group started to move in the direction of their two houses. "I didn't even get our beds made this morning."

"Wait'll she sees our house, " Auntie Georgie said. "Not what she's used to, I bet. Long Island, it's not." They laughed.

Uncle Archie was the only one of the older generation to take a swim. He went across the River and back, elbows angling sharply in his swift crawl. Helen's spike-heeled sandals sank into the lawn. She never took off her wide-brimmed black hat. I heard her low voice, recounting for Richard's aunt some anecdote about the fine family into which he was marrying. Her words were blurry, perhaps because that family—my family—had never been kind to her.

I have no memory of the rehearsal in the cavernous House of Hope church, nor of a subsequent cocktail party at Auntie Harriet and Uncle Bill's house in town. Was that because of the syrup?

The dinner that evening was at the stately old Minnesota Club, all marble and gilt, a stuffy men's club to which Uncle Herb belonged. I see myself in long periwinkle taffeta hugging the St. Louis aunts, my father's sisters, "so glad you could come."

"The flowers are really pretty, Cousin Gerry," I told her. "You've done so much for us."

I couldn't hear her frail voice. She had her eye on Richard's mother, our hostess for this dinner, who was engrossed in an agitated conversation with her sister over a much-folded sheet of paper. The seating plan. Richard's mother waved a limp hand over the beautifully-laid tables. "For seven!" she groaned.

Cousin Gerry walked over to them. "They're all set for seven!" she trilled. Richard's mother was shaking her head. "I spent hours figuring out who would sit where, at tables of eight; that's what I was told. This is absolutely desperate."

Bad marks for Cousin Gerry, I could tell. It was she who'd made all the arrangements for this party at St. Paul's fanciest club.

Presently we were all sitting down to dinner, me beside Richard, of course, with five of our favorite friends. At another table Richard's glamorous mother, apparently over her shock, was charming my father. Across the room, my mother looked anxious, I thought, as she leaned to hear what Richard's beaming father was saying. I could see Richard's youngest stepbrother Davy at a table with the little girls, my cousin-bridesmaids. Near the end of dinner, as our lemon mousse was being served, Davy, who had been well-coached, knocked on his Coke glass with a spoon. Heads turned as he climbed up on his gilt chair to serenade us with some then-popular nonsense song. Larry, our best man, was next, belting out his musical version of "The Owl and the Pussycat": ". . . and they danced by the light of the moon," he concluded to applause and whistles. One of the ushers sang about a "ski-yumper" from Norway, and Richard's oldest Emmet cousin followed with "The Wearing of the Green." Last and best of all was Richard, standing tall above me, singing, "Just One of Those Things."

There seemed to be a little confusion over in the corner, and I saw one of the St. Louis aunts leading the other out of the room. Fueled by champagne, and intending, I suppose, to uphold my family's end against all the song-ful Emmets, Uncle Bill attempted to recite an ostensibly comic riff on brave Barbara Freitchie: "Shoot if you must this peek-a-boo blouse . . ." Then he lost the words, and twice repeated, "this peek-a-boo blouse," before finally giving up amid a polite patter of clapping. There was more music, and we danced.

Richard and I had a minute alone together in the cool night air on the steps of the Lewises' house. "Sleep tight, my little mouse," he said. "And sweet dreams until tomorrow."

Upstairs in my narrow bed, I could hear my mother talking to Auntie Georgie. "Can you believe Gerry let that happen? Richard's ma was really in a swivet. And I can't blame her; she must have been furious: 'these stupid people out here; these mid-western hicks; they don't know how these things are done.' I'm sure that's what she's thinking. And it'll probably bring back her ulcer."

"Oh, Jeannie, it all worked out. Don't worry. Now go to bed; you need your rest."

"And then Jack's sister. That was so awful. Poor thing, she's not used to all that champagne."

The next morning, the Big Day: August 21, 1948.

"Stay in bed, Alan; you mustn't get overtired. Dena's bringing your breakfast up." My mother slipped a spoonful of syrup into me; I'd stopped fighting. "You don't need to do a thing, darling; just relax."

It was a long, boring day. "Just rest, dear. Stay in bed." I had no one to talk to. I had a book—*The Great Gatsby*—but I couldn't concentrate. Eddie'd been given certain responsibilities, so he wasn't around. The cousins—Piers, Genna, Janey, and Finlay—had been farmed out for the day. The grownups, I realized, simply wanted me out of the way. Late that morning, trapped and desperate, I tiptoed out into the hall.

"Just what do you think you're doing, Miss Allie?" Auntie Georgie happened to be coming upstairs at that exact minute.

"I thought I'd go up and take another look at our presents."

"Tch-tch; you're supposed to be resting." She winked.

Cousin Gerry and Great-aunt Katharine were giving a lunch for all the out-of-towners at Cousin Gerry's house at the lake. Uncle Herb came to my room to say good-bye. "Poor little Allie; you're the only one who's not invited." He patted me on the shoulder and planted a peck on my forehead.

My mother bustled in. "But Herb, you know she couldn't go. She'd get too tired, and besides, she and Richard can't see each other before the wedding. Good-bye, sweetie," she said. "We won't be gone long. You just stay right here and rest."

It seemed hours before Miss Stella arrived to button me into the wedding gown and arrange the veil. The wedding was set for five o'clock. "One more spoonful," said my mother. "She's very calm," I heard her telling my father.

"You look absolutely beautiful," he told me when I appeared. And then he and I were inside a black limo, and on our way to the House of Hope.

Our wedding was documented by the photographer in black and white. I have no memory of the wedding; those pictures are what I remember.

There I am outside the church, laughing, flirting—it looks like—with the ushers, while my mother in her long, gray dress, with an ostrich plume poking up from her little cap, reaches up to give my veil a tweak.

The wedding looks splendid. Nothing was the way I'd wanted it, not under the pines at the River, but in a big, unfamiliar city church. There I am, just inside the door, laughing and chattering with the satin-clad bridesmaids. I can almost hear Cousin Margaret's "Lohengrin" resounding from the organ. Now I'm on my father's arm, walking up the aisle toward my Richard.

The reception at Auntie Georgie and Uncle Herb's St. Paul house spilled over into their cramped urban back yard. But first everyone had to pass through the line-up in the big front hall. There's Richard clasping the hand of his first childhood friend, later a roommate, now his usher. Somehow

I doubt that they've ever solemnly shaken hands before. Richard's beautiful mother—Moo—is wearing a long, slim, flowered dress, with something small and white on her head. All the ladies wear hats. Here comes Auntie Harriet, under wide-brimmed straw. She and I are smiling at each other, she with that impish grin that means she's teasing me, as usual.

I see some of my old River pals. A grinning Margaret Harper in those brown and white spectator pumps. She's sitting on the porch steps beside Hank Grant, owlish in his wire-rimmed glasses and dark suit, a half-smoked cigarette between his fingers. He looks as old as his father. Mike Pettee's and Monnie's little sisters, in puffed-sleeve dresses, white socks, and patent leather Mary Janes, just look bored. Pat Shearer is missing; he, like Monnie, was off in some distant land.

Cousin Gerry looks triumphant, as if she'd brought off the whole event herself. She stands at the top of the porch steps, above the mob, substantial in a fluttery dress covered with pallid flowers, white gloves in one hand and a champagne glass in the other. Richard's grandmother, his aunts, and mine have corsages pinned to their dresses. Someone had thought to arrange that. Cousin Gerry, of course.

There is Xandra Kalman, ensconced in an armchair, a cigarette held to her crimson lips. A dotted veil covers half her face; her four-strand pearl choker doesn't quite hide the furrows in her neck. At her feet sit a trio of young men, apparently enthralled. Her plump little feet are hidden; I can't see if they're encased in those white shoes with curved heels that I still remember. Looking at the photographs weeks later, Richard's mother asked, "Who is that stout little woman with the marcelled hair? Dyed, surely."

"Oh, that's Mrs. Kalman," I told her. "She's—um—a friend of the family."

There's Eddie, looking all of sixteen, laughing with two of the other ushers. This was the first wedding he'd ever been to, and his heavy responsibilities were now over. He'd had to drive some of our wedding party here and there, and at the church Richard's ushers had expected him to tell them who was who.

Now here come the bride and groom, changed into our traveling clothes. We jump in the car with Larry, our best man, who is taking us to Union Station. Richard is laughing as I lean across him to wave. Wearing a dark hat with a feather that sticks straight up, I look like a happy, manic madwoman. Then we're off on a two-day train ride to Jasper Park in Alberta.

I shuffle through all the photographs one more time; none of them include even a glimpse of Helen. Sadness washes over me as I confirm once again that there's not a single picture of Uncle Archie, the best beloved uncle of my whole life.

Before they left St. Paul, one of the ushers dumped out all the Fuller Brush samples left from his summer job as a door-to-door salesman. In the front hall of the Fitzpatrick house where they'd stayed, he spelled out "Thank You" in brushes on the floor.

Uncle Archie in Mexico City – 1937

– THIRTY-ONE –

AFTER RICHARD AND I WERE MARRIED I no longer spent whole summers at the River. It was two years before we flew out for an extended visit. By then I was nursing our two-month-old daughter Caroline, whom we called Callie. My mother and my mother-in-law turned out to share the same idea as to how to travel with a child: "Be sure to ask her doctor to prescribe something for your trip." In phone conversations with each of our mothers, Richard and I heard the same message. "Just a little phenobarbital," my mother insisted. "That pink syrup. You know—just to take the edge off. It'll make the trip much more pleasant for you."

Dr. McDonald, our new pediatrician, looked stunned: "You mean . . . you mean you want to drug your child?" We didn't.

Everything at the River looked the same: the wide, calm water, with the Wisconsin hills on the other side covered with dark pines, light green maples lower down. Still paler willows and yellow-green marsh grass, lit by the setting sun, fringed the sloughs. From the hill behind us cool air descended into the dusky afternoon shadows.

All the aunts and uncles were at the River when we arrived. Everyone was intrigued with our baby. Uncle Archie's twins, Bruce and Laura, were eight years old; their sister Brenda was six. Finlay, the youngest of the Lewises, was eleven. The children formed a circle around me on the lawn while I nursed Baby Callie. We were an exotic spectacle. They all watched my mother give the baby a bath in a dishpan on the terrace.

Auntie Georgie had loaned us the Moses basket that her babies had slept in. Richard and I and Baby Callie shared my old porch. We hit a cold spell during the first week of our visit, and at night the temperature on the porch plummeted. My mother pulled extra blankets out of the wooden chest, the old Hudson Bay blankets that had been at the River forever. Mothballs rattled to the floor and rolled under our beds. "I don't want you to be cold," she said.

Auntie Georgie came over with the rabbit fur carriage robe that she'd used with Piers, Genna, and Fin. She and my mother undertook the task of keeping our baby snug and warm. "Remember, Jeannie, how we used to wrap them up? If you hold her I'll spread out that woolly blanket . . . keep her arms out."

I watched them roll up our baby like a sausage in a blanket. "She has on two warm sweaters," my mother said, tucking in the blanket. "Now she just needs a hat."

"I brought out one that Mother made years ago, when Piers was born."

"Oh, it's adorable," my mother said. "Typical; moth holes and all. But nothing's as warm as wool." She tied the ribbons under the baby's chin.

"Did you knit that white receiving blanket, Jeannie? Was it for Eddie?" Auntie Georgie laughed. "I never knitted one thing for our kids."

"Well, I made that yellow sweater for Callie," I said.

Archie and Helen and their kids were staying in the Big House with Auntie Georgie and Uncle Herb that summer. The Washburns were in their own house. My father—Jack—was there, too, now that he had more vacation time. We all went back and forth between the houses for dinner on many evenings.

One morning Auntie Georgie talked to my mother and me. "I feel anxious most of the time about Archie and his family," she said. "I don't know what's going to happen. Arch is always going off for days at a time, looking for work. And we all know what Helen's like. And now Herb has to go to Europe for the paper, and he wants me to go with him. So here we are leaving our kids and Archie's with them for two weeks. Am I crazy? Of course Dena's the one who'll really be in charge. And you're here. . . ."

But soon Helen was in trouble. "Could you and Jack come over, Jeannie?" I could hear her low voice on the phone. "I need some help."

"Helen, we're just about to have dinner, but . . . can you wait a little while?"

"What did she say?" my father asked. "Isn't Arch there?"

"No. Apparently he's gone out fishing. He had the kids all day, but when she's in her cups in the evening . . . ah, poor, poor Arch. All last week he was away, supposedly job hunting."

"How did Helen sound?"

"She's been hitting the bottle, I could tell."

"I'll go over," my father said.

"May I come with you?" asked Richard.

They walked out across the meadow in the deepening dusk. The whippoorwill was sounding off across the River.

I asked my mother, "Did Auntie Georgie and Uncle Herbert really think Helen would be up to taking care of their kids?"

"But you know, they all adore Archie—and so does Dena; she's pretty important. And two weeks didn't seem very long. But now . . . well, I don't know."

One night Uncle Archie came over to our house, still in his brown sweater and shorts, bare feet. "Do you want to go fishing tomorrow, Dick? I have to go back to Des Moines the next day. I'm pretty sure I'll land a job with this new company, selling adding machines and calculators. I'll be there all week. Quite a change, but I think it's going to work out."

"It's got to work out, Arch," my mother said.

The next day he and Richard went off up the River in the green canoe.

"He's teaching me to fly-cast," said Richard when they got home that afternoon. "We had a great time. Saw a lot birds, too. Heard the loon."

Uncle Archie opened the wicker creel, and pulled out a pickerel and two smallmouth bass. "Guess who caught these?" he called. "Jack, I've got to be in town, but call Gantenbein to take you out. He knows where the fish are, and he can help Dick with the fly-casting." Gantenbein was a locally famous fishing guide, who for decades had known the St. Croix River like no one else.

"Archie, I can't imagine a better teacher than you," Richard said.

Uncle Archie started his new job that Monday morning. Soon after he got back to the River the following afternoon, Helen took off in their car. He and the Washburns came over to dinner at our house that night. The weather had warmed up, and after dinner we all went out onto the lawn in the deepening dusk, swatting at mosquitoes.

"Hey, Dick, how about going out to see if we can get a few bass?" asked Uncle Archie. "Maybe a Northern pike. This is the time."

The two of them walked down to the landing. We heard the sound of the canoe being pulled over the sand into the water, and then the soft splashes of the paddles as they headed upriver. The rest of us went back into the house, switching on lamps and blinking in the brightness.

"Where do you suppose Helen went?" my father asked.

"Oh, Jack," said Auntie Harriet. "She's probably already on a bar stool in Osceola or Somerset, putting on the charm, getting some guy to pay for her drinks."

"It's hard to believe she'd go by herself—and that Arch would let her." My father was beginning to see how it was with Helen.

"She leaves the children?" I was horrified.

"Of course Dena's there now," Auntie Harriet said. "But when they're in town, who knows what goes on."

"H, Jack and I've been talking. This can't go on. It's not just the drinking. Bouncing checks, trying to borrow from people; she even asked Aunt Georgie Clark for money. We're thinking of telling Arch that we could have Laura come live with us. Georgie said they'd take Bruce. Helen keeps saying she can cope; she wants to keep the family together, but I have my doubts." My mother shook her head.

"But they shouldn't be split up," I cried. "What would Uncle Archie say?"

In October Richard and I and little Callie spent a weekend in New Jersey with my parents. I carried a couple of our old family photo albums out onto the terrace. "Have you ever seen these?" I asked him.

He hadn't. We spent an hour looking at small black-and-white snapshots secured with corner tabs to the black pages. I poured over pictures from our memorable, disastrous winter in Tucson: our bare, brown stucco house, the desolate wide street in front, the secondhand two-door Studebaker my mother had bought, and me and little Eddie on horseback, still looking relatively healthy, in our cherished cowboy outfits. "Why is that army cot out there?" Richard asked.

"For Eddie's and my sunbaths. Ugh."

One photograph from that year is of Uncle Archie standing on a cobbled street in Mexico City, a traveler at leisure, sporting snappy brown-and-white wingtip shoes. His hands are in the pockets of a natty dark three-piece pinstripe suit. He's half smiling, cigarette stuck in the corner of his mouth as usual. His forehead rises high above his glasses toward a receding hairline.

"I never saw him dressed up like that," I said.

"I wish we had a picture of Arch in a plane," my mother said.

"Did he fly? I never heard that."

"He wanted to have his own plane."

"Archie worked at Shearman Aircraft in Wichita for a year or so," my father said. "Probably the best job he ever had."

Richard studied pictures from the River, all of us over the years, we cousins stripped for our sunbaths on the lawn, or buckled into those loathed orange life jackets for a boat ride. Here we are lined up on the edge of the dock dangling our feet in the water, with Uncle Archie, our swimming coach, in bathing trunks, standing behind us. There is the old house—the Big House—and then our new house gradually taking shape. We see the dogs and all the aunts and uncles. There's skinny Eddie in shorts, no shirt, holding a limp fish, perhaps his first catch ever. And then we see Uncle Archie, fly-rod in hand, cigarette between his lips, with a string of bigger fish, probably salmon.

"That must be in Oregon," I said. "He went out there and bought land on the Rogue River. Great salmon fishing, he said, and hardly any people. I remember him raving about the Rogue River. Mother and Auntie Georgie told him he was crazy, wasting his money."

That night the four of us got talking about Uncle Archie. "Remember the summer he and that Al O'Toole were holed up in the Guest House? I think I was nine then. Uncle Archie couldn't even go swimming with us, or fishing. They were just in there multiplying, dividing, whatever, supposedly trying to beat the stockmarket. I hated Al O'Toole."

"Ugh, that old fraud," said my mother.

"No one can 'beat' the stockmarket," my father said.

"Then there were the years he spent traveling," I said. "I wonder where he got the money?"

"Oh, I'm sure he was selling off shares of the 3M he'd inherited; that was all he had. So foolish, so bad." My mother shook her head. "Dear Arch."

"Once he brought me a complete Heidi outfit from Austria: a red dirndl skirt with a flowered apron and puff-sleeve blouse, with a black velvet vest that laced up the front. It even had a wonderful green hat with a feathery plume. And he brought me dolls from all different countries. And we got stuff from Oregon, too: Indian moccasins and Indian dolls for me, all made of buckskin and beads."

"We should have hung onto that Indian stuff," my mother said.

A last picture of Uncle Archie – 1951

– THIRTY-TWO –

"ARCHIE TOOK A ROOM in St. Francis hotel and this day, Saturday Nov. 1, shot himself through the heart."

Auntie Georgie, keeper of the River Log, wrote this in the old black book in 1952.

It was Uncle Bill who called my mother in New Jersey at midnight with the news. All the next day she and my father tried over and over to reach Richard and me in Massachusetts. By the time my father's Air Mail-Special Delivery letter reached us, my mother was already landing in St. Paul.

"Mommy's very sad," Richard told Callie, who'd never seen me cry. She patted my back, while Richard held me. "Poor Mommy," she said.

"It was going from bad to worse these past two weeks," said my father on the phone. "Helen called us a few days ago, and said Arch had gone away; she didn't know where. We told you, Alan, that we'd offered to have Laura live with us, but Helen was still determined to keep them all together, despite everything. I never imagined this would happen. Never. Your mother will be able to fill you in—fill us in—much better than I can." He was struggling to talk about it.

When we finally reached my mother late that evening at Auntie Georgie and Uncle Herb's, she could scarcely stop talking. "Oh, Alan, I never, ever, ever thought this would happen. Who could have dreamed of such a thing? No one knew he was so near the deep edge. Our dear, dear Archie—we all loved him. Everybody loved him."

"Mother, tell us about it; we don't know anything; I have no idea. Please, please tell me."

"Oh darling, I didn't know either. We got Georgie's call, and I just came. She and Herb and H have been filling me in. I guess we're all in a state of shock. Of course we knew—your father and I knew the whole thing was a mess, but not this bad. I was just out here a month ago, the first week in October. Georgie and I stayed out at the River for a couple of days, so lovely and peaceful; we took the canoe out one evening. Of course I saw Archie then, too—the last time. Oh." She couldn't talk.

Then she went on, "He'd just been let go—fired—by Rice Motors. I don't know why; he blamed the boss, but he didn't seem that upset."

"But I want to hear about what happened yesterday, where and how he did it, and all. And about the twins. And Helen . . ."

"Alan, Georgie's feeling really terrible, maybe worse than any of us. She blames herself. But she's tried harder than anyone. Apparently he came over Wednesday evening to talk to her and Uncle Herb—just three days before—and they tried to talk sense into him, told him he ought to try getting back to selling trucks at GM, and that he should assume his responsibilities and stop depending on us and other people. Now she thinks that was just the last straw."

I learned that the day before Archie's death, Auntie Harriet and Uncle Bill were with Helen at the house she and Uncle Archie had rented. They were helping Helen pack up their things in order to move to some smaller, cheaper place. Archie was "away," according to Helen.

I never heard who in the family was first informed of his death. I have Auntie Harriet's anguished account of the suicide of the brother she adored, the sibling to whom she'd always felt closest. She'd read the note that Archie had left— "a long, thoughtful, un-self-pitying letter." Of the three sisters, only Auntie Harriet was a fly-fisher; she and Archie had often fished together. Remembering his "skilled, precise fishing," she wrote, "has brought me a sharp wrench of pain because it makes me think of how he killed himself. He did it with the same delicate accuracy, except that the gun misfired so he had to do it a second time. He went through the quite careful routine twice and the thought of this is almost too much. The decision, the planning, and preparation, the despair, the fear and the nerving yourself up—and then the gun misfired. He waited two weeks and then went back to the same hotel and tried again. He must have bought a new gun because this time it fired."

In his letter he said, according to Auntie Harriet, he believed the life insurance money would do more for his family than he could. "If I live," he'd written, "sooner or later that will be gone along with the rest." He felt he'd made a mess of his life, and that if he continued things would become even more awful, even worse than his suicide, for the three children he so dearly loved.

He sent his love to Helen: "You have been marvelous. I don't know how you put up with me for so long." Then, as Auntie Harriet wrote, "He had a few drinks, undressed except for his shorts, put towels down on the bathroom floor, closed the bathroom door, lay down on the towels, and shot himself."

From St. Paul later that week my mother wrote us about the funeral in the chapel at the cemetery. "Helen is wonderful," a rare favorable comment from one of Archie's sisters. Their three children had been at the service, the nine-year-old twins and Brenda, who was six. "You wonder what they are thinking—they made a touching sight, let me tell you. The chapel was packed with all his friends."

Auntie Harriet later described the last time she had seen Archie: "Another surge of pain has just hit, because I'm remembering his goodbye look. I've never called it that to myself before, but ever since his death I think I've known what it was . . . It was the afternoon of his 2nd, successful try. A warm Indian summer, late October afternoon. I can't remember what he said he had come to see me for . . . but I do remember being afraid he was going to ask me for another loan and that we'd end up in some terrible, frightening scene because we had all, we three sisters, agreed that these loans would have to stop.

"But Archie didn't ask, and he didn't stay long. When he left, I walked out to the car with him. The top was down and I went around to his side and leaned on the door. And its not easy to remember that the last thing I ever said to him was why, since he was broke and couldn't get a job, didn't he try driving a taxi for a while. I had been thinking about suggesting this . . . Archie was a superb driver; he liked people, and people liked him. I thought he'd be a success. People would over-tip him because they'd had fun; he'd make money and give himself time to catch up and breathe. But what made me think he could forget his pride . . . Archie driving a taxi? Why didn't I know it was unthinkable?

"It was then, not answering me, that he gave me his goodbye look, smiling in a way that's hard to describe. Rueful, a little amused, a little sad. A grown-up look, a kind look, a final look, not angry, not hurt, not 'don't be a fool.' But a look that put a period to what I had said. A simple, undramatic look. But final. Final and mature and sad.

"Then he raised his hand in a see-you-later gesture and, still without saying a word, nodded and drove away."

Callie with Auntie Georgie and her grandparents – 1956

– THIRTY-THREE –

WHEN I CLIMBED OFF the Burlington Zephyr at St. Paul's Union Depot, my mother and father were there with hugs for Callie and me. We went straight to the River in their Chevy station wagon. Richard flew out a week later. We spent a month at the River that summer, 1953, the summer after Uncle Archie's death.

Eddie had a job in construction. The first thing he did when he got home, hot and tired each afternoon, was to plunge into the water. Richard and I and Callie swam again, then, too. Callie, at three, wore a fat orange life jacket just like the ones Eddie and I as children had hated so passionately. But she was perfectly happy, bobbing near shore in a black inner tube.

Eddie took us out in the "Mrs. B," the little cabin cruiser he'd built in New Jersey. With cousin Finlay he'd brought the boat through the Erie Canal, across the Great Lakes, all the way to Otisville.

"I can't believe you came all that way," I said.

"I can't believe you built this entire boat yourself," said Richard. Now, in his spare time, Eddie was building a new dock at the landing.

"You just work, work all the time, Eddie."

He laughed. "Well, I guess that's what I like."

Aunts, uncles, and cousins were always at our house when we weren't walking over to visit them. The Lewises were in the Big House, as usual, and Auntie Harriet and Uncle Bill were in theirs.

We never saw Helen. She had gone out west, to Spokane—"to seek her fortune," sniffed Uncle Bill—taking eleven-year old Laura, and Brenda who was eight. Bruce, Laura's twin, was at the River with Auntie Georgie and Uncle Herb. He was to go to Spokane in August.

"Well, if it isn't our best, best great-niece, Miss Caroline, coming to call." Auntie Georgie took Callie by the hand, while Richard and I sat talking with Uncle Herb. Bruce, clutching a comic book, appeared from the far end of the porch, and Fin, now fifteen, came to say hello.

It was a warm day, and the porch was just as I remembered. In the heat the wicker chairs gave off a sweet smell like baking bread. Uncle Herb puffed on his pipe. "Is it three years since you were here? That's too long. How does it seem?"

I was conscious of a huge hole in the family, but I wasn't going to say that. "It's just the same; same old River."

Richard and I walked around slowly with Callie, looking at everything, the tennis court, the old tool house, the sharpening stone that we used to pedal as if it were a bicycle, the silver poplar where we had our tree house, and the big maple by the River where we kids used to perch in a fork about fifteen feet in the air. Crossing the narrow plank footbridge over the marshy patch of cattails and touch-me-not, we went to visit Auntie Harriet and Uncle Bill in their house beneath the pines.

"Well, my darlings, come in and see your old auntie. Hello, Callie; you are a treat to see, especially in your brand new espadrilles." Callie looked down at her new shoes, given to her by Auntie Georgie. "Your bad Uncle Bill isn't here; he'll be sad. But we're all coming over to your house tonight. That's the plan." She looked as glamorous as ever, I thought, with her auburn hair drawn loosely up, a white halter top and flared shorts that left bare her smooth shoulders and long legs.

"It seems really strange not to have Janey here," I said. "Or Genna."

"Ah, they're both almost grown up, waiting on tables at Glacier Park Lodge. Can you believe it? Janey says their feet are killing them, in those flimsy little ballet slippers."

We laughed. "Auntie Georgie told me. But I don't blame them for refusing to wear the hideous old-lady oxfords that they were told to get."

"No one around here ever wears any shoes, as far as I can see. Except this smart young lady." She lifted Callie onto her lap.

"And Richard." I looked down at his brown legs, white socks, and dark blue Topsiders. Auntie Harriet's toenails were painted the darkest mahogany red I'd ever seen; mine were their own natural pale. "I only go barefoot at the River; nowhere else," I said. "I used to be so proud of the tough bottoms of my feet. Like leather."

"Yeah," said Auntie Harriet. "But I remember many, many trips up to old Dr. Simensted in Osceola, all those times one of you stepped on a rusty nail or a fish hook."

"Piers always said we'd get lock-jaw. He loved to scare us."

She and Uncle Bill, and Auntie Georgie and Uncle Herb came over for dinner that evening. My father brought drinks for everyone out onto the lawn. The sun was still bright across the water, on the Wisconsin shore. Eight of us—Eddie was out with Phylis Fitzpatrick—sat at the long trestle table in the big, airy living room, over roast chicken, rice, and the first corn. Mary Ann, the cook that year, passed a napkin-covered basket of her delicate blueberry muffins. Even before we'd finished dinner, the talk veered toward what was uppermost in my mind. And, as it turned out, not surprisingly, in the minds of all of us.

"Why, oh why?" Auntie Georgie shook her head in anguish. "Do we think he really believed the kids would be better off without him?"

"How much do we blame Helen?" my mother wondered. "He must have known she couldn't cope—with or without him."

"She tried to do her best, I think," said my father.

"Oh Jack, you're so naive," exclaimed Auntie Harriet. "I don't blame you, but you and Jeannie off in New Jersey haven't been living with it every day, like the rest of us."

My mother said, "Maybe because we haven't been so much in the thick of it all, our perceptions might be more realistic."

"Jeannie, I know what you're going to say," Auntie Georgie spoke as if quoting my mother. "'Call in the professionals.' But those kids are family. Herb and I would give Bruce everything we've given our own kids."

"Jack and I offered to take Laura, but none of you thought that would solve anything."

Auntie Harriet said, "And now they're all racketing around in Spokane, of all places."

Uncle Herb took his pipe out of his mouth. "They'll be back soon enough. Helen will never make a go of it."

We moved to the soft chairs and the sofa at the other end of the room. It was dark now. From across the River we could hear the whippoorwill start on his peaceful, monotonous, wild call.

"Archie loved those three children more than anything in the world. That I know," Auntie Harriet said.

I spoke up. "He always had a special way with kids. Long before he had his own. Eddie and I and all of us knew that. He was a great teacher, so patient. He taught all of us to swim, and the boys to fish."

"Bruce is already a great fly-fisherman," Uncle Bill said. "He's hooked; even ties his own flies."

"Uncle Archie was always encouraging us to try new things, things we might be scared of, like swimming in the water tower. You used to get mad at him sometimes, Ma. And you too, Auntie Georgie. Afraid we'd get hurt. But he was our pied piper; we would have followed him anywhere."

"He didn't have such a great time himself, growing up," my mother said. "Faddie was always after him. He never did well in school, which used to infuriate Faddie. 'You should be at the top of your class,' he'd say. 'You're not trying.'"

"Oh, poor Arch." Auntie Georgie groaned. "But he was a great athlete. I remember watching him and Scott Fitzgerald when they were on the Academy football team. Neither one of them was very big, but they were fast."

Auntie Harriet said, "I remember Archie once told me, 'If only Faddie hadn't always expected the worst of me. That just made me balky and stubborn.' Faddie was always telling him to do this, do that, measure up, be responsible, be a man, and Archie just couldn't stand it."

"Well, of course he was the only boy, so Faddie piled a lot of chores onto him. And let's face it, sometimes Archie was lazy. He had a bad temper, too. Faddie'd have to remind him over and over to shovel the snow, cut the grass, bring in the wood, get the ice from the ice-house." My mother sighed.

"The ice house," echoed Auntie Harriet. "That was one job Archie really hated. He used to get me to help him sometimes. You had to dig down in the sawdust, and pry up those big cakes of ice with a crowbar or a shovel, then grab them with the tongs, and lug them inside."

The three sisters were recalling the days before the rest

of us had come onto the scene, before they were married, before I was born. We just listened, let them talk.

"Don't forget that ghastly pump," my mother said. "A battle every day to get it going—Archie'd get mad and kick the darn thing. He always put off his chores, so when Faddie got out here on the six o'clock train after work, he'd be faced with some crisis. We'd be out of water or out of wood, or no ice in the icebox."

"Then there'd be a furious scene with Archie," Auntie Harriet recalled. "I was terrified by those quarrels. You were older, Jean, so you probably didn't get as upset as I did."

Then my mother remembered something else. "One time when he was about fifteen Archie told Georgie and me that twice he and Gus Schermeier had hitched rides on freight trains all the way to Duluth and back. He made us promise not to tell. Faddie would have really had a fit."

Auntie Georgie said she thought their father had counted on Archie's success to compensate for his own sense of failure. "Faddie always felt he had disappointed his father. He once told me that old D.W. used to take him out to the stable at least once a week, and beat him with his buggy whip."

"Well, I adored Faddie," my mother said. "That dear man. But to tell the truth, his own career wasn't exactly stellar, flitting from sheep ranching to gold mining to laying out railway lines and selling mining machinery."

"He never made much money," Auntie Georgie said. "We were always the poor relations, remember? "

"How could I forget?" asked Auntie Harriet. "The MacLarens were the worst; so patronizing. I hated it. Aunt Katharine trying to give us 'useful' things."

"But at least Faddie had his degrees," my mother said. "Unlike Archie. And he was never fired from anything."

"Faddie was such a snob, Jeannie. So different from Arch. He was so stuffy, so rigid about honor, breeding, tradition,

what gentlemen do and what they don't do. And so proud."
Auntie Harriet groaned.

"Oh, H, I know. But it was the same with us, at least with
Georgie and me; you were so young you probably got off
easy. 'Ladies are always modest, no low-cut necklines, never
leave the house without first putting on your gloves.' He had
so many rules. And Mother didn't care a bit."

"It sounds like a Victorian upbringing," I said.

"Actually, Archie was like Faddie in a lot of ways," my
mother went on. "Rolling stones, both of them. And each of
them convinced he wasn't measuring up to his father. Archie
looked like Faddie, too, with the high forehead and good
Ingersoll nose."

"Archie's hair was more reddish, though, like Georgie
and me," Auntie Harriet said. "But fly-fishing was always a
bond between Archie and Faddie. They really had a good
time together. Remember how they'd come back full of
stories, kidding each other? When Faddie died—right after
we heard—Archie came out to my sleeping porch, where I
was already in bed. He sat down beside me, and hung onto
me with his head against mine, and he cried and cried. Deep
shaking sobs."

My mother and I walked over to the Lewises' house one
morning. Rigo, their German Shepherd, lay in the sun by
the steps. We sat out on the porch with Auntie Georgie,
listening to the thunk of balls on the tennis court, where Fin
and Eddie were playing doubles. Now with a husband and a
child of our own, I felt old and grown up, sitting there with
my mother and my aunt. I heard Eddie's voice, "Good shot."

"Herb just called from the office, and guess what: the

kids are coming back." We knew Auntie Georgie was talking about Helen's children.

"Well, that didn't take long," my mother said. "I'm not surprised."

"Laura called collect, Herb said, asking for train fare back to St. Paul for the three of them. I'm sure Helen put her up to it. There's no one to look after them, Helen can't find work, and she's broke."

"And probably drinking again, too," said my mother.

"We have to send the fare," Auntie Georgie told my mother. "That means the three of them will be staying with us, but you'll have to share the expense. They've got to be in school, and at least in St. Paul they have us, and people who knew Arch and the whole situation."

"We really have no choice. Of course, H says they're fed up with bailing Helen out."

"Helen told Herb that if she comes back she might take the training course at St. Catherine's College, so she could get a job teaching art in a parochial school. Herb has his doubts."

"Oh, Georgie, I don't know. Maybe she could do it. She always said she'd had a year there once. But how's she going to pay for it?"

"And what have they been living on? She and the three kids were all sick off and on, all winter, ever since Archie died. By the time she went out west she was looking a little better, her skin and her eyes were clearer, less of that drinking look. She told Herb on the phone that she could earn three-hundred and twenty dollars a month after she gets trained. But meanwhile she'll need to use the last of the insurance money to live on."

"And meanwhile," my mother said, "we're all still paying our share of the funeral expenses. She said she'd pay one quarter . . . Oh good, here comes H."

Auntie Harriet was ready for a swim, in her black and white bathing suit.

"You'll never guess what we're talking about," Auntie Georgie said.

"Well, what can we do?" said Auntie Harriet when she'd heard Helen's news. "We can't dictate to her."

My mother said, "She'll have to go talk to Benno again when she decides to come back. Thank the Lord for Benno. He's our friend, now, as well as our lawyer, and he knows the whole situation. He's the only one she listens to."

"Herb and I talked to him in June," Auntie Georgie said. "She'd shown him all her old bills—food, phone, light, everything. She'd spent way too much on Christmas, as we suspected. She told Benno she was withdrawing a thousand to pay the bills, but that wouldn't come close to covering them. That would leave her with four-thousand of Archie's last insurance policy."

Auntie Harriet said, "I hope Benno told her to leave that alone, at least for now."

"Do you think Helen realizes Benno talks to us?" my mother asked. "Of course he's worked for us forever, and we're the ones paying him, after all."

"Do we all know about the bad checks?" asked Auntie Harriet.

From the court I heard a girl's shrill voice: "Our game!"

"I think it started three years ago," Auntie Georgie said. "Helen tried to cash a check she'd written in Osceola. She signed it with Archie's name in her handwriting; somehow it found its way to me, and I sent it on to Benno. When he confronted her with it, he thought she'd probably say Archie'd written it, but no, she owned up. Then she even told him of another check she'd forged last summer. Archie'd already told us about that one: she was very anxious for Bruce to go to the Academy, and that was supposed to pay for his tuition."

"Oh, that's so pathetic," Auntie Harriet sighed. "Of course she wanted Bruce to go where Archie went."

"And where Piers went," said my mother, "and Fin's there now."

"But, oh, she must have been utterly desperate," I said. "Poor Helen."

"Herb and I are taking the notes for the last two loans we gave Arch as bad debts against our income tax. You should all do that, too. Benno says we can't claim the earlier notes 'cuz they were signed by both of them, but the ones last fall were signed by just Archie."

"This is so sad and hopeless and terrible, " Auntie Harriet said. "Archie's getting lost in all this mess."

They were silent for a minute. Then my mother said, "Let's talk about him for a change. I'll never forget that ghastly year in Tucson, and how dear and supportive and wonderful he was. He probably saved Alan's life, bringing that serum for Dr. Birnberg."

"You were wonderful, too," I murmured to Auntie Georgie.

She patted my knee.

"Do we still have his letters somewhere?" Auntie Harriet asked. "They were marvelous. He was so happy that winter, driving around Mexico, all by himself, hundreds of miles through the mountains on terrible, narrow, winding roads. There were hardly any people, just tiny villages where they'd practically never seen an automobile."

Dena came out with a tray of ice tea. The ice cubes clinked in our glasses. I could hear the sounds of a long rally out on the court, and Eddie saying, "Your serve, Fin."

My mother said, "He landed on his feet in Mexico City, remember? He met up with a convention of Junior League ladies from Texas. They'd all left their husbands at home, so they adopted Archie. He saw the sights with them, played tennis, swam, danced . . ."

"And then he found Frank Kluckhohn, who'd been the *Times* correspondent in Spain. Herb knew Frank; they'd worked together. He got a Pulitzer for his dispatches from

Spain, but also a death sentence from the Fascists. So the *Times* sent him to Mexico to cover Trotsky." Auntie Georgie got up to open the screen door for Rigo.

"Arch, I remember, stayed with the Kluckhohns," my mother said. "He told us he was Frank's 'typewriter boy' when they went to interview Trotsky."

"He was Frank's photographer, too, with his Leica," Auntie Georgie said. "I remember him telling us how they had to pass through cordons of Mexican police and soldiers to get in. The Trotskys were living with Diego Rivera and his wife, Frida Kahlo at Coyoacân. According to Archie, Trotsky had a little fling with her; don't be shocked, Allie."

"I'm not." She was teasing me.

"Well, poor old Trotsky didn't last long before the Soviet thugs got him, bashed him over the head with a mountain climber's pickaxe."

I said, "Then Uncle Archie and the Kluckhohns climbed the highest mountain Mexico, Mount Popocatepetl. I remember in Tucson I used to love to say that word. Uncle Archie drove all the way to Tucson from there when I was in the hospital. I was too sick to remember that part."

"I even get sad remembering happy things." Auntie Harriet's eyes filled. "I've got to go for a swim. Come on, Allie."

My mother dabbed at her eyes with a linen handkerchief. She turned to put her arms around me. "I think we should all go in."

"Our darling, happy-go-lucky Arch," Auntie Georgie said. "Footloose and fancy free, tooling around Mexico in the old Green Car—well, it was new then. Was that really only fifteen years ago?"

After that they stopped talking about Archie. Over the next few years the sisters hardly even mentioned his name. He was just gone. His children were very much a part of the family, especially for Auntie Georgie and Uncle Herb. Helen's role in her children's lives faded gradually, but the sisters were involved with her ups and downs, too. Auntie Harriet grew more detached.

Those three children were loved and cared for, but left with a thousand unanswered questions and a wall of silence.

*My mother, Auntie Georgie, Richard, my father, and
Uncle Herb on the lawn. Callie looks at the camera – 1956*

– T H I R T Y - F O U R –

"WHY ARE THEY GOING out there now?" I asked
my mother on one of our last days at the River. "Is this
a vacation?"

"Well, no, not really. I'll tell you later. But it's still hush-
hush, so don't say anything." Auntie Harriet and Uncle Bill
were taking a trip to California.

Auntie Georgie walked across to our house the next
morning after breakfast. "Oh, Jeannie, we have to talk. Let's
take the canoe; you and I haven't done that for ages."

"May I come? I'm a good paddler."

Richard helped us flip the old green canoe, and slide it
into the water. He and Callie and my father waved us off.
Auntie Georgie, wearing her straw coolie hat, sat in the
middle. My mother was proud of her modest skill with the
stern paddle. I took the bow. We made our stately way up the
River, so different from Richard's vigorous pace when he and
I canoed together.

"Oh, Jeannie, I'm already feeling desolate. I'm sure they're going to end up moving to California for good, and I can't bear it."

"What do you mean?" I asked. "I know they love La Jolla, but Uncle Bill's job is here, and they have their River house, and the house in St. Paul . . ."

"I can tell you, Alan," my mother said. "They don't want everyone talking until they make up their minds. But Uncle Bill's been having trouble with his father. Old Mr. Washburn got remarried, and now he's down on Bill and his brother, in favor of the second wife and their two boys. The father's literally forcing Bill out of the company, cutting his salary, maybe disinheriting him."

"He may have done that already," Auntie Georgie said. "The tough part about working in a family business."

"And if Bill tells his father he's leaving, then Mr. Washburn is sure to cut him out of his will. But you know, Georgie, this is probably Bill's last chance while he and H are still young enough to make a go of it with the California job."

"Does he actually have a job lined up there already?" I asked. "Watch out for that deadhead, Ma."

"Yeah, I see it. Well, Bill's had an offer from someone he knows, in advertising. That's what they're going to see about on this trip. Look at all the fish jumping; H ought to be here."

"Or Uncle Archie."

Auntie Georgie sighed. "I don't even want to think about their moving, but we sure don't want it talked about till it really happens. If Helen hears about it, it'll be all over town."

"And we don't want to get the kids upset. And they would be, the twins especially," my mother said.

"But, oh, I feel bereft," cried Auntie Georgie. "I'll be losing a brother and a sister in the same year. Unlike you, Jeannie, H won't keep coming back. Without Archie, there'll be nothing for her to return to, except me. She has no feeling for St. Paul, and she says none for the River."

I protested. "But they love it here. I know they do. Why wouldn't they? It'll never be the same without them."

"Oh, sweet Allie, you're right; it won't be," Auntie Georgie said. "But you just have no idea. Families are so complicated. I'll miss H so much; I just can't bear it. But she's always considered me the big, bossy, older sister, ever since she was a little girl."

"Well, you've always tended to belittle her, Georgie, and Bill, too," my mother said. "You know that's true. You've always said they were too frivolous, spent too much on fancy cars and stuff. And that Bill was a lightweight, never went to college. And you and Herb were so critical during the war, when he took that job at Lockheed 'so he wouldn't be drafted,' you said, but it was important defense work."

"I know, I know, Jeannie; you're right; it's true. You're making me feel worse than ever."

My mother went on. "And H is really having success as a writer. "What's so terrible about *Redbook* and *Ladies' Home Journal?* It's quite something that they publish her stories. And now that radio play she did from one of her *McCall's* stories, with what's-his-name, that famous actor."

"Oh Jeannie."

I turned around. Auntie Georgie's face was buried in a towel.

Then we heard the hum of an outboard. My father and Richard were approaching in the old motorboat. Callie in her orange life jacket was waving to us. Richard pointed to the sunny sandbar. They putted to shore, and we paddled over to land beside them on the narrow beach for our picnic: tomato sandwiches, devilled eggs, and a thermos of lemonade.

My mother stayed at the River into October. She kept Richard and me—home in Massachusetts—up-to-date on what was going on with Helen and the children. Her vague hope of somehow making a go of it out west had fizzled with her steady drinking and no possibility of a job. "Now she's back in St. Paul," my mother reported. "She says she's on the wagon, and looking for a place where she can have the children with her. She's registered at an employment office, hoping for maybe a receptionist job with a doctor or a dentist."

Two of my mother's old St. Paul friends were social work professionals. They both urged my mother to seek help from the experts at Family Service. Auntie Georgie was resistant. "Oh, Jeannie, this is family. The last things we need are cold, clinical, so-called experts. Outsiders."

But my mother kept pushing. "I told Georgie that she'll be the one who'll have to work with Family Service; I'm leaving the River next week. We really need Georgie on board."

That next week, before she went east, my mother said on the phone that she and Auntie Georgie had had a long session with Mrs. Hoffman at Family Service. "She was not optimistic about Helen's ability to care for her family. We talked about placing the kids in a foster home, as opposed to having the court take over the guardianship. Mrs. Hoffman thinks Helen might agree to a foster home. And Family Service can help Helen with her bills. She'd have to pay, say, fifty dollars a week to Family Service, and they'd distribute it among her creditors. But Helen would have to keep up her end, or it won't work." My mother sighed. "So there are a lot of ifs, but at least maybe we're getting somewhere, not just drifting."

"Are the kids with Helen now?" I asked.

"The girls are, off and on, but Bruce is with Georgie and Herb at the moment. Mrs. Hoffman feels they should all be together; that it's not good for Bruce to be singled out. But Georgie insists on keeping him." Mrs. Hoffman was becoming indispensable.

That winter, the news we heard about Helen was not good. She was drinking again. The girls sometimes found her passed out on the floor when they came home from school. But then she'd stop; for weeks she'd be sober, gentle, kind, the perfect mother. Richard and I talked and talked about Archie's children; "They're my cousins," I said. One night after Callie was in bed, Richard asked me, "What do you suppose Helen would say if we offered to have the girls come to us?"

"We could tell her we'd take them until she was on her feet again."

"Bruce seems to be settled in with Georgie and Herb; at least for now."

"I bet Callie would love to have Laura and Brenda."

"And we have room now, in this house." We'd moved recently from Cambridge to an old farm in the country. I wrote my parents a letter suggesting that the girls come to live with us. No one took our offer seriously. I guess they all thought we were just too young.

Before the next spring, Mrs. Hoffman had found a foster home for Helen and Uncle Archie's children. Patsy and Bill Petersen had two younger children of their own. The state of Minnesota paid them some minimal amount for looking after the three Ingersolls.

It did not work well for Bruce, now thirteen. He was resentful, unhelpful, and hostile to the Petersens. After a year or so he went back to Uncle Herb and Auntie Georgie. She wished they could have all three. "Oh, Jeannie," she lamented to my mother, "Archie's kids are family; they shouldn't be farmed out like this. Oh, the Petersens are nice enough, but so limited. I didn't see one single book in that house. And when I think of all that Herb has to offer them . . ."

"Georgie, that just sounds snobbish. I know we can't make it perfect. The girls wouldn't be happy in New Jersey with Jack and me. This is the best we can do; we've got to try to make it work."

"Jeannie, you ought to have Laura; this is what families are for."

"Oh, Georgie, you've heard Mrs. Hoffman. She knows what's best for the three of them; that's her job."

Family was the heart and center of Auntie Georgie's life. She was distressed and embittered by my mother's blind faith in professionals. They didn't agree on this, ever.

Auntie Georgie was a passionate reader. Reading books was central to her existence, as central as prayer in the life of a cloistered Trappist monk. Uncle Herb too, was a devout reader, as well as a writer and editor. Their children and all of us cousins fell to some degree under the literary spell. The Petersens, on the other hand, both college graduates, may not have been constant readers, but they didn't drink.

Having Bruce in the house was not always a piece of cake for Auntie Georgie. As she wrote to my mother, "After living with half-educated, uncultured foster parents, Bruce has poor grammar, barbarous pronunciation . . . and he's a bad sport on the court, uses bad language, and annoys Dena by rummaging around in the icebox at all hours. And we can't afford to alienate her. Why is he so immature?"

Bruce at thirteen, in Massachusetts with Alan and Callie – 1954

– THIRTY-FIVE –

WE DID NOT GO OUT to the River that next summer, 1954. The only news of my Ingersoll cousins that reached Richard and me came from my mother's letters and the occasional phone conversation.

"Oh Alan," my mother said. "Now that school's out, Georgie's finding it hard having the three kids, and sometimes Helen, too. She's taken them with her to Devil's Lake a couple of times, but we've got to figure out a permanent solution."

Richard and I talked about it. "Maybe now Georgie would consider letting Bruce, at least, live with us," he said.

After much back-and-forth discussion in the family, my thirteen-year-old cousin Bruce came to spend the month of July with us in Massachusetts. All three of us—Richard, Callie, and I—loved having him. He was bright, brave, cheerful, outgoing, and seemed happy to be with us. He quickly made friends with a boy his age whose family we knew. To us he seemed so old, compared to our four-year-old Callie, that we allowed him complete freedom to explore the fields, woods, and streams for miles around. Richard and I were inexperienced as parents, and Bruce was uniquely adventurous. It didn't occur to us to say no, or even to worry about him. (Other parents we talked to expressed amazement at Bruce's independence and resourcefulness.)

Fishing, that's what it was. He'd fished with his father since he was four. The first day he was with us he fashioned a rod from a slender tree branch. I took him to buy line and some little hooks. He dug worms in the garden. After breakfast most mornings, off he'd go, all by himself.

Hours later he'd come back, smiling and happy, sneakers wet, blond hair rumpled, scratches and mosquito bites on his arms, holding up a forked stick from which dangled two or three pretty little fish. "One rainbow, two brookies," he announced to Callie and me.

"Where did you get them?" I was amazed. "I never knew we had trout streams around here."

"Oh, there are streams all over; mostly small, but one's pretty big. I found some really good pools. Tomorrow I'll catch more."

Callie and I watched him clean his fish with one of our kitchen knives. "We can have them for breakfast," I said. "I never learned to fish, but your father showed me how to cook them."

"Bruce, you're wonderful," Richard said when he got home that evening. "I'd love to know where you went." We hadn't been living for very long in this rural setting, and Richard still hadn't explored the countryside as thoroughly as he soon would.

Later, when we were getting into bed, Richard and I looked at each other. "He's so like Archie," he said. "It's amazing."

"He is. Isn't it wonderful? Aren't we lucky to have him here?"

Bruce had been with us for almost two weeks when one evening the phone rang. I picked it up to hear Helen's low voice. "I'm going to be in Massachusetts next week for my new job, and I'd love to come see you, and see Bruce."

I clenched. "Of course, Helen," I squeaked. "When would you get here?" Richard could see my face, pinched in anguish. Helen had always been kind to me, but now all I heard were the troubles for which she was blamed.

She didn't ask to speak to Bruce, who was already in bed. "She's coming here," I said. "On Friday. I told her we'd meet her at the station in Concord; maybe she'll even be on your train. Oh, I'm scared; I really dread this."

"What is this job, anyway?"

"She says she'll be selling ads in all these little towns in western Massachusetts, where some church groups have ordered cookbooks of their favorite recipes. She has the name of who to meet in each town. She has no car, so she'll have to go around by bus. Do you believe it? She made it sound real: Turners Falls, Millers Falls. She'll be here till Sunday." I put my head in my hands.

"Don't worry, Alan. We'll manage; it'll be fine."

Bruce expressed no surprise to hear that his mother was coming. I, on the other hand, was tied in nervous knots for the next two days. I made up a bed in our downstairs guest room; I cooked chicken and rice; I baked a pie with our rhubarb. "We're not going to serve any wine or whiskey," I told Richard. I made two big pitchers of iced tea.

While she was with us, Helen was calm, low-key, and domestic. Sitting on the porch, in a flowered blouse and the tan skirt of her one summer suit, she shelled peas from our garden. I let her use my sewing basket to mend Bruce's clothes. She gave Callie a haircut. We lent her our car to go sightseeing in Salem with Bruce. She changed the sheets on his bed, ran the dirty ones through the washer, and hung them on the line.

Before she'd arrived, Richard had said, "I don't think it's up to us to try giving her advice."

I agreed. We just listened.

"I'm going to quit this job soon," she told us. "It's impossible. Last week I was in Illinois peddling these cookbook ads. They give me my orders each week, so I never know where I'll be sent."

"What will you do then?" I asked.

She and Richard and I were sipping coffee after dinner. I thought Helen's face looked puffier than I remembered. Her dark hair, still pulled to the top of her head, had strands of gray. She was sewing a patch over a rip in Bruce's blue shirt. "Probably caught on a fish hook," she said. "I'm used to that." She went on: "I have to be back in St. Paul by the first of August, because my apartment's been sold. I'm going to try to find a place where the rent's not too high, and where I can have my children again. You'd be surprised, a lot of places don't allow kids."

We just nodded. That certainly sounded like a reasonable dream, but considering all the circumstances, it seemed unlikely to come true. She said nothing about finding another job. Her future seemed as cloudy to us as it probably did to her.

"She couldn't have been nicer," I said to Richard after her visit.

"She was really making a huge effort. But what struck me is how sad she is. Did you feel that?"

"Oh, I do. It's pathetic; it's terrible. Now I feel awful that I've been so suspicious and antagonistic—even though there were good reasons. . . ."

What Helen's visit revealed to us with stark clarity was her relationship to Bruce and his to her. They adored each other. My carefree, fearless, independent cousin changed radically as soon as his mother arrived. Richard and I were surprised, shocked, and profoundly saddened. Bruce reverted to behaving almost like a baby. "Mama," he called her, as he clung to her, hugging her all the time. He seemed to wish he could climb onto her lap. I felt uncomfortably embarrassed for him, this big thirteen-year-old boy.

When Richard and I were finally alone that first night, we were able to talk about Bruce. "This almost kills me," I said. "When you think of what it means."

"Seeing him with his mother like this really shows what an aching void there is in his life. I had absolutely no idea."

"Everyone—Ma and Pa, Auntie Georgie, Uncle Herb, all the friends—everyone's been saying that the whole thing, Uncle Archie dying and everything, hasn't affected Bruce so much. Or at least that he's taken it all in his stride. But he has not, not at all."

"I just don't see how he can take it much longer," Richard said. "Being tossed around, from place to place, here and there. He's got to have some kind of security soon."

"Poor, poor dear Bruce. It seems as if only his mother and his sisters could give him that, now. But of course it's unlikely that Helen will ever be the firm rock that he needs, even though she's so sweet, and obviously means well . . ."

"We haven't seen as much of Laura and Brenda, so we don't know whether they're as lost inside as Bruce."

"I bet they are. But I don't understand why Auntie Georgie with all her motherly instincts doesn't see this. I'm afraid she dislikes Helen too much, and blames her for Archie's death and all. Well, of course Mother's pretty rigid, too."

Richard, sitting on the side of the bed, took off his shoes and socks. "I can see it would be hard for them to admit that Helen could offer the children anything good."

Our outlook on the situation was entirely changed as a result of Helen's visit during Bruce's month with us. We discussed it from every angle. "Somehow, Alan, we have to tell your parents what we think, and how it looks to us."

"It may not do any good, but, yes, we have to tell them what we've seen and what we think. The only way I can do it is to try putting it in a letter."

Bruce, Brenda, and Laura Ingersoll – 1957

– THIRTY-SIX –

WHILE BRUCE WAS WITH US we'd spent a long weekend on the Vineyard visiting my mother-in-law. Richard and Bruce went on the water one day with a professional fisherman. They came home with more than enough bluefish for dinner. Saltwater fishing was new to Bruce. "Boy, there sure are a lot of big fish out there," he exclaimed. His face and arms were pink. I felt responsible: "We should have made you wear long sleeves, at least. And a cap."

It was wrenching to say good-bye to Bruce. Richard drove Bruce, Callie, and me into Boston to put him on the train to Chicago, from where he'd take the Zephyr to St. Paul. Uncle Herb was to meet him. Like his father, Uncle Archie the railroad buff, Bruce had no interest in going by air.

We laughed and talked all the way into the city. But at the station Callie finally realized what was happening; our dear Bruce was leaving. She threw her arms around his waist.

"Don't go 'way." She began to cry.

"Bye Bruce; bye Bruce. Come home soon." Callie waved until he was on the train and it began to move. We three stood there, Callie still waving, until the Lake Shore Limited disappeared around a bend.

"We'll miss him, won't we Callie?" Richard said. "Maybe he'll come to visit us again. We hope so. But our house isn't his house. He can't live with us all the time."

"He has to be with his mommy," I told her. "And with his sisters—can you remember their names? And Auntie Georgie wants to see him, too. We'll see them all when we go out to the River."

I knew that wasn't going to happen for another year, at least.

Our house seemed too quiet, too empty without Bruce. I wrote to my mother at the River, telling her about our time with Bruce, about Helen's visit, and how our outlook had changed. "I know you'll probably say she just charmed us the way she has all of you in the past, and that we've gone over to her side. We have, in a way, but finally I don't think Richard and I have any illusions about her. We just realize that the situation is even tougher than it seemed before, but I guess you and Auntie Georgie and Uncle Herb knew that all along." My letter crossed with one to us from Uncle Herb, saying he appreciated our at least "wanting to help with this one difficult aspect of 'family.'"

On the phone I told my mother that Richard and I did not think Bruce and his sisters should be permanently separated, "if there's any way they could all be together with their mother."

"But Alan, Helen just cracks under strain. And she has no money sense; none."

"Well, I can imagine her panic when she was in Spokane with the children and running out of money. . . ."

"Well, that was completely her own fault."

"Ma, you don't seem to hear what I'm saying."

"They're not going to pay any attention to what you and I think," I told Richard.

"There's no easy answer," he said.

My mother called a few days later. "Helen is taking all three kids up to Devil's Lake this weekend. She wanted to come here after, and stay with us at the River, all four of them, over Labor Day."

"So are they coming?"

"Oh Alan, we're trying to get packed up for the drive home next week, closing the house . . . there's just so much to do. I told her we would take the two girls for a couple of nights, but I can't have them all. And then Helen launched into a nasty, venomous tirade . . . it was ghastly. I could tell she'd been drinking."

I tried to imagine her Devil's Lake weekend with the children. Bruce would have been fishing, Laura swimming with Brenda, and Helen: what? Probably cooking, being quiet and loving, and then as the sun sank behind the trees, pouring herself a drink. Maybe drinking with people in the other cabins, sleeping late in the morning. I had a nightmare memory of my one visit to Devil's Lake, when my mother and Auntie Georgie had taken me along to see Helen, and then left me all alone after dark. I'd been about twelve then, close to the age that Bruce, Laura, and Brenda were now.

A month later, my mother related Helen's story that a successful businessman—"a Mr. Frank something"—had asked her to marry him. He'd take on the three kids, buy a nice house, settle down—all lovey-dovey. But no one believed it.

"It always sounded too good to be true," said Auntie Georgie. "It's over now anyway. That poor devil, he probably never knew what a close call he'd had."

I spent a few days in New Jersey with my parents that fall. My mother showed me a letter she'd had from Helen. "What do you make of this?" Helen wrote that she'd had a tempting job offer. "A very prominent pharmaceutical firm wants me to be their northeast regional sales manager," she'd written. "Of course it would mean a lot of traveling; that's the bad part. I'd be away from my kids. But I would get to see Alan and her husband, and of course you and Jack, which would be marvelous. I haven't decided whether to take it or not. I'd definitely need a new car first, and some snappy business suits, hats, and all, maybe a nice alligator bag. . . ."

"Where would she get the money for all that?" I wondered.

"That's the point. She may be making the whole thing up; I wouldn't be surprised. Why would this big company want her? Your Pa and I are so fed up. He thinks she's paving the way for another appeal to us for money. Oh, I pray she doesn't come here."

Auntie Georgie telephoned that evening. I could hear my mother's end of one of the long, bitter phone conversations that they had in those years. "Georgie, we can't just keep lending her money; it must be a couple of thousand by now. We'll never get it back, for one thing. And it doesn't change anything; it's just throwing money into a pit. Jack says, 'No more.' The kids will be better off without her; you know that."

My mother was the tougher of the two sisters; Auntie Georgie was more tolerant. She had finally accepted that Helen was probably incapable of ever making a home for her three children. But still Georgie clung to her emotional belief in family. "I hate having Archie's kids brought up by strangers, those Petersens," she said. "Herb and I can keep Bruce; I wish we could have them all."

"It's the best we can do, Georgie. Jack and I are too old, anyway. I know Alan and Richard have offered, but it shouldn't fall on them. They're just starting their family. You've heard what Mrs. Hoffman says . . ."

Mrs. Hoffman, the caseworker at Family Service, had been trying to help Helen manage her expenses, and pay off her unpaid bills, bit by bit. "She doubts that Helen will change," my mother reported. "She'll talk about getting a place so she can have the three children, but Mrs. Hoffman doubts that'll ever happen. Meanwhile, she'll take and take from us, anything we'll give. It's up to us to set limits."

With each new crisis, my mother and Auntie Georgie argued. Each sister clung to her own idea of how to cope with Helen and what was best for the children.

"Boy, was Harriet ever smart to get herself and Bill far away from all this. I write her; I try to keep her informed. But she really doesn't want to hear, says there's nothing she can do, anyway." My mother took a deep breath.

"I hate to hear you quarreling with Auntie Georgie," I said. "You need each other."

"You're right, dearie, we do. But don't worry. Georgie's finally gotten to trust Mrs. Hoffman. So she and I can disagree about some things, but it's okay, it really is."

Richard and Callie at the River – 1953

– THIRTY-SEVEN –

IT WAS THE FIRST TIME in years that I'd laid eyes on Janey, Auntie Harriet and Uncle Bill's child. Auntie Georgie and Uncle Herb were giving a big family party at the River the night before their daughter Genna's wedding. After dinner, out on the lawn under the starry sky, we all clapped as our cousin Janey did a wild, barefoot flamenco dance with clicking castanets. This turned out to be the last time I would ever see Janey.

She and Genna were exactly the same age. They'd been inseparable as children—"the little girls"—blonde, curly-haired Janey and Genna with those enormous brown eyes.

Genna's real name was Georgiana after her mother. Her wedding in the summer of 1956 was almost a replay of Richard's and mine: ceremony at the House of Hope Church followed by a reception at the family house in St. Paul. Five-year-old Callie was a flower girl, as was my eleven-year-old cousin Brenda, both of them dressed in white with blue sashes.

But this wedding was different, too. I couldn't help thinking of those who were missing now: Uncle Archie, of course, for one. But Auntie Harriet and Uncle Bill, Janey's parents, were not at Genna's wedding. After they'd moved to California and sold their River property to Auntie Georgie and Uncle Herb they never came back to the River. I missed my young, fun-loving aunt and uncle.

Janey hadn't been there for a long time either. Now everyone was worried about her. She was alienated from her parents and unhappy with her life. She'd confided in Piers, telling him of her involvement with the multi-ethnic, multi-everything "Beat Generation" in San Francisco, marijuana parties, long nights, a psychiatrist, and someone falling off the roof.

"Janey was always rejected by her parents, even when she was a baby," said Auntie Georgie a day or two after Genna's wedding. She and my mother and I were walking up the hill with the dogs to put letters in the mailbox. "To them she was just a nuisance; there's never been any real rapport there."

"I didn't know that," I said. Then I remembered how Auntie Georgie used to criticize her little sister Harriet: "H and Bill care about nothing but parties and fancy cars," she'd say. "Poor little Janey."

"Have I ever told you about the month I spent out here one spring with Genna?" Auntie Georgie asked now. "I was waiting for Finlay to be born that summer. Gen was four. She and I were alone together. We walked, picked wildflowers, paddled on the cold River, read aloud by the fire, slept in the same bed, and were happy. I remember how H was amazed. She kept saying that she could never do that with Janey. She said, 'She'd be bored to death and so would I.'"

"I'm not sure I would have enjoyed it, either," murmured my mother.

"Harriet was not close to Janey," Auntie Georgie shook her head. "If you cannot be close to your child when she is four, whenever can you be?" (Janey moved from California a year or two after Genna's wedding, to a cold-water Bowery walk-up in Manhattan, where she took up painting. She studied physical therapy, moved to Santa Fe, and died in her fifties, possibly from a slow leak of carbon monoxide in her little adobe house.)

We saw all the cousins that summer, as they came and went. I had come out before Richard, who had only two weeks vacation. Callie was made much of by doting grandparents and by Auntie Georgie and Uncle Herb. We had Henry then, too, an agile one-year-old who had to be watched every second. He took a shine to teen-age Bruce, who lived with Auntie Georgie and Uncle Herb. Henry was like a little gnat, trying to follow Bruce everywhere.

I slept on my same old porch, hearing the trickling stream and the familiar night sounds. When the screech owl called at two in the morning, Henry ran screaming and trembling to me, asking for Papa.

One day Callie and I took the canoe into Lily Lake. The water was so low in the slough that we often had to drag the boat. I was ready to give up, but Callie was determined. She collected clams for Crow, the wild bird that Auntie Georgie had tamed. "He loves them," she said. We both loved the silence, a flock of ducks, a Black-Crowned Night Heron right off our bow, and an enormous flapping Great Blue. "It makes it better 'cuz it's so hard to get here," said Callie.

Archie and Helen's daughters, Laura and Brenda, lived with the Petersens, their foster parents, but they were often at the River, too. Helen had recently moved to Chicago. "She says she hasn't room for the children," Auntie Georgie told my mother and me. "She doesn't want them, and none of them want to live with her."

One day Helen came to take the three children up to Devil's Lake for a few vacation days. According to Uncle Herb, she gave them an earful while they were with her, saying "Archie's family owes you an education and money to live on. It's up to them."

Helen, brought up as a Catholic herself, began insisting on a Catholic education for her daughters. The Petersens were Protestants, perhaps a drawback in Helen's mind. "Laura and Brenda should go to Villa Maria in Frontenac, where I went," said Helen in her low voice. "I want them to board there and be taught by the Ursuline nuns." She got her way.

Benno Wolff, the lawyer, had arranged a trust fund to provide some modest financial help for Bruce, Laura, and Brenda as they headed toward college. Helen tried to have their money sent to her instead. No, said Benno, under the terms of the trust she couldn't do that.

Helen kept saying she was coming to see Bruce play football, but she never did. Sometimes during school vacations the three children would take the train to Chicago to visit Helen and her new husband, Ted. He was a salesman. They lived modestly. After seven or eight years Ted died in an accident. Helen was found unconscious a week later. Her death from pills and alcohol was deemed a suicide.

Richard, Henry, Callie, and Will – 1959

– T H I R T Y - E I G H T –

WHEN NEXT WE CAME TO THE RIVER we had three children. Henry, the middle one, was four. "Oh, I remember this place," he said as we walked over to see Auntie Georgie. "I know the way." He came onto the porch, sat down, swung his legs around and said, "I know this house. I've been here before."

"How could he remember?" My mother was dubious. "He was only a year old."

He spent much time at Auntie Georgie's. He invited himself for lunch, and insisted on having his nap right there on the old hammock-swing. She offered him nips of coffee, and Dena plied him with her heavy fried doughnuts.

"He shouldn't be having coffee, Georgie," said my mother. "And all those doughnuts just spoil his appetite." My mother never knew that Auntie Georgie let Henry try a few puffs from her Kent cigarette.

Auntie Georgie's half-tamed wild pet crow dove at Henry, who screamed in terror. "Don't worry, Henry; Crow just doesn't know you yet. Here, hold out your hand." She placed a grape on his palm. Crow plucked it up. Henry shivered, laughed. "More! Crow wants more grapes," he cried.

Our youngest was Will, almost two. He didn't speak, but my father and I were convinced he was a young Mozart because he could sing—or at least hum. We all persuaded him to perform for us. His favorites were from South Pacific: "Ditez-moi, pourquoi, la vie est bel-le . . ." hummed wordlessly, right on key. Uncle Herbert tipped back in his chair, and roared with delight. "He's so handsome," murmured Auntie Georgie.

Henry was scared at night. I'd light a candle against the darkness. He and Callie learned to row, taking turns with the old wooden boat. They wanted to play tennis. Callie asked Uncle Herb for a lesson. "Well, sure," he said. "Come on out to the court."

He was a natural teacher. He taught her as well as little Henry, who wouldn't be left out. "I wish I could have my own racquet." Callie said.

We didn't see Bruce that summer. He was a fly-fishing counselor at a camp in Wyoming. "The fishing here!" he wrote. "Fantastic. I truly caught a trout a minute." He made sure every boy got at least one fish, then cleaned enough fish for lunch, built a fire, and fried the trout in butter with a splash of orange juice.

"Oh, he sounds so much like Uncle Archie," I said when Auntie Georgie read us his letter. "That passion for fishing—and his way of teaching."

He and Laura, his twin, had graduated from their high schools that year. Laura would attend Macalester College in St. Paul. Bruce had wanted to follow Finlay, Auntie Georgie and Uncle Herb's youngest, to Harvard. He'd always looked up to Fin, two years older. Bruce had been accepted and offered a scholarship at Harvard, but not enough to pay the entire cost. "He told Harvard he needed an eighteen hundred dollar scholarship," Uncle Herb said. "But he didn't quite make it. So he'll go to Carleton."

"Well, Carleton is supposed to be very good," my father said. "And they've offered him a full scholarship."

Uncle Herb knocked the ashes out of his pipe. We were all sitting on their porch that evening. "All three of them have been promised scholarship money from the Bremer Foundation," he said. "But only if they go to colleges in Minnesota."

Richard and I walked home at dusk through the meadow. "Why aren't they treating Bruce the same way they treated their own children?" I asked. "Something's not right."

"They've done a lot," Richard said. "Your parents, too. I guess maybe they feel enough's enough."

"I don't understand. It makes me sad."

"Yes."

While Bruce lived at Georgie and Herb's, Laura and Brenda often stayed with them, too, for holidays, vacations at the River, and frequent weekends. Auntie Georgie adored Brenda. "She's like a certain star," Auntie Georgie said. "We talk, we understand with our spirits, and we read to each other. Then, for no reason, down comes mysterious laughter and helpless giggling. And meanwhile, Bruce is talking about atomic power with Herb. It all makes me wonder why these three children do not live with us."

But she couldn't have done it; that time was past. Something was terribly wrong with Auntie Georgie. Now, five years after Archie's death, her balance was off. She noticed it; we all did. She was unsteady on her feet, and even with a cane she often fell. She'd had to give up the long walks she'd always taken with her dogs. But to me she still seemed as cheery as ever, ready to listen, ready to talk. Carefully, slowly, she made her way down to the water to swim. "The River is cold," she wrote in a letter to my mother that September, "and coated with froth in which myriads of leaves float and obstruct me while I am desperately swimming, and when

I have swum upstream enough so that I feel warm, then I try the coldest thing of all, put my whole head under and swim home."

With Uncle Herb she made repeated trips to the Mayo Clinic for evaluation and endless batteries of tests. Her illness remained a mystery: "a degenerative disease of the nervous system, which may worsen." It worsened.

"The doctors haven't really found anything," my mother said. "So it must be psychosomatic. I'm sure of it."

My mother was anguished and frightened by Georgie's mysterious decline. But that winter Auntie Georgie was still able to travel with my mother to visit Auntie Harriet and Uncle Bill in La Jolla for the first time. Auntie Georgie hated leaving Uncle Herb and the dogs and the Ingersoll children. But she loathed gray, frozen St. Paul, where she was now confined to the house except for the afternoon walk, clinging to Uncle Herb's arm, around the block with the dogs. "I hate the houses," she wrote, "their dinky yards, the icy streets. . . ."

La Jolla was a world away. She and my mother stayed at a posh little inn not far from Auntie Harriet and Uncle Bill. They lay in the hot sun, and swam every day in the pool. The visiting sisters were feted at party after party, in what Auntie Georgie lampooned as "this old people's gala wonderland."

"No one has anything much to do," wrote Georgie. "Everyone lives in a palace with a pool, everyone comes from Owatonna or Saranac or Greenville . . . everyone outdoes his best friend in snobbery."

But they worried about Harriet. Bill's work in advertising was not going well. After having been brought up by a rich father who'd led him to believe he'd inherit the family business, he'd been cut out entirely. "Gold was always shining in his young eyes," wrote Georgie, but now he seemed pitiful, wary, and faded. Harriet's little fortune from her mother was long gone. "H wears worn clothes, looking superb always with her high head, and they don't drive a Cadillac any more. Harriet, so slender and fair, was always the "pretty hopeful"; now she's faced with this diminution. But "their house is more snug, in better taste even with the stuffing coming out of the chairs than any of the satin-covered lounges we have seen here." And Harriet was the one who consoled and encouraged Bill. Georgie decided to rewrite her will to leave a small something to her little sister.

Auntie Georgie seldom wrote or spoke of Uncle Archie, but from La Jolla she wrote that, much as she missed Uncle Herb, she was not looking forward to plunging back into "that dreadful St. Paul to be shut up again on the second floor, in the old blue room, the room most identified with our family life, with Archie's life since he came there so often in his many agonies and where at last I refused to listen."

She and Uncle Herb had decided to embark on a major remodeling of the old St. Paul house on Fairmount Avenue, the house where their three children had grown up, the site of my wedding reception and Genna's. Most of the houses along the streets on the hill in St. Paul, the neighborhood where my mother's family and all their friends had always lived, were solid, ponderous structures from the 1890s and early 1900s. Beautiful they were not. But they belonged together. Each house covered most of its lot, its modest half-acre. There was a comfortable harmony along these avenues.

Auntie Georgie, always a rebel, a nonconformist, was not afraid to make her own mark on their neighborhood. More and more confined at home now, she wanted congenial surroundings in which she could be as cozy and comfortable as possible. They hired a prominent St. Paul "moderne" architect, Magnus Jemne, who seemed to have felt no compunction to blend in with the rest of Fairmount Avenue.

The old front porch was ripped off, interior walls knocked down. Demolition and rebuilding went on for months. Auntie Georgie focused on the new, bright upstairs sitting room, lined with bookshelves, a fireplace, and silvery gray walls "the color of gossamer." Here is where she read *Anna Karenina* aloud to Brenda or *Les Misérables* to Bruce, read André Gide and Bellow's *Seize the Day* to herself, talked and laughed with family, or sipped a highball and smoked another Kent cigarette with friends. A deck opened off this room, offering a view of the street and into the neighbors' trees.

A year later she wrote Piers, "I grow weak, inept, stumbling . . . I have not been outside for five weeks." Her condition was worsening; she often fell. She couldn't even turn over in bed. They put in an elevator big enough for her new wheelchair. She tried not to speak of her despair: "How can one live helpless?" she asked in a letter. Only in reading could she forget her fear.

Cedar Bend
(photo by Andrew Summersby)

She and Uncle Herbert were reading Faulkner's *Sanctuary*. "The River is sanctuary for me," she wrote. Now she worried that the River would be impossible. "We'll make it work," promised Uncle Herb. They had Willard, the carpenter, install grab bars in their River house. Uncle Herb got a small walker so she could move around. She relied on Bruce to help Uncle Herb with her care. He helped lift her, ran errands, did kitchen chores. "I couldn't be here without Bruce," she told my mother. He and Uncle Herb together even got her down to the water's edge, where she slid in and swam hard against the current, close to shore.

So pleased was she with the alterations to their house in town that she and Uncle Herb had architect Magnus Jemne design changes to the old River house. There were new bay windows in the living room. The end of the long front porch facing the River, where we'd always sat in the grapevine shade, lost its old cozy intimacy after it was enlarged and modernized with an industrial steel column running up through the middle. The old brick steps and Gangie's once phlox-filled flowerbeds gave way to a small metal-railed deck.

Auntie Georgie clung to the hope that her doctors would finally discover the cause of her illness and fix it. She endured spinal taps, hypnosis, parathyroid surgery; she was willing to try anything. Auntie Harriet wrote in anguish from La Jolla: "My God, Georgie, what in hell is it? Truly I cannot bear it. Reading your letter, and Genna's and Jeannie's, I began swearing and crying and pounding the table." But she did not come to Minnesota. Georgie's visit to La Jolla three years earlier was their last time together.

I was in the middle of the Atlantic Ocean when Auntie Georgie died. With Richard and our three children returning on a Cunard liner after a month in Ireland, I knew nothing. At home I found a letter from my mother telling me of our great loss. She hadn't wanted to "spoil our vacation" by cabling me or even calling. There was no funeral for me to attend, no nothing. There was no funeral at all, no memorial service. Auntie Georgie's life was just . . . over.

Callie and Henry in the old green canoe – 1959

– THIRTY-NINE –

UNCLE ARCHIE had taught his children not to be afraid of taking chances. Like him, they didn't shy away from risk. When they were learning to swim, he taught them as he'd taught all of us. He'd have them jump off the dock and swim upstream, against the current, a fair distance to that big black boulder along the shore. "Don't give up," he'd shout. "You can do it."

Laura once told me that their father had often encouraged them to support each other. "Stick together, kids." I often noticed that they did stick together, in foul weather and fair, more so than the children of some more stable families.

Laura switched from Macalester to St. Catherine's, a Catholic college in St. Paul. She was the only one of the three who adopted their mother's Catholic faith. Laura studied art, and later taught at schools around St. Paul. With her husband Jim, she did the hands-on restoration of their old house in the city. Later they moved to a house on the River, in the nearby village of Marine. Laura worked hard to make it perfect. I remember her almost compulsive neatness; in the bathroom, even their toothbrushes were kept out of sight.

Laura's narrow face was framed by smooth blond hair. Luminous gray-blue eyes focused her intense gaze. She leaned close when we talked, as if our conversation was the most important thing in the world right then. She wanted to know about my life, and she wanted to hear everything I could tell her about her mother. "No one else talks about her," Laura said.

The aunts and uncles had given Laura a trip to Europe the summer of her graduation from college, so it happened that like me she was far away when Auntie Georgie died. Laura was heartbroken. Georgie had always been the warm, welcoming, loving, forgiving, anchoring center in Laura's young life, as she had been for Bruce and Brenda.

My mother had always been especially fond of Laura. They became even closer when Jim's job took them to New Jersey for several years. Laura and Jim and their little ones lived near my parents, and came over often. That was a happy interlude for my mother. "Laura's such a wise person," she said. "We talk about everything under the sun: about art— she really knows a lot—and of course about family. She wants to hear everything about our growing up, the early days at the River, and, of course, about Archie."

Laura and Jim had two children. They gave their daughter a family name: MacLaren. Their whole family skied. I never saw their house at Big Sky, Montana, but I can imagine it: beautiful mountain views, minimalist decor, everything clean, perfect, and neat as a pin.

Laura had just turned sixty when she got sick. Something went wrong in her lungs. She spent many weeks in the Mayo Clinic. Her doctors made a supposedly therapeutic hole in one lung. It didn't work. It didn't heal. She told me on the phone from her hospital bed about the book she was reading: *The River of Doubt,* by Candice Millard, an account of

Theodore Roosevelt's disastrous expedition through dense jungle up an uncharted tributary of the Amazon. Roosevelt was determined to forge ahead, wouldn't think of turning back. Several people died, and Roosevelt himself barely survived. "Don't give up," I remembered Laura quoting her father. "You can do it." But Laura didn't make it.

Ten years earlier, as a festive way of celebrating her fiftieth birthday, Laura had decided to do something brave. During a picnic up the River, she'd climbed out onto the railroad bridge, and with a jubilant yell, jumped into the roiling water below, a feat that I'd always connected with Uncle Archie. A year after their mother's death, her two children made that same leap off the bridge, in memory of her, scattering Laura's ashes onto the River.

Bruce, Laura's twin, lived with Auntie Georgie and Uncle Herb until he went off to college at Carleton. He got along well with cousin Finlay. They spent a lot of time together in St. Paul and at the River. "Bruce had a slightly second-class status in our house," Finlay says. "Because of Dena." Dena, the bossy, indispensable cook-housekeeper, had been with the family since Finlay was born. Fin was her adored pet, waited on and fussed over. For Dena, Bruce was always a changeling. She resented him, complained about him, and treated him, as Auntie Georgie put it, "with subtle malice" because he was not Fin.

Auntie Georgie thought that Bruce's interest and endless talk about trains, and his passion for fishing were his ways of identifying himself with his father. Once when he was fourteen, she'd told me, he sobbed and pounded his pillow after losing a four-pound bass that he'd played on his line for ten minutes.

One summer when they were both in college, Bruce and Fin drove out west to Washington to work for Weyerhauser

Lumber. They were assigned the extremely dangerous job of "Choker-Setters." Working deep canyons in steep terrain, they spent their days attaching cables to huge logs. Each log was then dragged out of the matrix of other big logs, swinging crazily so one end or the other might suddenly come at you, as they were hauled up onto logging trucks. Off duty, the two cousins spent their weekends trout-fishing in the Cascade Mountains.

Bruce was determined to prove himself to Uncle Herb. He wanted his uncle to think well of him. He also hoped to earn the respect of his cousin Piers, the older son in that family.

Right out of college Bruce went into journalism, Uncle Herb's profession. He worked first for a news bureau, then for the *Chicago Tribune.* He moved to the *Minneapolis Tribune*, where he met and married Trish, a colleague at the paper. I saw them often the summer they spent at the River in a little house just downstream from what had been Auntie Harriet and Uncle Bill's. Trish was assigned to the women's page of the paper—a feature still alive and well in the 'sixties. She tried out new recipes on us, some of which my mother copied into her own spiral-bound cookbook. The recipes are still there, but the marriage ended.

Bruce went on to the University of Wisconsin, where he earned a graduate degree in the new field of Environmental Journalism, and was hired as an investigative reporter by the *Chicago Sun-Times* in their Washington bureau. To report on the leak at Three Mile Island in 1979, Bruce made his way into the core of the plant, entirely unprotected. I can imagine his determination to get the story, and his dismissal of the risk. That exposure undoubtedly later caused his fatal illness, a rare form of cancer. In my mind I can see Bruce's father, Uncle Archie on our lawn—awed, amazed, and elated—when that first atom bomb was dropped on Hiroshima. He sensed that we were entering a new age.

His optimism now seems misplaced, as his own son became a casualty.

At *The Wall Street Journal*, Bruce continued his investigative journalism, delving into the revolting horrors inside huge poultry processing mills, or uncovering the flagrant pollution of rivers and streams by certain major mining and manufacturing companies. He dug into the nasty institutional bias that denied black farmers the benefits to which they were entitled. A colleague likened him to Clark Kent: "Thick glasses, soft-spoken, and an easy manner," and then Bruce would put on his Superman suit: "When he got his teeth into something he would not let go." After he was happily married to Carol, they bought an old house on the River, not far from Laura's. They named their son Archie; their daughter is another Brenda.

Eventually Bruce's illness caught up with him. Unable to find a match for a bone marrow transplant, his treatment options were exhausted. His white blood count had dropped precipitously, and his strength had declined when he called Finlay to take the day off and go fishing with him on the Susquehanna River. Fin knew what that meant. They rented a little flat-bottomed boat and fished for small-mouth bass. When Bruce got too tired, they went ashore, had a beer and a hamburger, and drove home to Washington. That was Bruce's last fling. They'd been on a river, even though not our River. Bruce was sixty. Six months later he was dead.

We all sang, "Shall We Gather at the River" at his funeral. Everyone cried.

> *Yes, we'll gather at the river,*
> *The beautiful, the beautiful river;*
> *Gather with the saints at the river*
> *That flows by the throne of God.*

Bruce and Laura's sister, Brenda, three years younger than the blond, blue-eyed twins, has big, dark, wide-apart eyes and brown hair. "Absolutely beautiful," my mother said. "Now, who does she take after?" Nobody said so, but probably it was Helen.

Unlike Laura, Brenda was miserable at their Catholic boarding school. She begged to return to her foster family, the Petersens, and attend the local school. She remains close to them still.

After college she, too, became a journalist, writing for Chicago papers and later the *Detroit News*. Unlike Bruce and Laura, she was never able to have her own house at the River. She regrets her father's surrender of his inherited share of the River property, their birthright. I am sure they all felt that. They may have thought that the three sisters had talked him out of it, taking advantage of his unsettled state and his need for money. We'll never know. Brenda loves the River as much as any of us, and is nostalgic for childhood summers in the family compound. "I've always wanted to have my ashes sprinkled under those tall pines," she told me one day, pointing to the grove by the house that was once Auntie Harriet and Uncle Bill's. "Overlooking the River."

St. Croix River
(photo by Andrew Summersby)

– F O R T Y –

RICHARD EXPERIENCED THE RIVER in his own way, swimming against the current, going out early alone in the canoe, exploring the sloughs, keeping an eye and an ear on the birds and other wildlife. Neither the tennis court nor the motorboats were of interest to Richard. When I canoed with him I sat still and silent, the bow paddle across my knees, while he looked at the great crested flycatcher on an overhanging maple branch.

Checking his battered *Peterson Field Guide* at breakfast one morning, he told my father he'd seen a prothonotary warbler in the slough behind the Shearers' island. "A prothonotary warbler!" exclaimed my father. "That's a new one." Uncle Herb was impressed, too.

Sometimes Richard and I fished for bass from the canoe. One day he came home with a fish such as no one had ever seen. After comparing it to drawings in Eddie's fish book, Richard concluded he'd caught a Freshwater Drum. "What?" Piers was skeptical. "I've lived here all my life, and I never heard of a Freshwater Drum."

On our one-night camping trip that summer, we pitched a claustrophobic pup tent on an island upstream. All night, in the penetrating mosquito whine, we made futile swats at the sides of our own heads. Finally asleep, I was startled awake in the first gray light by the snort and stomped hoof of a deer just outside our frail shelter.

I'm standing on the lawn above the River. Everything looks almost the same as it did when I was a child—probably little has changed from the days when my mother and the aunts and Uncle Archie first saw it. I hear the murmur of the waterfall, the soothing sound that used to put me to sleep on my porch. The steep dirt road still clings to the cliff edge as it descends. After passing the shaded clay tennis court, you finally glimpse the wide River. Then you arrive at the old house, which now belongs to Auntie Georgie and Uncle Herb's children. Auntie Harriet and Uncle Bill's house is theirs, too. Eddie owns the house our mother built.

Across the River from where I stand, the Shearers' compound has vanished without a trace, leaving that watery island to the cardinal flowers, swamp maples, warblers, herons, and turtles. Most of the houses along the River at Otisville still belong to the same families—children or grandchildren of the people I knew.

I look at the canoes—green, red, yellow, and one silvery metal—flipped over in a row by the landing. Clumsy pontoon boats have taken over a good chunk of the beach. We never used to have those. But there are now more canoes than ever on the River. Noisy outboards no longer shatter the Sunday quiet, and there are none of those buzzing little speedboats so beloved years ago by certain teenage boys such as Eddie.

The River didn't just happen to stay the same. It took an Act of Congress. Two senators from the bordering states— Walter Mondale of Minnesota and Wisconsin's Gaylord Nelson—worked for years to have the St. Croix designated in 1972 as a Wild and Scenic River. That's why I'm not seeing a bunch of new houses along the river, or more timber cutting, or any commercial anything.

Uncle Herb once wrote to Richard and me on this subject of change. "The River has been at its best this year," he said. "The trees and grass and shrubs were never better, as many perfect days as could ever be expected and, oh yes, the tennis court is in professional shape. Only now I measure my tennis not in sets but in minutes. Now there we have it. The River is the same but we aren't. What changes is us."

The River is low now, at the end of summer, giving us a strip of beach at the landing where we swim. The water flows in two deep channels, running parallel to the shorelines, but in the middle of the River the water is shallow enough for me to touch the sandy bottom with my toes.

Every spring the River still floods. Some years it spreads over the meadow, up to the edges of the lawn. It drowns the little stream below what had been my sleeping porch. I've never been there for the record high waters, but I've often seen it wide and deep. Auntie Georgie described one spring flood: "The River from where I look is as wide as the land and comes full to the green shore, the May green shore and woods colored now as never else in the green that is May, with its shades, light, flowers—unborn like broadtail fur from a lamb and wet with tiny rain dropping on the river flow and going slowly by all pitted and flat and wimpled and the river leans away to go under the far banks and the shape of the Wisconsin hills . . . the trees bend down and lay their ungrown leaves in the high water."

Richard always treasured those times of high water when he and I, or he alone, could explore the winding sloughs in the green canoe, skimming along hidden green channels that at other times are half-blocked by fallen trees and branches. We glide past willows, ferns, and cardinal flowers. Maple trees lean over us. Next winter some will fall, making passage difficult once again. But now we're floating over the fallen logs in this secret world, a million miles from anywhere. An otter plops into the tea-brown water, frogs chirrup, the pileated woodpecker makes a drumbeat on a dying tree, then calls a warning as he flies off. A tall heron languidly flaps his wings as he makes his dignified escape from two intruders in a canoe.

The big sugar maple by the River bank looks sad now and lonely. I used to climb up the tree to a fork that made a secure perch, where, hidden by leaves, I could hear and observe the life of my River family. Auntie Georgie once described this tree on an autumn afternoon: "I think I am alone to watch the blazing hills and our maple tree which stands with black trunk bearing down pillows of leaves so yellow and red cascading to the ground and swaying to each wind in deliberate caressing grace." Now the maple tree is dying. Its upper branches are bare and broken. "That's the way they die," Piers tells me. "From the top down."

"So we beat on, boats against the current, borne back ceaselessly into the past": the final sentence of Fitzgerald's *Great Gatsby*. From the lawn I look down at the shore. Purple joe-pye weed and yellow sneezeweed grow along the water's edge among a scattering of those black boulders dropped by the melting glacier long, long ago.

But my past here is less remote. I think of my grandparents—Faddie and Gangie—who found this place and made our sanctuary.

And then, of course, I think of my mother and father, the aunts and uncles, the cousins, the children. I look at the rings on my fingers: the emerald ring that Auntie Georgie helped my father pick out when he'd asked my mother to marry him. And my grandmother's gold wedding ring, passed on to my mother and then to me. I slip it off and look inside: "Edmund to Jeannie – September 8, 1892." I decide that I will give this ring to my daughter Callie when next we're together. It's time.

Fifty years ago, when she came home to the River after yet another of her fruitless sessions at the Mayo Clinic, Auntie Georgie wrote, "How could there be another place all lonely and shining under a hill, a house so warm and barking and wiggling with dogs and joy, a house so closed, personal and alive and welcoming and empty as this? In the night sky the dipper is in the right place and the stars are where I expect them. And so in the firelight of home at last."

ABOUT THE AUTHOR

Alan Emmet grew up in Minnesota and New Jersey. She received her bachelor's degree from Radcliffe College, where she also did graduate work in landscape history and design. She has worked as a preservation consultant for the National Trust and other organizations. Her book *So Fine a Prospect: Historic New England Gardens* was named a Notable Book by the *New York Times*, and acclaimed by *Martha Stewart Living*. Her novel, *The Mr. & Mrs. Club*, is set in the 1950s. Alan Emmet's articles have been featured in Conde Nast's *House & Garden*, *Garden Design*, *Harvard Magazine*, *Architectural Digest*, and other national periodicals. She lives in Massachusetts, where she continues to write and cares for her well-known historic garden.

CPSIA information can be obtained at www.ICGtesting.com
Printed in the USA
BVOW08s0535150916

462060BV00001B/13/P